Adam Ferguson and the Idea of Civil Society

Edinburgh Studies in Scottish Philosophy

Series Editor: Gordon Graham
Center for the Study of Scottish Philosophy, Princeton Theological Seminary

Scottish Philosophy Through the Ages

This new series will cover the full range of Scottish philosophy over five centuries – from the medieval period through the Reformation and Enlightenment periods, to the nineteenth and early twentieth centuries.

The series will publish innovative studies on major figures and themes. It also aims to stimulate new work in less intensively studied areas, by a new generation of philosophers and intellectual historians. The books will combine historical sensitivity and philosophical substance which will serve to cast new light on the rich intellectual inheritance of Scottish philosophy.

Books available

Adam Ferguson and the Idea of Civil Society: Moral Science in the Scottish Enlightenment, Craig Smith
Adam Smith and Rousseau: Ethics, Politics, Economics, edited by Maria Pia Paganelli, Dennis C. Rasmussen and Craig Smith
Essays on Hume, Smith and the Scottish Enlightenment, Christopher Berry
Hume's Sceptical Enlightenment, Ryu Susato
Imagination in Hume's Philosophy: The Canvas of the Mind, Timothy M. Costelloe
Thomas Reid and the Problem of Secondary Qualities, Christopher A. Shrock

Books forthcoming

Eighteenth-Century Scottish Aesthetics: Not Just a Matter of Taste, Rachel Zuckert

www.edinburghuniversitypress.com/series/essp

Adam Ferguson and the Idea of Civil Society

Moral Science in the Scottish Enlightenment

Craig Smith

EDINBURGH
University Press

Edinburgh University Press is one of the leading university presses in the UK. We publish academic books and journals in our selected subject areas across the humanities and social sciences, combining cutting-edge scholarship with high editorial and production values to produce academic works of lasting importance. For more information visit our website: edinburghuniversitypress. com

© Craig Smith, 2019, 2020

First published in hardback by Edinburgh University Press 2019

Edinburgh University Press Ltd
The Tun – Holyrood Road, 12(2f) Jackson's Entry, Edinburgh EH8 8PJ

Typeset in 11/13 Adobe Sabon by
Servis Filmsetting Ltd, Stockport, Cheshire,
printed and bound by CPI Group (UK) Ltd, Croydon, CR0 4YY

A CIP record for this book is available from the British Library

ISBN 978 1 4744 1327 5 (hardback)
ISBN 978 1 4744 7453 5 (paperback)
ISBN 978 1 4744 1328 2 (webready PDF)
ISBN 978 1 4744 1329 9 (epub)

The right of Craig Smith to be identified as the author of this work has been asserted in accordance with the Copyright, Designs and Patents Act 1988, and the Copyright and Related Rights Regulations 2003 (SI No. 2498).

Contents

Preface

This volume is the result of a research project that began in 2004 when I was fortunate enough to be awarded a British Academy Postdoctoral Fellowship to work on Adam Ferguson's idea of civil society. It has been undertaken in the supportive atmospheres of the Department of Moral Philosophy at the University of St Andrews and the School of Social and Political Science at the University of Glasgow.

Most will acknowledge Ferguson is a complex and apparently somewhat disordered thinker, and I found myself exploring a number of different avenues into his thought down the years, each time attempting to make sense of his intellectual project. This book takes the form it does because of my desire to understand Ferguson's own conception of his project and to use this understanding as the context through which to explore his views on the idea of civil society. Ferguson has also been accused of being a derivative thinker who attempts to stitch together elements drawn from a wide range of intellectual sources. There is a sense in which the present book might be thought to do the same: it attempts to draw together the various strands of interpretation of Ferguson's thought and to place them into a unified whole. As a result, I owe thanks to those who have pioneered the various interpretative approaches to Ferguson, in particular to Richard Sher, David Kettler, David Allan, Lisa Hill and Iain McDaniel. My pursuit of this has been greatly aided by the fact that two other scholars were working on their own, equally holistic, readings of Ferguson at the same time. And so, for many chats and conference panels where I have tried out versions of these ideas, I thank Jack Hill and Katherine Nicolai, who I'm sure will recognise the puzzles shared by us all.

Over the last decade or so I have profited immensely from conversations with the wider circle of Scottish Enlightenment scholars, particularly James Harris, Thomas Ahnert, Alexander Broadie, Nicholas Phillipson and Maria Pia Paganelli. My largest debt remains to Christopher J. Berry, whose guidance and advice have proved invaluable down the years and to whom the volume is dedicated.

Series Editor's Introduction

It is widely acknowledged that the Scottish Enlightenment of the eighteenth century was one of the most fertile periods in British intellectual history, and that philosophy was the jewel in its crown. Yet, vibrant though this period was, it occurred within a long history that began with the creation of the Scottish universities in the fifteenth century. It also stretched into the nineteenth and twentieth centuries for as long as those universities continued to be a culturally distinctive and socially connected system of education and enquiry.

While the Scottish Enlightenment remains fertile ground for philosophical and historical investigation, these other four centuries of philosophy also warrant intellectual exploration. The purpose of this series is to maintain outstanding scholarly study of great thinkers like David Hume, Adam Smith and Thomas Reid, alongside sustained exploration of the less familiar figures who preceded them, and the impressive company of Scottish philosophers, once celebrated, now neglected, who followed them.

Gordon Graham

List of Ferguson's Works

The following abbreviations of Ferguson's works in the editions listed will be used throughout:

Analysis	(1766) *Analysis of Pneumatics and Moral Philosophy*. Edinburgh: A. Kincaid & J. Bell.
Black	(1997) [1805] 'Minutes of the Life and Character of Joseph Black MD', in G. Y. Craig (ed.) *James Hutton and Joseph Black*. Edinburgh: Royal Society of Edinburgh, pp. 107–17.
Correspondence	(1995) *The Correspondence of Adam Ferguson*, 2 Vols, ed. Vincenzo Merolle. London: William Pickering.
Essay	(1995) [1767] *An Essay on the History of Civil Society*, ed. Fania Oz-Salzberger. Cambridge: Cambridge University Press.
Institutes	(1994) [1769] *Institutes of Moral Philosophy*. London: Routledge/Thoemmes Press.
Lectures	*Lectures on Pneumatics and Moral Philosophy 1774–1783*. Edinburgh University Library Research Collections.
Manuscripts	(2006) *The Manuscripts of Adam Ferguson*, ed. Vincenzo Merolle. London: Pickering & Chatto.
Militia	(1756) *Reflections Previous to the Establishment of a Militia*. London: R. & J. Dodsley.
Natural Philosophy	(1760) *Of Natural Philosophy*. Edinburgh.

Price
: (1776) *Remarks on a Pamphlet lately published by Dr Price* . . . London: T. Cadell.

Principles
: (1973) [1792] *Principles of Moral and Political Science*, 2 Vols. New York: AMS Press.

Rome
: (1856) [1783] *The History of the Progress and Termination of the Roman Republic.* New York: J. C. Derby. University of Michigan: Historical Reprint Series.

Sermon
: (1746) *A sermon Preached in the Ersh Language to His Majesty's First Highland Regiment of Foot* . . . London: A. Miller.

Sister Peg
: (1982) [1761] in D. Raynor (ed.), *Sister Peg, a pamphlet hitherto unknown by David Hume.* Cambridge: Cambridge University Press.

Stage
: (1757) *The Morality of Stage Plays Seriously Considered.* Edinburgh.

Introduction

I am ambitious to show that there is a science of manners or of Ethics, no less than of Jurisprudence or of Politics, and for this purpose would willingly point out a method, by which to derive the offices or duties of a virtuous life from principles at once so comprehensive and unquestionably evident, as to enable every person to fill up the detail for himself. (*Principles* 2: 321–2)

Adam Ferguson (1723–1816) is well known as a major figure in the Scottish Enlightenment. While he is not as famous, nor as highly rated, as his friends David Hume and Adam Smith, he has maintained a place in the history of ideas that has become indelibly linked to the early development of sociological thought and, in particular, to the idea of civil society. The aim of the present study is to try to place Ferguson's overall intellectual project in its proper setting, the better to appreciate what Ferguson actually meant when he talked about moral science and civil society.

There are two common issues which emerge in serious treatments of Ferguson's thought: that he disagreed with Hume and Smith on important political issues (particularly that he was more sceptical about commerce), and that his work is less consistent and systematic than that of his friends.[1] In what follows I will take issue with both of these tendencies. I do not wish to argue that Ferguson agreed with everything his contemporaries say, nor that he was totally consistent across his career. Instead, I want to argue that the *way* in which Ferguson has been read has predisposed readers to see him as more sceptical of commerce and less consistent as a thinker than is actually the case. The fact that he has been read in this way is completely understandable given Ferguson's, at first glance, very different views on commercial society and the fashion for recovering civic republican themes that dominated early modern intellectual history in the latter half of the twentieth century. However, both of these tendencies involve placing Ferguson in a context defined by one particular aspect of his thought. The aim of the present study is to open up the consideration of Ferguson and to consider other aspects of his thought.

I am far from the first scholar to attempt a more holistic reading of Ferguson: David Kettler (2005), Lisa Hill (2006) and Jack Hill (2017) have all sought to do justice to Ferguson's overall body of work in their books on his thought. In what follows I am engaged in much the same kind of project that they develop: an attempt to identify the consistent position that lies beneath the apparent contradictions in his thought.[2] It is worth stating clearly, at this early point, the two central claims that I hope to demonstrate. The first is that Ferguson does have a coherent and life-long intellectual project: the creation of a practical moral pedagogy based on a secure moral philosophy which was, in turn, grounded in a scientific observation of human nature. The project is that of every serious moral philosopher from Aristotle to Francis Hutcheson, but significantly it is not the project of much moral philosophy after the eighteenth century. This change in what we consider the nature of philosophy to be has, I will argue, obscured what Ferguson was trying to do. And where his project is appreciated it is viewed as quaint and indeed hopelessly old-fashioned moralising.[3] Ferguson is often damned with the faint praise of being a moralist rather than a moral philosopher and while this is true to an extent, it represents a failure to understand that moral philosophy and moralising were (and perhaps even should be) linked activities. Even in those studies that take Ferguson seriously, like those of Richard Sher and David Kettler, the temptation is to excuse the tensions in Ferguson's thought by regarding him as a moralist (Sher 1989: 241) or an intellectual (Kettler 2005: 222) rather than a philosopher.[4] But as Gordon Graham (2007) has argued, the understanding of the nature of philosophy in eighteenth-century Scotland saw practical moral education as central to its task, so it is not so much that Ferguson was a poor philosopher, it is more that we possess an impoverished understanding of philosophy.

This book makes the case for reading Ferguson as a moralist deeply concerned to place his moralising on a secure 'scientific' basis. It may not be a project that modern philosophy has much time for, or one that ends up saying anything startlingly original, but it does represent a coherent and (relatively) consistently pursued project. Moreover, as Richard Sher (1994) has shown, it is a project that lies firmly in the mainstream of the Scottish Enlightenment and the Moderate literati. The argument of the first three chapters of this book will seek to reconstruct the three main elements of Ferguson's conception of moral philosophy before using this as the appropriate context through which to approach his discussion of the idea of civil society.

The second major interpretative point that runs through this book is that our reading of Ferguson has been systematically distorted by the context in which he has been discussed. The main source of this has been the dominance of *An Essay on the History of Civil Society* in studies of Ferguson. While this is understandable as it is the book that made his name and which was most widely read in his lifetime, it has had an unfortunate impact in placing a focus on some aspects of Ferguson's thinking which appear there, but are less significant elsewhere in his writing. As Jack Hill (2017: 32) has recently argued, the tendency to stress the *Essay*, rather than the *Roman History* or the *Institutes*, or perhaps most significantly the *Principles*, has created something of a false impression of Ferguson in the mind of intellectual historians.[5]

One further feature has reinforced this tendency and is a product of the fact that Ferguson has been chiefly read for what he says about politics. The focus on republicanism and civic humanism that dominated much history of political thought for much of the later part of the twentieth century stressed these themes in Ferguson's writing.[6] But in doing so it tended to foreground the *Essay* and set Ferguson up as a useful sceptical foil for the more commercially inclined Hume and Smith in accounts of the political thought of the Scottish Enlightenment.[7] Reading Ferguson in the light of an axis plotted on wealth and virtue gives one the impression that there are significant tensions between the two in his work and that his overall project is to favour ancient virtue over modern commerce.[8] Whatever the truth of such a reading, it is clear that it pushes the reader in a direction that sees Ferguson 'in context'. The question is whether this 'context' is the appropriate context. I want to argue here that it is not, and that if we want to appreciate Ferguson we need to understand how he saw his project and how it related to his personal commitments.

My aim is not to suggest that the *Essay* is unimportant for an overall interpretation of Ferguson's thought. I accept that, compared to his other works, it has been more influential and widely read. But this very fact skews our reading of the whole of his work.[9] The question before us is whether there is a systematic theory in Ferguson's *oeuvre*, and whether we obscure that system when we read the Ferguson of the *Essay* as the definitive Ferguson.[10] Read in his own right and across his works, a very different impression of Ferguson emerges. Jack Hill, David Kettler and Lisa Hill have all pointed to this in their studies of Ferguson and each has gone some way to dethroning the *Essay* from our appreciation of Ferguson. The present study attempts a more complete version of this, not by ignoring the *Essay*, but by placing it, and in particular its highly wrought style, within the overall system developed from the earliest pamphlets to the final manuscript essays. Doing this allows us to defuse some of the tensions that appear to rend Ferguson's work. It is also worth noting that the history of the *Essay* itself saw it morph, in Ferguson's own words in a 1758 letter to Gilbert Elliot, from a 'paper on refinement' to a 'Dissertation on the vicissitudes incident to Human Society' (*Correspondence* 1: 15).[11] John Robertson (1985: 201–2) has suggested that the impetus behind the *Essay*'s composition was Ferguson's involvement in the debates over a Scottish Militia in the 1750s and 1760s rather than his move to the Edinburgh Moral Philosophy Chair, as suggested by Richard Sher. In this sense, when Alexander Carlyle referred to the *Essay* as a 'college exercise' (Robertson 1985: 202; Hill 2017: 63) he did not mean that it was prepared as part of the preparations to lecture on moral philosophy, but rather that it represented a literary exercise akin to a student's essay rather than a scientific or philosophical work. The *Essay* stands apart from Ferguson's other writings not because there is anything necessarily contradictory about the content, nor because it represents an early as opposed to a later work (after all the *Analysis* and *Institutes* pre-date it), but rather because the *Essay* is an essay.[12] The difference between them is a result of the form and purpose of the *Essay* being distinct from the systematic nature of his other writings.[13] Ferguson's career-long obsession with militias obviously invites civic humanist and republican readings, and it would be fruitless to ignore this central aspect of his thinking, so in Chapter 6 we will consider Ferguson's views on military matters and attempt to understand them within the context of his thought as a whole.

The focus of historians of political thought tends to lead them to stress the political context of the time as an explanation of why a thinker is interested in particular issues, while the focus of a historian of philosophy tends to lead them to approach a thinker through their engagement with the classics of philosophy, and in particular with the relation of a thinker to the ancient schools. Both of these approaches can be illuminating and display the influence of events and predecessors on the way a thinker approaches a particular issue. Each such study seeks to place its subject in his proper intellectual and political context and together they add to our appreciation of the thinker at hand. It is the nature of the academic article – and even the monograph – that we focus on a particular interpretation or element of the author's work. This advances scholarship on particulars, but if we mistake each individual piece for a comprehensive account of the thinker in question we end up with a series of one-eyed accounts of our subject.[14] The object of the present study is slightly different: it is to identify Ferguson's basic method and then to use that as the 'context' within which he discusses commercial civilisation. My focus is not on providing a comprehensive intellectual biography of Ferguson (though that is something we could do with), rather it is to pin down his understanding of philosophy and use that as a way to approach his thinking.

I want to examine what I will call Ferguson's 'project' as a whole and to understand what he, himself, understood that project to be, then look at how he undertook it and why it took the form that it did. My aim is to cut beyond the notion of Ferguson as a contradictory or inconsistent thinker by avoiding readings which illuminate particular aspects of his thought at the expense of obscuring the project as a whole. Obviously one part of this will include a claim about what Ferguson's project was and how it appears in his major works. I will argue that it is the combination of a moral science, a moral philosophy and a moral pedagogy that characterises Ferguson's thinking.[15] Ferguson was at the heart of the Moderate establishment of the Scottish Enlightenment and his project represents the core project of that group: Ferguson was engaged in the self-conscious creation of a social ethic for the recently emerged Scottish middle class.[16] His philosophical and educational endeavours were driven by the need to shore up the new British state and, even more crucially, to provide an ethos and education for the class of students who would go on to run the polity and emerging empire. There is an extensive literature by Colin Kidd (1993, 1996), Linda Colley (2009) and others who have examined the creation of a sense of British (or North British) national identity during Ferguson's lifetime.[17] I want to be clear that this is not really the sort of argument that I want to run here. I do not see Ferguson as being particularly interested in shaping the content of national identity. Indeed, he provides us with a generalised sociological account of the development of national sentiment or spirit without interjecting specifically British content, and if he is being consistent to this he would presumably believe that such identity would arise gradually over the next few generations.

The view advanced by Nicholas Phillipson (1981) that the Scottish Enlightenment is best understood as an identity crisis of the Scottish elite following the trauma of the Union of Parliaments, one where the literati attempted to create a social ethic of politeness to replace direct political activity, strikes me as persuasive,[18] but with two significant caveats. Both Phillipson and Rosalind Mitchieson refer to this as a response to an identity crisis and a trauma – indeed Mitchieson (1978: 77) goes so far as to describe the Scottish obsession with improvement as having stemmed from a sense of national humiliation at the country's perceived backwardness. First, I see little evidence that the Union was traumatic for the Scottish literati. They lost nothing from it. Their social backgrounds meant that none of them would have been a part of the active polity of the old Scottish Parliament. Their elite status stemmed from their place in the Church, the universities and the law, and their decision to make their careers there did not stem from the absence of a political alternative following the Union, an alternative that would never have been open to them in any meaningful sense. Rather the Union represented an opportunity for the literati, the first real opportunity for the emergence of a genuine middle class in Scotland.[19]

Second, it seems far more likely that if there was a trauma that motivated the political thinking of the Moderates then it was the chaos of seventeenth-century Scotland's civil and religious wars and the death throes of the Stuart challenge in 1746. I want to suggest that Ferguson's interest lies in the character education of an elite officer class who would be able to secure the pragmatic management of the new British institutions. He is trying to provide the intellectual and educational apparatus that would be critical to producing the sort of gentleman able to take his place in the 'polite elite', as Alexander Broadie (2001: 88) would have it, moving the British project forward.[20] Yes, they would be patriots, but the identity that they would be patriotic about would emerge organically like all national sentiment. Ferguson was far more concerned that the right sort of person was in place to make the right decisions in the public interest. His project links a notion of moral science to the creation of a very particular training programme directed at the very specific needs of the Scottish, Hanoverian, Unionist, middle and upper classes.[21] That such a programme also spoke to posterity and to abiding moral concerns should not diminish Ferguson having worked on it at a particular time and with a particular set of commitments.

It is in the light of these personal commitments and this philosophical and educational project that we will come to better understand Ferguson's thought. Critical discussion of Ferguson tends to view him through one of four main intellectual contexts: Stoicism, Republicanism, as a forefather of sociology or as the only highlander among the main figures of the Scottish Enlightenment. Each of these readings has merit, but none in itself captures the whole of Ferguson's project, and by considering each of them in the light of our chosen approach we will come to better understand the impact that each of them has on his thinking.

Stoic

By far the most pervasive reading of Ferguson has been that he is best understood as a 'Roman' thinker, more specifically that his thinking is shaped by Roman history and Stoic philosophy. His publications, not least the *History of the Roman Republic*, bear this out. Quotations from Cicero, Marcus Aurelius and Epictetus are littered throughout his works and we will discuss these in closer detail in Chapter 4. Whatever Ferguson took from Stoicism, it must be clear to any reader that the Stoicism that he advocated was not that of the Greek Stoics with their advocacy of retirement from the world and indifference. Ferguson's Stoicism, if we can call it that, was the product of a Scottish education steeped, in particular, in Cicero.[22] Latin, and particularly Cicero, formed the backbone of the Burgh school system that Ferguson passed through (Camic 1983: 153–5), and Ferguson seems to have continued to engage with his work throughout his life. Jane Fagg (2008: 45), in her analysis of Ferguson's use of Edinburgh University Library, notes his extensive borrowing of Cicero in the 1770s, while the general outlook of the Moderate clergy has been characterised as a 'Ciceronian spirit' (Phillipson 1981: 38).

Christopher Brooke's recent study of the influence of Stoicism in early modern thought has made the case for the careful use of a notion of 'Ciceronian Stoicism' (Brooke 2012: 41–2). Brooke points out the close fit between this notion and both the natural law arguments developed by Grotius and Pufendorf and the moral philosophy developed by Shaftesbury and Hutcheson.[23] This context seems to be the most accurate way to understand Ferguson's relationship to ancient thought, as a Ciceronian rather than a Stoic.

But even with this modified version of the Stoic aspect of Ferguson's thinking in place there are still issues with placing him full-square in the Stoic tradition. The most comprehensive study of Ferguson's relationship to ancient philosophy has been undertaken by Katherine Nicolai.[24] Nicolai's central claim is that, far from being a doctrinaire Stoic, Ferguson is a modern eclectic. Modern eclectics regard the ancient schools as potential sources for ideas rather than as the locus of authority. By mixing and blending elements from different ancient schools as they appear to help us to understand the phenomena of modern life, the modern eclectics were able to place themselves within the longer tradition of philosophy, but also to remain true to the advances in modern science. This interpretation, emerging from the engagement by Pufendorf and Christian Thomasius with the history of philosophy, rests on the idea that the modern thinkers conduct their own observation-based examination of the world and draw on ancient sources as additional evidence or as a way of illustrating their own ideas.[25]

This interpretation has the virtue of being consistent with Ferguson's own self-assessment in the *Principles* (1: 7) where he denies warping the truth to fit Stoic principles. It also fits nicely with recent work on Hume and Smith which self-consciously downplays the tendencies of earlier historians of philosophy to attempt to read the Scottish Enlightenment as straightforward utilitarians, deontologists, Stoics, Epicureans or virtue theorists.[26] But it is worth stressing an additional feature of this approach that is, perhaps, best captured by Adam Smith's statement that the schools have only bordered on the truth on account of their 'partial and imperfect view of nature' (Smith 1976a: 265). An accurate account of moral experience will be based on observation, but it will also have to encapsulate the elements of truth revealed by the other, partial accounts. An accurate account of moral experience, something which for Ferguson was vital to the development of a viable normative moral philosophy, will have to incorporate, or at least account for, the truths of the other theories while going beyond them. This was clearly what Smith was doing when he added Part VII to the 1790 edition of *The Theory of Moral Sentiments*. It will be the contention of this book that Ferguson is engaged in much the same project as Smith, assessing ideas from the Schools in his pedagogical writings and showing his readers the various strengths and weaknesses that he sees in them in the light of their conformity with the lived experience of moral judgement, but that he believes his theory succeeds where Smith's fails (for more on this see the section below on Smith).

In the case of Ferguson, the eclectic reading also has the particular virtue of accounting for why so many critics have been troubled by his apparent inconsistencies.[27] In his original study of Ferguson David Kettler (2005: 124) referred to him as 'eclectic and opportunistic'. Kettler's point was that Ferguson's project was driven by the social role that he hoped his ideology would fulfil rather than by a commitment to philosophical consistency. The tensions in Ferguson's thought have been accounted for by viewing it as an 'amalgam' (Kettler 2005: 152), or a 'mosaic' or 'patchwork' (Hill 2006: 35), composed of elements drawn from distinct philosophical traditions which are then stitched together into an unstable and messy union.

However, the idea that a system of thought is inconsistent or messy because it does not fit into a preconceived notion of philosophical consistency understood as resolution into the teachings of one school of philosophy is the wrong way of looking at this. Ferguson's thought is not cherry-picking the thought of others, it is an attempt to make a consistent system while recognising the distinct, but partial, truths of other thinkers. Ferguson – and I would argue Hume and Smith – simply were not interested in doing philosophy in the monomaniacal fashion. For them eclecticism is a strength because it reflects the reality of moral experience. Ferguson's eclecticism is not supposed to sacrifice consistency for 'complementarity' (Kettler 2005: xiv) because it needs to do this to prove useful, it is trying to find a way to make what is observably the case into a consistent philosophical system. Ferguson starts from the position that the observation of moral life tells us that there are various modes of moral experience, and understanding these modes is necessary to understand what a consistent moral philosophy for human beings will look like. That philosophy is tempted to sacrifice this for the sake of consistency with a predetermined set of ideas is a failing of the philosophical method in Ferguson's view.

We can see a clear example of this in the discussion of the place of natural law in Ferguson's thought. One of the less commented on elements in Ferguson's thinking is the influence of natural law thinking (Haakonssen 1996; Forbes 1982). When Ferguson has been mentioned in the literature on the place of natural law thinking in the Scottish Enlightenment he has been placed with Hutcheson, Reid and the Moderates as working in a tradition derived from Pufendorf (Haakonssen 1996; Poovey 1998: 371 n. 42), as opposed to that derived from Grotius supposedly apparent in Hume, Smith and Millar.[28] It is worth expanding on this to get a more accurate picture of Ferguson's relationship to the jurisprudential tradition. As John Robertson points out, the general approach of the Scottish Enlightenment fits into the project of trying to find an 'empirical basis for natural law' (Robertson 1985: 75) which they inherited from the seventeenth century; but it is also the case that the approach sat particularly comfortably alongside the Christian Stoicism of the Moderates and was easily adaptable to the classroom teaching of moral philosophy.

As we will see in Chapters 5 and 6 the influence of Protestant natural law is apparent in Ferguson's conception of civilisation, but so too is that of a much older version of the method, that of Aristotle. Ferguson makes a number of allusions to Aristotle in the *Principles*, and these allusions include both discussions of his views and the use of some key concepts in Ferguson's own analysis. For example, he discusses the 'scale of Being' (*Principles* 1: 11–17) and the distinction between animals and humans in the light of Aristotle before modifying his position with argument from more recent authorities such as Buffon (*Principles* 1: 130; see also *Institutes* 13, 18–19). The teleological and perfectionist positions are also outlined using Aristotle (*Principles* 1: 17, 21, 71, 95), as is the view of virtue as a mean (*Principles* 2: 155–7), and the discussion of skill is directly Aristotelian (*Principles* 1: 227). Aristotle is a significant background influence on Ferguson precisely because of his self-conscious 'scientific' approach to the foundation of moral philosophy. Studying human nature before formulating arguments about how individuals ought to act is one of the key commitments that Ferguson makes and, to the extent that he saw Aristotle as engaged in a similar exercise, without the benefits of the modern scientific method, he recognised the similarity between their projects.[29]

The natural jurisprudence elements in Ferguson's thought are also related to the interpretation of him as inconsistent. The project of merging the languages of the civic tradition and the jurisprudential tradition is typical of the mainstream social thought of the Scottish Enlightenment.[30] Robertson (1985: 12) points out a variety of tensions between the different elements of the civic tradition and the jurisprudential tradition, not least the conflicting languages of public duty and private right. As a result, a systematic approach to moral philosophy that seeks to combine the two intellectual traditions faces the danger of introducing potentially incompatible conceptual languages. But as M. M. Goldsmith (1988: 594) pointed out, there is no reason in principle why it should be impossible for the two approaches to be reconciled in a workable practical ethics, a point made even more likely if, like Ferguson, you reject the basic argumentative form of both traditions (the social contract and the great legislator myths).

Republican

Ferguson's reputation as a 'Scots Cato' comes from his deep engagement with Rome and it has come to serve a particular interpretation of him as part of a republican tradition of thinking about politics.[31] The image of Ferguson as the 'most Machiavellian' (Pocock 1975: 499) of the Scots has been influential in many interpretations of his work. Though part of the aim of the present volume is to suggest that this has been overplayed by a focus on the *Essay* and a tendency to read him as a foil for Hume and Smith's more favourable view of commercial society, there is no getting away from the many aspects of the purported tradition which are apparent in Ferguson's thought. This observation, however, requires some serious qualification. The first has to do with whether or not it is, in any meaningful sense, one tradition. The disparate elements of republicanism and civic humanism are certainly in the air, but it is not obvious that they cohere in a helpful way. John Robertson (1985: 9–11) discusses this question and comes to the view that there are important differences of opinion leading him to adopt the more generic term of 'civic' to describe it. This point is accepted by Pocock himself in his identification of different threads of the tradition and, of especial interest for our present study, of the existence of a 'Ciceronian and Stoic' and a 'Catoian and Machiavellian' thread (Pocock 1983: 247). These threads might develop quite different responses to key political issues thus blurring the usefulness of the term and, in the case of Ferguson, placing the Scots Cato in the rival Ciceronian and Stoic thread.

The second major qualification is whether Ferguson fits comfortably with any of the lines that have been identified for the transmission of these ideas from the ancient Romans to Machiavelli and then into English thought. The usual line pointed to here is the issue of the militia and the arguments concerning it made by Harrington, Fletcher of Saltoun and others. The main issue with this view is that there is remarkably little evidence for such a chain of influence in Ferguson's case. Indeed, as we will see below, there is significantly more evidence for a line of influence coming to Ferguson from France in the person of Montesquieu or from his own direct reading of Roman history and personal experience of military life.

My aim here has not been to deny that Ferguson has concerns about commercial society, nor is it to downplay the influence of republicanism and humanist ideas on his thinking – we will return to each of these ideas later in the book. Instead, it has been to see these in a slightly different context from that which has dominated the recent literature on him. Likewise, I do not suggest that we should completely ignore the *Essay* and those passages of high rhetoric where he lauds simpler societies and their virtues, but these concerns need to be set against the other, far more frequent, if less emotionally wrought, passages where he sides fully with the modern British commercial state and with his conception of civilisation. Ferguson's interest in republican or civic humanism is not, then, backward looking, nostalgic or a 'rear-guard' (Sher 1985: 398; 1989: 244, 263–4), nor is he operating at the 'limits' (Robertson 1983) of the civic tradition. As David Allan (2006: 118) observes, he does not want to go back to the ancient republics because he saw that circumstances had changed.[32] It's also unclear whether the ideal of the republican tradition traced by Pocock in the period of the British Civil Wars ever really mapped onto the lived experience of politics at the time, or even if it did, whether Ferguson would be attracted to the sorts of thinker who would make that argument or the sort of polity they envisaged.

In Ferguson's case, it is not really so much that he feared that the civic, political ideal was losing out to a commercial, individualistic idea of the good life, rather it is that he saw in the example of Rome and in particular Cicero a vital element in a successful political order. Science and the evidence of history demonstrated that elements of the civic tradition captured something important about social life and Ferguson sets out to explore what that was and how it might be made to serve the larger goal of securing the British state.

Donald Winch (1978: 38) has suggested that Ferguson's republican ideas come, not from Machiavelli or the English thinkers who interest Pocock, but rather from another source: Montesquieu. Winch's suggestion is backed by the presence of numerous direct citations of Montesquieu in Ferguson's work, and the near total absence of direct allusions to Machiavelli (or even his source Livy).[33] Ferguson is famously fulsome in his praise of Montesquieu stating: 'When I recollect what the President Montesquieu has written, I am at a loss to tell, why I should treat of human affairs' (*Essay* 66) and even continues with a modest statement of his project of disseminating ideas, a project more appropriate for Ferguson as a man 'more on the level of ordinary men' (*Essay* 67).[34]

As we move through the following chapters the influence of Montesquieu on many of the central elements of Ferguson's thought will become obvious.[35] For the moment it is worth noting that they are methodological in the self-conscious attempt to be scientific, that they are conceptual in the use of the idea of spirit, that they are substantive as in the celebration of Britain's mixed form of government and that both thinkers are preoccupied by the lessons of the fall of the Roman republic. However, Harold Laski's jibe that Ferguson was a 'pinchbeck Montesquieu' (Laski 1920: 115–16) is also wide of the mark as Ferguson develops or enlarges on many of the points that he draws from Montesquieu and draws on more diverse sources besides.

Sociology

The deep influence of Montesquieu leads us to the next major interpretative tradition applied to Ferguson. The first major book length study of Ferguson, William Lehmann's 1930 volume, began a tradition of reading Ferguson as an influential founding father of sociology.[36] This reading sees the most interesting aspects of Ferguson's thought being those which were picked up by later thinkers. This is particularly true of his 'conflict sociology' (Hill 2001), his doubts about the division of labour (Mizuta 1981; Meek 1954) and his apparent pre-figuring of Marxist arguments about alienation (Meek 1967; Hamowy 1968; Skinner 1982; Brewer 1986; Benton 1990).[37] But it is also – and perhaps more basically – due to the early formulation of the study of society as such that forms the basis of his understanding of his own project.

Understanding Ferguson's influence on later thinkers is part of placing him in context, and understanding that he has been read in different ways at different times reveals as much about the context of the readers as it does about Ferguson. But, as we noted above, readings like this stress the elements of a thinker's work that echo and speak to his reader's own concerns. The development of sociology as a self-conscious discipline accelerated in the mid-twentieth century, and it seems natural that thinkers in both that and the Marxist tradition should seek to trace Ferguson's influence on the development of their disciplines. One obvious consequence of this for Ferguson studies has been that his concerns about commercial society have been foregrounded to an extent that may have led to a distortion of his overall views. As this study is concerned with understanding Ferguson within the context of his own academic project our focus will be on his own formulation of his ideas on society rather than how he has been read and absorbed by others. Again, I do not wish to argue that Ferguson has no concerns about commercial society, but rather that those concerns are not directly those of the sociological tradition any more than they are those of the republican tradition.

Highland

The final major interpretative approach stresses Ferguson's status as the only Highlander among the main thinkers of the Scottish Enlightenment. His Highland birth has invited a series of speculations on the degree to which this biographical detail might help explain certain elements of his thought.[38] Ferguson's scant mentions of the Highlands do not reveal a great deal. He refers to himself in a letter to James MacPherson of Ossian fame as a 'bastard Gaelic man' (*Correspondence* 2: 351; Fagg 1995: lxxi; Brewer 2007: 115; Buchan 2009: 32), in an apparent attempt to downplay his ability to act as a potential support for the authentication process for MacPherson's poems. There is no explicit discussion of the Highlands – or indeed of Scotland – in Ferguson's published work, so interpretations that dwell on this aspect of his biography are necessarily speculative.[39] Perhaps the most developed of these is Michael Fry's (2009: 22) argument that the Highlands lie 'beneath' Ferguson's philosophy. Fry's reading accepts that Ferguson may have been ambivalent about the Highlands, and was certainly averse to accepting a parish there, but that the themes of martial virtue and the sympathetic portrait of 'barbarians' and 'savages' invite such speculation. Michael Kugler (1994, 2009) goes further than Fry. In his view the Highland society with its tight bonds and martial virtue is close to an ideal for Ferguson and something which underpins his criticism of modern civilisation. This interpretation fits neatly with arguments that see Ferguson as an influential voice in the development of Romanticism, particularly German Romanticism (Merolle 2009; Oz-Salzberger 1995).

This reading has been criticised by John Brewer (2007) who argues that the Highland speculations have been overplayed. Brewer argues that the true impact of the Highland upbringing needs to be understood by way of Ferguson's status as a representative of the Protestant, Presbyterian, Hanoverian order in a part of the country where that was not the majority view and where Episcopalianism, Jacobitism and even Catholicism were widespread.[40] Ferguson and his family, despite his father's ancestry, were outsiders in the Highlands of the 1720s and 1730s.[41] The impact of a Highland childhood, Brewer persuasively argues, would have deeply affected his view of Highland culture. Jack Hill (2017: 3–10) takes up this theme in his recent study of Ferguson and argues that there is a Highland influence, but that it is not the dominant feature of his intellectual biography. Equally important, according to Hill (2017: 19), were the fact that his father was a Presbyterian minister, that he supported the Union and the Hanoverian succession and that, along with the Regality court and prison, he represented law and authority amid the wildness of the Highland scenery.

Ferguson was clearly the product of a Scottish education system and was exposed in that education to particularly Scottish intellectual traditions.[42] But this experience needs to be considered in the light of who he was, who his family were and where he ended up settling during his career. Ferguson was, as David Allan notes, 'a Hanoverian clergyman and military officer' (2006: 8), he was the son of a Calvinist minister, his friends were the Moderate literati of the Kirk who were, to a man, Unionists, Hanoverians and 'Improvers'. The key to understanding Ferguson is not that he grew up a Highlander, but that he grew up a Hanoverian in the Highlands.

The Consummate Moderate

In the analysis that follows in the rest of this book Ferguson's thought will be characterised by a set of commitments that he broadly shared with his fellow Scottish literati. Ferguson was, in a sense, addressing the same intellectual problem that faced every Whig in the eighteenth century: how to move a radical and oppositional system of thought forward once it had secured political dominance.[43] This is the project behind much of Hume's political thought, but it is, I will argue here, even more deeply embedded in Ferguson's world-view: what happens when revolutionaries become the establishment doesn't just affect the arguments used to support the Hanoverian state, but it also shapes Ferguson's wider conception of education and politics. Re-tooling the philosophical education of the new British elite was Ferguson's conscious lifelong project and it places him at the heart of the establishment.[44]

Richard Sher, in his seminal study of the Moderates, stresses the middle class and professional background, the political conservatism and the educational focus of the group. Ferguson, on this reading is best understood as part of the 'didactic tradition of Whig-Presbyterian moral philosophy' (Sher 1985: 241).[45] Thought of in this way, rather than as a foil for Hume and Smith, or a thinker exploring the outer boundaries of the civic tradition, we get a clearer view of his commitments and how they shape his intellectual agenda.[46] One caveat needs to be added to this reading. Some of those who have discussed the Scottish literati's views in this light have suggested that they are, at bottom, arguing for a form of aristocracy (Forbes 1975) or even 'nobility' (McDaniel 2013b: 155). This, I think, is a mistake. However vague the term 'middling ranks' (Berry 1997: 104) might be in its application, it is clear that Ferguson's understanding of it included the emerging middle classes like his fellow literati. A major part of this project is the creation of a system of moral philosophy which would underpin the education of the newly emerging Scottish middle class to take their place in society and understand the role expected of them.

One additional feature of Ferguson's Moderate context is worth highlighting. Ferguson's political thought has been described as a form of 'Whig-Presbyterian conservatism' (Sher 1985: 17; Hill 2006: 227), and this seems an apt characterisation of the view outlined above.[47] However, significant voices in the historiography of the period have suggested that Moderatism ossified into a form of complacent belief in the inevitability of progress that was only upset with the events of the French Revolution. In Ferguson's case I think that this reading is a mistake. As Anna Plassart (2015) has pointed out, Ferguson's politics are consistently conservative and do not change in response to events in France (an issue we will return to below). Ferguson does not become increasingly conservative with age or in response to increasingly radical forms of politics: he never had any time for that sort of thing. His reputation for pessimism about commercial society arises, I will suggest, from a career-long recognition of the fragility of the British settlement and indeed the fragility of civilisation itself. Ferguson's thought is directed at developing solutions to the problem of fragility.[48] If, in the common eighteenth-century image, the British constitution is a balance, then it needs to be understood as a balance that could easily be upset. Ferguson saw his task as finding ways of ensuring the stability of the British social and political order, and he maintains this project from his earliest publication to his final letters.

This also, in part, helps to explain why Ferguson has been read among the founding fathers of liberalism (Kalyvas and Katznelson 1998, 2008; Hill 2006). Readers who take this view, such as Hayek (1967) and Hamowy (1987, 2005), stress that Ferguson's contribution to the development of liberalism lies in his work on the ideas of unintended consequences and gradualism – ideas shared by classical liberalism and British conservatism through the shared influence of Edmund Burke. I have discussed Ferguson's place in this tradition elsewhere (Smith 2006), but it is worth pointing out in this context that Ferguson's conservatism is a Whig conservatism. His is not the sort of directionless conservatism criticised by Hayek (1960); instead, he wants to conserve a political system that provides stability after a long period of political upheaval, but which, at the same time, represents a system which defends a particular conception of liberty and civilisation.

Ferguson's Life

A brief survey of Ferguson's biography will help to underline this description of his commitments. The details of Ferguson's career show us a picture of a consummate member of the Scottish Enlightenment, an ambitious, Moderate, middle-class intellectual and public servant. Adam Ferguson was born in 1723 at Logierait in Perthshire. Son of the Reverend Adam Fergusson, the minister of the parish, Ferguson junior was the product of a family descended from minor gentry and distantly connected to two of Scotland's most influential families (the Houses of Argyle and Gordon). He was raised in genteel poverty, part of a large and devout Presbyterian family. The young Adam was educated at the parish school before attending Perth Grammar school (from 1732) and St Andrews University (from 1738). Ferguson's early education followed the classic template for the Scotland of his day with the school education providing a deep foundation in the classics and the undergraduate study adding more advanced Latin and Greek together with mathematics, moral philosophy and natural philosophy along the traditional Scottish generalist lines. Ferguson appears to have been destined to follow his father into the Church and began divinity studies at St Andrews before moving to Edinburgh in 1742.

At Edinburgh Ferguson found himself among a group of young scholars who would go on to form the backbone of the Scottish Enlightenment and the Moderate literati: William Robertson, Alexander Carlyle, Hugh Blair and others studied alongside him; Joseph Black was a cousin; and Adam Smith and David Hume would become friends. By the time Ferguson's ordination was rushed through, under the patronage of the Duchess of Atholl so that he could accept the offer of the chaplaincy to the newly raised Highland regiment (the Black Watch), he was already integrated into the social network that would become the Scottish Establishment. Ferguson spent the years 1745 to 1754 in the army and served in Flanders, Ireland, England and France (the Highland Regiment was deliberately kept away from the restless Highlands). We have no detailed evidence of how much engagement Ferguson actually experienced (the story of his leading the Charge at Fontenoy being sadly apocryphal), but the early military experience seems to have had a deep impact on his thinking.

By 1756 Ferguson was back in Edinburgh and spent the next few, very lean, years in search of a permanent position. At this time it seems his friends despaired of him settling in one place. He made some desultory attempts to find a parish before he turned his attention from the ministry to other potential career paths, taking on Hume's old position as Librarian of the Faculty of Advocates, a position he soon left to serve as a tutor to Lord Bute's sons.[49] He finally secured a measure of stability when he became the unlikely choice for Professor of Natural Philosophy at the University of Edinburgh in 1759, a position he dedicated himself to with some success until the Chair of Pneumatics and Moral Philosophy became vacant in 1764. Ferguson then embarked on a professorial career that saw him become one of the most influential and popular teachers in Scotland. His publications from this period – the *Analysis* (1766), the *Essay* (1767) and the *Institutes* (1769) – built his literary reputation.

During his time in Edinburgh Ferguson was a central figure in the literati clubs, playing a particular role in the Poker Club established to advocate for a Scottish Militia (a near life-long obsession of Ferguson's). He was involved in politics and in Church politics, serving in the General Assembly of the Church of Scotland on several occasions.[50] He was an active participant in various pamphlet wars including the Douglas controversy, the militia debate, the American crisis and the controversies around Ossian, and generally acted as a supporter of the established social and political order.

Biographies of Ferguson frequently mention his home at Sciennes which became known as Kamchatka for its distance from the homes of his friends and their favoured taverns (though the nickname was also perhaps a reference to both Ferguson's stinginess in heating the property and his famous adoption of heavy fur clothing in the aftermath of his stroke). But Ferguson only moved to Sciennes in 1786. Prior to this he spent most of his married life in Argyle Square: this puts him far closer to the heart of Edinburgh's social life, and though he may have spent vacations at his farm at Bankhead in Lothian, he seems to have been deeply embedded in the life of enlightened Edinburgh.

His time in the moral philosophy chair was interrupted twice: in 1774–5 he spent time as a tutor to the Earl of Chesterfield at Geneva and London, while in 1778–9 he was in America as secretary to the Carlisle Commission.[51] The later years of his professorship were taken up in writing *The History of the Progress and Termination of the Roman Republic* (1783) which, though its reputation has since been eclipsed, was a standard history of the period and admired by both Gibbon and the young John Stuart Mill. He retired from active teaching in 1785 to take the nominal post of Professor of Mathematics, relying on a proxy to cover teaching duties. His retirement was spent exercising his interest in scientific agriculture, developed during his long tenancy at Bankhead, first at Niedpath castle (1795–6) and then Hallyards (1796–1809), and working on the final statement of his lecture course which appeared in 1792 as the *Principles of Moral and Political Science*. Ferguson spent his last years in St Andrews where he died in 1816.

Almost every source we have which talks about Ferguson's personality points to the same outstanding features: that while he had the air and manners of a gentleman he was quick tempered and argumentative, that he was prone to 'fits of impatient restlessness' (Fagg 1995: xxxiii), that he was ambitious (seeking to become Principal of Edinburgh University in 1762 and Governor of West Florida in 1766) and careful with money, that he could appear prickly and thin-skinned because he was careful of his reputation and precious of his integrity to the point of bloody-mindedness, and that he was devoted to his family and friends. The apparent stroke that he suffered in 1781 does not appear to have slowed him down – indeed twelve years later at the age of seventy he embarked on a trip through Europe to Italy, and he continued even in near blindness and great old age to maintain an interest in affairs as his daughters read the latest news to him. He married late and had a large family. Much of his later correspondence is a record of his attempts to use his influence in the patronage networks that dominated Scottish life to secure positions for his sons (Adam, Joseph, James and John). These letters are revealing because they show the extent to which Ferguson understood his own lifestyle to be precarious. Ferguson was never a wealthy man, but he was secure and able to live what, for the time, was a respectable upper-middle-class lifestyle. That his early life was characterised by financial insecurity was perhaps something that always stayed with him. His life was that of a man who was ambitious, and who wanted to have a career, but it was also the life of someone who knew how the world worked and what had to be done to secure one's place in the established order. He was a man who recognised the reality of the world he lived in and the need for a man to find a place in which he was able to provide for his family and play his part in society. Ferguson served the government interest as a pamphleteer, electioneer and diplomat. While militia advocacy was his clearest political commitment, he was always careful to ensure that his advocacy of this cause was not mistaken for opposition to the established government or constitutional settlement.

There has recently been some attention paid to Ferguson's views on the French Revolution (Fagg 1995; Kettler 2005; Plassart 2015; McDaniel 2013b). This is understandable as Ferguson's long life means that he was one of the few members of the main generation of the literati who was still active enough to record his response. Some surprise has been expressed at the mildness of Ferguson's response to the Revolution and the puzzle of why he was not more against it. As Jane Fagg (1995: lxxxii–lxxxiii) points out he only seems to disapprove of it to the extent that it threatens a war that threatens British interests. But the deeper issue may not even be that, for by the time of the *Principles* in 1792 and the later correspondence on the rise of Napoleon, Ferguson is clear in his general view on the revolution as a matter for the French except in so far as it threatened British interests. This need not be too much of a puzzle, for despite his conservatism and general distrust of radical reform, Ferguson was underneath it all a Whig – a conservative Whig, but a Whig nonetheless. His worries are not about the fate of France, but about how that fate affects the balance of power in Europe and, though with far less urgency than some contemporaries, whether the example of the French Revolution would strike inspiration at home.

Ferguson's modern biographer Jane Fagg (1995: xxxii) has suggested that his restlessness led him to participate beyond the academy, but that this participation was at the expense of his scholarly efforts. While there may well be an element of truth to this, it is a truth that is revealing about Ferguson's attitude to the academy. As we will see, Ferguson possessed a very particular vision of what the learned should do. In particular, his view of the role of the philosopher was one that stressed active engagement and practical usefulness. Moreover, he stressed the idea that the skills necessary for a successful life were to be acquired in active participation, so the idea of scholarly retreat was anathema to his notion of the role of the philosopher.

Ferguson and the Scottish Enlightenment

At this point it is worth making some observations about Ferguson's relationship to the established views in the Scottish moral philosophy of the time. Ferguson's most obvious debt is to Francis Hutcheson.[52] Hutcheson's blending of elements from the thought of Cicero with parts of the natural law tradition and the ethic of politeness from Shaftesbury has obvious echoes in Ferguson's own thought. It is also significant that when Ferguson came to set up his own lecture course in Edinburgh the dominant models of how to do this would have been those of Hutcheson (in his published *System of Moral Philosophy*) and Ferguson's own teacher William Cleghorn. The structure of Ferguson's lecture programme appears to be even closer to that of Hutcheson than the Glasgow curriculum adopted by Adam Smith.[53]

There are, however, some major differences between Ferguson and Hutcheson. First, Ferguson's political philosophy may appear close to Hutcheson in its conclusions, but they differ radically when it comes to method. Ferguson utterly rejects the idea of contractualism, a central element of Hutcheson's Whiggery. Second, on an even more fundamental level, Ferguson does not see much to be gained by conducting the subsequent examination into moral judgement in terms of a moral sense akin to that of Hutcheson.[54] Ferguson's worry is that by referring to the moral faculty as a 'sense' we are led to a common mistake – the mistake of regarding normative moral philosophy as reducible to philosophy of mind. Ferguson is not really interested in going deeper into the link between philosophy of mind and moral judgement. There is no real point in arguing about the term moral sense if we accept that moral judgement is a fact. There is more to moral judgement than a psychological description and, moreover, there is only so far that philosophy of mind can penetrate before becoming pure speculation. Instead we should accept the fact of moral judgement as a principle of science that cannot itself be explained and build on that following the success of Newton's method on gravitation.[55]

Like his contemporaries Ferguson saw himself as developing a scientific approach to the study of moral subjects. His conception of science is broadly conventional, a blend of Bacon, Newton and in Ferguson's case overtones of Aristotle and Buffon.[56] It was no doubt bolstered by his time in the natural philosophy chair at Edinburgh, and the published content of his lecture outline suggests a particular reliance on experimental examples to illustrate his principles which fits soundly with the approach being developed across the Scottish universities at the time.

Despite the background influence of Aristotle on his overall project, the destruction of the scholastic system by modern scientific methods was enthusiastically accepted by Ferguson, and his decision to base moral philosophy on empirical moral science involves abandoning the search for primary causes in physiology. We must settle for considering things as 'fundamental in nature' (*Principles* 1: 76) and building on them. The mode of his argumentation here bears affinities with Thomas Reid. While it may be an exaggeration to call him a common-sense philosopher along with Reid and the Aberdeen coterie, he is nonetheless a professed realist and committed empiricist.[57] On the key issues of perception (*Institutes* 45, 49–50; *Principles* 1: 86), belief in testimony (*Principles* 1: 83–5, 91; *Institutes* 124; *Analysis*: 15), ordinary language (*Principles* 1: 82, 84) and rejection of scepticism and the theory of ideas (*Institutes* 50–4; *Principles* 1: 75), Ferguson adopts positions nearly identical to Reid or directly derived from him.[58]

For Ferguson there is simply no reason to doubt the validity of the information provided by our senses. As with the rejection of the moral sense, Ferguson's worry is that the course of philosophy can be misdirected by the adoption of a conceptual language which promises access to knowledge of the deep operation of the human mind. Once we set off down this path, no matter how deeply committed to empiricism, we open the door to conjecture and, ultimately, to a pointless scepticism. But as dependent as Ferguson appears to be on Reid, he also develops these basic positions in a very particular direction. He is quick to separate out what he sees as two distinct areas of philosophical enquiry: enquiry into the operation of the human judgement and enquiry into the content of morals. As he puts it as early as the *Institutes* (and thus presumably only influenced by Reid's *Inquiry* which was published in 1764):

> In consequence of this vague use of the term moral, any theoretical question relating to mind has been substituted for moral philosophy; and speculations of little moment have supplanted the study of what men ought to be, and of what they ought to wish, for themselves, and for their country. (*Institutes* 84)

This latter task – what men ought to wish – is the subject matter of moral philosophy for Ferguson.

What humans do blame is different from what they ought to blame and 'the subject of morality has been greatly perplexed by the blending of these two questions together' (*Institutes* 109).[59] Ferguson's point is that moral science as a distinct activity can provide us with a history of moral opinions and with an account of human nature which will serve as the basis for a moral philosophy of what a creature such as man should be. The facts of what is done do not prevent us from choosing what is better. The combination of moral science with moral philosophy will allow us to pursue the good while avoiding potential errors of opinion in morals. In Ferguson's view this is one place where ancient philosophy has the advantage over modern philosophy. While modern philosophy has correctly adopted the scientific technique as a secure means of enquiry, it has gone astray in jettisoning some of the old ideas such as that of a *summum bonum* and a systematic normative framework of morality that flows from it. The problem with the search for a *summum bonum* was not so much the very idea of such, but the method by which ancient philosophy sought to find the ultimate good.

Ferguson consistently argues that moral philosophy involves finding a standard against which to judge men. Moral science provides us with a secure basis upon which to moralise only if it is based on careful observation:

> As observation is the first voluntary effort of our distinctive nature, the defect of it is likely to mar the advantages to be reaped from thence: – If we overlook in the objects around us, the circumstances in which they concern us, if we are ignorant of their consequences, and thus unprepared for the scene in which we are destined to act, our lives are likely to be a series of error, folly, and disappointment. (*Principles* 1: 94)

This is vitally important because Ferguson believes that humans are capable of moral reflection and of reforming their views. Our character, in his view, can be shaped by clear reflection grounded on knowledge of human nature as it has been lived. 'It is not in vain, therefore, that man is endowed with a power of discerning what is amiss or defective in the actual state of his own inclinations or faculties.' Man may be 'formed by himself' (*Principles* 1:

225). The combined task of moral science and moral philosophy is for man: 'To know himself, and his place in the system of nature' (*Principles* 1: 306). This core methodological commitment is important to grasp because Ferguson seems to have developed it in response to the moral philosophy of two of his closest friends, David Hume and Adam Smith. In setting up the discussion of his objections to Hume and Smith he argues that they are both guilty of a mistake which stems from the structure of their philosophical method.

Hume

While the details of Ferguson's critique of Hume's scepticism broadly follow the Reidian position, the lessons which he draws from this become the basis of one of his key methodological assumptions.[60] According to Ferguson, Hume is guilty of two main errors in his moral philosophy. The first of these mirrors the point above about confusing descriptive philosophy of mind and prescriptive moral philosophy. Hume's scepticism is a product of his commitment to the theory of ideas and when he comes to admit that his scepticism bears little relation to ordinary life he ought, in Ferguson's view, to have concluded that there was an error somewhere in his argument.

> The Sceptic, indeed, sometimes affects to distinguish the provinces of speculation and of action. While, in speculation, he questions the evidence of sense; in practice, he admits it with the most perfect confidence: But speculations in science are surely of little account, if they have not any relation to subjects of actual choice and pursuit; and if they do not prepare the mind for the discernment of matters, relating to which there is actual occasion to decide, and to act, in the conduct of human life. (*Principles* 1: 91)[61]

The charge is that Hume, despite his commitment to the experimental method, has allowed his philosophy to become detached from reality, though we should also be clear that Hume himself was well aware of this feature of his thinking, and indeed his scepticism is always mitigated by the fact that he acknowledges that it has little effect on the ordinary course of life. What is interesting from our point of view is that Ferguson, while criticising Hume on this point and seeking to retain the hope of detailed and reliable philosophical enquiry, is also aware of the benefits of scepticism within certain bounds. It is one of the benefits of scepticism that it keeps the claims of philosophy modest and realistic.

The second charge is levelled by Ferguson against both Hume and Adam Smith, and that is that they have both failed to provide an adequate account of moral judgement because they have both sought to redescribe a complex phenomenon under a single principle. In the *Discourse on Moral Estimation* Ferguson argues that they are guilty of 'tending to explain away distinctions of the utmost importance to mankind turning zeal for morality into a mere selfish Intent or into a mere Coincidence of sentiment which may take place among Knaves and Fools as well as honest Men' (*Manuscripts* 64).

This is especially interesting as he sees both Hume and Smith as having levelled the same objection to Clarke's moral theory which they regard as 'unfit to explain the phenomenon of moral approbation' (*Principles* 2: 117). Hume and Smith are, according to Ferguson, guilty of mistaking descriptive philosophy of mind for prescriptive moral philosophy, of being content with the identification of an explanatory principle rather than a principle to guide judgement. However, this problem is compounded by another, and that is that both Hume and Smith have identified a principle that fails as an explanation of moral experience.

Ferguson's criticism of Hume depends upon the meta-level argument that he is substituting utility for 'its constituents' leading us to 'risk misleading the mind from its principal object' (*Principles* 2: 121). Hume's account of the development of moral belief leaves out too many universally recognised aspects of that experience, such as the urge to judge a person's character and actions in terms of merit and demerit arising prior to any concern about the usefulness of the action. Hume's division into agreeable and useful behaviours thus becomes an unnecessary complication that does not accurately track moral judgement. In an extended discussion in *Principles* 2 (118–20; see also 25), Ferguson offers a range of objections to reducing morality to utility. Among these are: that we approve of things that have no private or public utility, that we approve of past actions which can have no present utility, that utility neglects intentions and focuses on external and observable consequences and the fact that we admire attempts to do well that are frustrated or fail. And it is here that we see where Ferguson wants to take this argument. Ferguson's point is that it is benevolence that is the source of our moral approbation of individual actions. What follows, though ostensibly a discussion of Hume is, in fact, an attempt to clarify the disparate elements of benevolence and utility that appear in Hutcheson's work.[62] Benevolence, not utility, is a candidate for the *summum bonum* and Ferguson's sparring with Hume here is one of the ways in which he approaches the central assertion of his moral philosophy.[63]

Hume also appears in two late essays, with his views on utility being addressed in the *Country Walk Discourse* (*Manuscripts* 53); this is interesting because it shows not only that the argument continued to preoccupy Ferguson, but also because a whole series of the later essays deal with happiness, benevolence and utility and how they might be distinguished from each other, identified for what they are and related to other aspects of moral experience.

Smith

In many respects Ferguson is similar to Adam Smith in the overall methodology that he adopts.[64] Both are eclectic, observational and basically empirical in their approach to moral psychology. *The Theory of Moral Sentiments*, like much of Ferguson's work, accepts the reality that there are distinct and possibly conflicting elements to how humans think about morality. The difference is in the response to this fact adopted by either thinker. Ferguson's main – and repeated – criticism of Smith is that sympathy cannot account for all moral experience. While Ferguson is happy to admit to the role of sentiment and sympathy in moral experience (*Principles* 1: 125; 2: 17), to borrow the Smithian imagery of society as a mirror (*Principles* 2: 92), and of the central importance of the distinction between praise and praiseworthiness for the development of conscience to illustrate his account of socialisation (*Principles* 2: 92–3), he is unwilling to accept sympathy as a master principle. Of course, the problem with this is that sympathy is not a normative master principle for Smith. It is not the *summum bonum* that gives the content of morality but rather the psychological explanation of how we undertake moral judgement. And here Ferguson falls back on the original meta-level criticism that Hume and Smith mistake explanatory philosophy of mind for moral philosophy.[65] What is particularly curious about this line of attack is that in the *Institutes*

(115) Ferguson cites Smith's *Theory of Moral Sentiments* with approval precisely because Smith's approach involves criticising theories that seek to reduce morality to one principle.

Ferguson raises a series of objections to Smith's account of sympathy (*Principles* 2: 123–6), not all of which are particularly convincing. He begins by adopting a similar strategy to that apparent in his criticism of Hume, that sympathy misses some important element of moral judgement.

> There is sympathy, as well as utility, without approbation; and there is approbation without either; for we sometimes have an idea of what we ought to have done, or to have felt, as very different from the part we actually take in the feelings of other men. (*Principles* 2: 125)

Indeed it is precisely on those occasions where we know we would not be able to act in that way that we most admire heroic actions. This leads Ferguson to accuse Smith of violating Newton's principles because he provides a more convoluted rather than a simpler account of moral judgement.

Another set of objections revolve around the fact that sentimentalism in general is too arbitrary to form the basis of morality. In the *Principles* he asks us what happens when two people are in sympathy, but the rest of the world disagrees: 'in what manner is that sympathy itself evinced to be right' (*Principles* 2: 124)? There is no external standard provided beyond the potentially accidental concurrence of the sentiments of individuals.[66] This leads Ferguson to the view that Smith is being led astray by his commitment to providing a descriptive theory.[67] Sympathy is 'by no means a safe or an adequate principle of estimation' (*Principles* 2: 126). It tends to produce a circular theory which fails to provide a reliable criterion of morality for moral philosophy:

> If sympathy is admitted as the principle of moral estimation, it is evident that we admit, as a standard of good, what may itself, on occasion, be erroneous and evil, or what ought not to be esteemed beyond what is just and proper; limits which presuppose that there is a prior standard of moral estimation, by which even the rectitude of sympathy itself is to be judged. (*Principles* 1: 162)

Smith compounds this with his introduction of the impartial spectator which Ferguson describes as little more than admitting that what is morally virtuous is what a morally virtuous man would approve of as morally virtuous.

Conclusion

In a sense, all of the main interpretations of Ferguson are partly in the right – Ferguson is a product of Scottish, British, European, modern and ancient influences. He can't help but be that, and the stress of each critical interpretation argues the case for the importance of their favoured aspect. Reading Ferguson as part of a school, whether civic humanist or republican or Stoic obscures other elements of his thought, the natural jurisprudential or the early modern scientific for example, just as picking some elements of his biography, his Highland birth rather than his Edinburgh adulthood, can create a false impression of biographical determinism which foregrounds some aspects of his thinking. Similarly, reading him as a step on the way to romanticism, sociology, Marxism or liberalism illuminates some facets at the expense of obscuring others.

As should now be apparent the interpretation offered here is in part an attempt to correct the tendency to read Ferguson as in some important way a critic or opponent of commercial modernity. That he saw problems with the society around him is not in dispute, but the problems that he saw came with proposals for how they might be avoided or ameliorated. Ferguson did not want to go back to some earlier era, not even to Republican Rome or Sparta as is often supposed. The question that preoccupied him was how to deal with contemporary problems. And this preoccupied him precisely because he was trying to provide a useful education to the people who would have to deal with them. Ferguson's overarching aim, if such he ever had, was the preservation of the British commercial state and the benefits of stability and wealth which came with it. Times change, circumstances change and societies change with them. Ferguson's deep appreciation of history and of the unpredictable and spontaneous nature of social change predisposed him to the view that the best way to preserve a state was to educate its leading citizens in such a way as to provide them with the tools to adapt and preserve the state in reaction to change. In doing so Ferguson brings together a series of influences and it is not in the domination of one of these, but in their deliberate combination, undertaken with an eye to the problems he identified, that we find a more comprehensive view of his philosophy. By placing Ferguson in the mainstream of the Scottish Enlightenment, by understanding his system of moral philosophy as a whole, by dethroning the *Essay* from its privileged position and by looking at Ferguson on his own terms rather than as a foil for Smith and Hume or an anticipation of Marx, we have a very different view of him.

Before we move on to our discussion of the elements of Ferguson's moral science it is important to point out something about the critical terminology used here. Ferguson himself, as was common for the period, uses the terms science and philosophy interchangeably, but for the sake of analytical clarity I have instead adopted a tripartite distinction which seeks to emphasise the distinct and interconnected elements of Ferguson's overall method. The chief reason for this mode of presentation should become apparent as we go along: it is that some of the confusion in Ferguson's thought comes from his shifting use of conceptual vocabulary through his works. If we aim to get a more solid purchase on what, conceptually, is going on, we need to impose a certain order on Ferguson's prose. In doing so I am not distorting, or even reconstructing Ferguson's methodology – rather I am pulling out distinct elements of it that the reader might better understand the operation of the whole. Ferguson's system has three main elements that operate together and each of them will be covered in a chapter. What I refer to as moral science is the identification of the different elements which are, in fact, related to human moral experience, the study of how they do in fact interact through the study of self, society and history. What I call moral philosophy is the normative application of this to arguments about how human beings ought to act. Moral science informs moral philosophy because it provides us with reliable systematic knowledge of what human beings are and how they interact in society. Finally, what I call moral education is the application of moral science and moral philosophy in a practical pedagogy which prepares the student and reader for practical moral decision-making. In the rest of the book I will spend three chapters outlining the three elements of Ferguson's approach before using this model of his overall approach to understand his discussion of civilisation, civil society and commerce in the remaining two chapters.

Notes

1. For readings that approach Ferguson through a comparison with Hume and Smith on commerce see Winch (1978: 175) and Sher (1985: 237; 1994: 394–8); for approaches that compare Ferguson to Hume and Smith in terms of philosophical sophistication see Graham (2013: 512–13). The idea that Ferguson's thought is characterised by tensions and contradictions has a long pedigree. Leslie Stephen (1902 v. II: 215) described him as 'a facile and dexterous declaimer whose rhetoric glides over the surface of things without biting into their substance. He expounds well till he comes to the real difficulty, and then he placidly evades the dilemma.' For considerations of the tensions, paradoxes, contradictions or inconsistencies in Ferguson's thought more generally see: Fagg (1968: 104), Hill (2006: 27, 40; 2009: 107–8), Camic (1983: 55), Allan (2006: 1), Forbes (1967a: xix) and Elazar (2014: 772). Some others are more euphemistic in making the same point – see, for example, Ronald Meek's description of the *Essay* as 'provocatively complex' (1976: 150). David Kettler expends a great deal of effort in an attempt to dispel the 'wobble of improvisation' (Kettler 2005: xv) that he believes characterises many of Ferguson's arguments and attempts to patch up the tensions between different parts of his thinking.

2. Katherine Nicolai (2011: 175) and David Kettler (2005: 153) are correct to suggest that Ferguson maintains what is basically a consistent position on the essential elements of his thought from the beginning to the end of his professional life. This study is not primarily a developmental one that traces Ferguson changing his mind. The differences that appear in his various writings are differences of expression and of emphasis rather than a move from youthful to mature positions. In their respective books Lisa Hill states that her aim is to 'organise and arrange these pieces more systematically and to counter claims that his thought lacks any system' (2006: 33) while Kettler (2005: 290) describes his approach as 'an attempt to reconstruct the logic of Ferguson's situation and to assess both his orientation and his role in the light of such a reconstruction.'

3. Perhaps the starkest example of the impact that the changed nature of philosophy has had on Ferguson's reputation is Roy Sorenson's (2002) confession of his ignorance of Ferguson until he stumbled across his grave. But even here Sorenson moves his discussion swiftly onto Hume and Smith and deeper questions of exclusion from the canon.

4. Kettler adopts a reading of Ferguson based on 'complementarity' (2005: xv) which he derives from his reading of Ferguson as primarily an intellectual creating an ideology from building blocks drawn from other thinkers. The resulting system is not particularly elegant in a theoretical sense, but it manages to do the job Ferguson expects of it.

5. For a criticism of this view see Kugler (2017) who cautions against displacing the *Essay* from its place in our understanding of Ferguson's intellectual development.

6. Among the many civic or republican readings of Ferguson are Robertson (1985), Sher (1989) and Sebastiani (2011, 2013: 50). Berry (2013: 154) is more sceptical and argues that while Ferguson is sympathetic to republicanism, he does not subscribe to it in detail as he displays no nostalgia for past glories. This view is shared by McDaniel (2013a: 11) who believes that Ferguson is actually a critic of eighteenth-century republicanism.

7. For example, J. G. A. Pocock's (1975, 1999) discussions of Ferguson focus almost entirely on the *Essay*. Examples of Ferguson being discussed as a foil for Hume and Smith include Arbo (2011), McDowell (1983), Sher (1989) and Berry (1994: 147 n. 3).

8. For examples of the reading of Ferguson as a sceptic on commerce (when held up next to Hume and Smith) see Sher who read Ferguson as providing a 'rear-guard civic moralism' (1994: 398), Forbes (1966: xiv–xv; 1967: 44) who argues that Ferguson doubts the notion of progress, and Allan (2006: 68) who suggests that Ferguson shows 'a substantially greater degree of ambivalence than most of his immediate Scottish circle'. Kettler (1977: 439) and Hill (1997: 683) both regard the situation as more complex than simplistic optimist versus pessimist readings, while Plassart (2015: 125) argues that Ferguson was generally positive about commercial society but at the same time saw it as greatly flawed.

9. This point has been raised by, among others, Camic (1983: 55–6), Nicolai (2014: 200) and Bello (2017: 13–14).

10. Perhaps the most obvious example of a similar systematic partial reading can be found in Hume studies, where the interest of contemporary philosophers in certain arguments from the *Treatise* have hindered attempts to understand Hume's work as a whole – a tendency that has only recently been redressed in the literature. See Harris (2015).

11. The *Essay* was clearly received as a didactic and moralising piece. Lord Kames wrote to Mrs Montagu in 1767 that the aim of the

Essay was to 'wean us from selfishness and luxury, the reigning characteristics at present of all commercial nations, and to restore the
manly passions of heroism, generosity, and love of our species. The
aim is noble; but the disease, I doubt, is too far advanced to be cured
by any characters that can be formed with ink' (*Correspondence* 2:
546).

12. A point noted by Pocock (1999: 330), who places it in the genre of
'moral essay'.

13. Recent work on books and readership in the Scottish Enlightenment
have made a convincing case that authors and publishers were well
aware of the impact of various different styles of presenting their
material to their readers (Phillips 2000; Sher 2006; Allan 2008;
Towsey 2010). This suggests that Ferguson was aware of the style of
the piece when he chose to call it 'An Essay'.

14. David Allan (2008: 24) has noted that appreciation of Ferguson's
body of work has fared particularly badly on this front.

15. This represents a different tripartite division from that recently
adopted by Jack Hill (2017: 53) who divides his analysis into physical
science, moral science and moral discipline.

16. A point made variously by Murdoch (1980) and Camic (1983).

17. See, for example, Simpson (1988), O'Brien (1997) and Allan (1998).

18. A view shared by Kugler (1996; 2009: 128–9) and Moore (2005).

19. Ferguson clearly identifies himself with Scotland and the Scottish
interest in a number of places (*Correspondence* 1: 146) but he
sees no contradiction between this and loyalty to Great Britain
(*Correspondence* 1: 108). Lisa Hill's (2006: 10) speculation that
Ferguson was 'resigned' to the Union is based on no real evidence
other than an assumption, one shared by John Robertson who does
not draw the same conclusion, that Fletcher of Saltoun was a significant influence on Ferguson's thought. Similarly, Richard Sher's
contention that a tension exists between Scottish nationalism and
British patriotism in the first edition of his book (1985: 17–18) is
misplaced as the Scottish interest could easily be advanced with
the British system – the phenomenon of unionist nationalism later
developed by Walter Scott arguably became the dominant political
position in Scotland for most of the nineteenth and twentieth centuries. Sher's later argument that Scottish nationalism can be identified in the debate over Ossian and the promotion of John Home's
Douglas (Sher 1982) also seems wide of the mark. In both of these
cases the Scottish interest is being advanced within Great Britain not
against it. The sentiments of cultural Scottishness at no point lead

any of the literati to consider political independence for Scotland. Part of the issue with both of these errors is that they arise from an assumption that nationalism as a political phenomenon exists in any meaningful sense at that time. National sentiment, as Ferguson clearly knew, existed, but the emergence of a contemporary concept of nationalism post-dates the eighteenth century. For a discussion of the impact of twentieth-century Scottish nationalism on the study of the Enlightenment see Wood (2015b).

20. The use of gentleman here is quite deliberate. Silivia Sebastiani (2013: 146) rightly notes that Ferguson's conception of politics is entirely masculine and that Ferguson appears almost entirely uninterested in the status of women. It is worth noting though that Ferguson provides no argument or justification for this, it is simply one of his basic assumptions. To underline this aspect of his thought I will deploy the masculine as a generic throughout. For discussion of the role of gender in the Scottish Enlightenment see O'Brien (1997, 2009), Moran (2000), Rendall (2008) and Sebastiani (2013).

21. Fania Oz-Salzberger (2003: 168) has characterised Ferguson as a mixture of 'neo-Roman' and 'adamant Whig'.

22. Ferguson has been read as a 'Christian Stoic' (Sher 1985: 176) or as a purveyor of 'naïve stoicism' (Raynor 2009: 51) or 'liberal-Stoicism' (Hill 2009: 107). Fania Oz-Salzberger (2008: 154; 216 n. 48) refers to this as Ferguson's 'Ciceronian mindset'. Allan (2006: 22–4) makes a similar point about the active nature of Ferguson's thought and the influence of Cicero.

23. The identification of this chain of influences underpins the reading of Ferguson as a Christian Stoic. For a discussion of this see Kugler (2009: 126) and Skjönsberg (2017: 8). Jack Hill (2017: 174) offers a more sceptical reading of this as he notes that there is little trace of orthodox Christianity in Ferguson's work after the *Sermon*.

24. Matthew Arbo (2014: 102) and Jack Hill (2017: 174) have both raised doubts about the usefulness of reading Ferguson as a Stoic. Making a more general point Christopher Berry (2004: 457) has suggested that stoicism was so pervasive in the early modern period that unpicking its influence on the overall thought of the period would be next to impossible.

25. Nicolai (2011: 109) points out that Ferguson's experience in Natural Philosophy would have made this approach familiar to him.

26. See, for example, Garrett and Hanley (2015) or Garrett (2014).

27. See, for example, Knud Haakonssen (1996: 7).
28. Fania Oz-Salzberger (1995: xiii) makes the case for the influence of both Grotius and Pufendorf.
29. For a discussion of Aristotle's influence on Book 1 of the *Principles* see Hill (2017: 103 n. 37).
30. See Berry (1997), Plassart (2015: 8–9); Kalyvas and Katznelson (1998: 174), Skjönsberg (2017: 28).
31. See Nicolai (2011: 30) for a discussion of the coining of this description by Lorimer.
32. A view shared by Anna Plassart (2015: 145–51) who reads Ferguson as part of the republican tradition, but as free of nostalgia.
33. References to Montesquieu in Ferguson's work include: Montesquieu listed with Harris, Hutcheson and Shaftesbury in relation to scepticism (*Principles* 1: 8); Montesquieu and Mandeville sharing the view that 'whoever would govern mankind' should shape 'their conception of what is excellent' (*Principles* 2: 2); citing natural sociability as the basis of politics (*Institutes* 41; *Essay* 21), the forms of government including the distinction between monarchy and despotism (*Institutes* 43–5; *Essay* 252) and the virtue of mixed constitutions (*Price* 10; *Rome* 418); citing *Spirit of the Laws*, Book 1, on the distinction between the laws of the intellectual system and the physical system with both understood as natural but law as an object of choice implies discretion (*Institutes* 81); on political law (*Institutes* 282); on comparing constitutions (*Institutes* 296); cited as support for the rejection of arbitrary government (*Institutes* 318); quoting Persian Letters (*Essay* 42); quoting Montesquieu on Rome (*Essay* 83, 145; *Rome* 13, 20); criticising Richard Price's reading of Montesquieu's conception of civil liberty (*Price* 4, 5, 8, 9); citing Montesquieu approvingly (*Manuscripts* 62, 111).
34. In his biographical sketch of Joseph Black (102–3) Ferguson refers to a family connection between the Blacks, who resided in Bordeaux and were in the wine trade, and Montesquieu.
35. For discussions of the relationship between Ferguson and Montesquieu see Lehman (1930: 142, 185–8), Chitnis (1976: 95), Sher (1994), Mason (1988), Moore (2009) and most prominently Broadie (2012).
36. For other examples of the approach see Bryson (1945), Benton (1990), MacRae (1969), Swingewood (1970), Kettler (2005) and Brewer (1986, 1989, 2007). For a sceptical view see Forbes (1982: 193) who argues that much needs to be added to Ferguson's thought before anything recognisably like modern sociology becomes

apparent. Lisa Hill (2007) and Jack Hill (2013) are similarly sceptical of Marx's reading of Ferguson.

37. Fostered in part by Marx's own references to Ferguson in *The Poverty of Philosophy* and *Capital*, for a discussion of which see Hill (2013).

38. For example, Duncan Forbes (1967: 41) notes that although Ferguson does not mention the Highlands in the *Essay*, the interest in primitive societies does invite speculation on the influence of his upbringing on his thought, while David Allan (2006: 5) notes that his upbringing made him different from his fellow literati, and his peers certainly referred to his Highlander status when they discussed him.

39. Beveridge and Turnball (1997) have argued that Ferguson's failure to mention Scotland stemmed from a widespread sense of 'inferiorism' among the literati. The desire to avoid parochial examples and at the same time to remind a wider British audience of the backwardness of Scotland has been linked to the phenomenon of Anglicisation and the Humean project of purging written work of Scotticisms. This view has been criticised by John Brewer (2008: 7–8, 20) who stresses Ferguson's willingness to state his love for Scotland in his *Correspondence*. It is also worth noting that both Smith and Hume were happy to use Scottish examples in their work, as were Millar and Robertson. The cultural cringe reading of twentieth-century nationalist-inclined cultural critics seems misplaced in this respect.

40. Ferguson's father and his often tempestuous career are covered by Jane Fagg (1994). Denise Ann Testa (2007: 3) provides perhaps the most detailed account of Ferguson's Highland childhood, and cautions against a binary division between Highland and Hanoverian, concluding that Ferguson was both a Hanoverian and a Highlander, and was no less a Highlander as a result.

41. Though David Kettler (2005: 322) perhaps exaggerates when he says that Fergusson senior was 'furiously hostile' to the religion and politics of his parishioners.

42. A point made by David Allan (2008: 24, 36) and Alexander Broadie (1990).

43. Or as Ian Clark (1970) would have it, how to move from protest to reaction.

44. David Kettler (2005: 57) argues that Ferguson's closeness to the interest of the establishment made him close to being a 'court philosopher'.

45. Agreeing with Sher, John Robertson (1985: 165) suggests that the new elite in Scotland was a combination of Edinburgh lawyers,

country gentry and urban oligarchs who were, post Culloden, able to enforce the rule of law, but whose outlook was ultimately 'parochial' (Robertson 1985: 240).

46. In addition to Sher, the case for reading Ferguson as closer to mainstream, establishment positions has been made by Skjönsberg (2017: 2–3) with relation to political thought and Haakonssen (1996: 64) with relation to moral philosophy.

47. See also Kettler (2005: 4), Allan (2006: 113) and Fagg (1968: 144).

48. This view has also been taken by Kalyvas and Katznelson (1998) who suggest that Ferguson is seeking a 'prophylactic' for the problems of commercial society, while Sebastiani (2015: 330) continues the medical imagery by seeing Ferguson as diagnosing and then seeking to cure the ills of modernity.

49. Jane Fagg (1995: xxix) suggests that Ferguson's departure from the clergy was not the result of a rejection of the teaching of the Church but rather an awareness that his interests lay elsewhere. His biographer John Small suggests that his limitations as a preacher may have made this move inevitable: 'he was deficient in the gifts necessary for the popular preacher' and 'his sermons were elaborate disquisitions showing more acquaintance with systems of philosophy than with the wants of common hearers' (Schneider 1980: vii). There is also the possibility raised by Brewer (2007) and Testa (2007: 116) that the need for Gaelic ministers would have meant that Ferguson would have most likely ended up in a parish too far from Edinburgh for his taste.

50. Richard Sher (1985: 128) points out that Ferguson served in the General Assembly thirteen times between 1762 and 1785.

51. See Raphael (1994) and Raphael et al. (1990) for a discussion of Ferguson's work as a tutor.

52. See Taylor (2014), Lehmann (1930: 192) and Merolle (2006: xviii) who all see the influence of Shaftesbury mediated by Hutcheson as central to Ferguson's thought. Carey (2015: 65) points out that the combined influences of Cicero, Marcus Aurelius and Shaftesbury form Hutcheson's intellectual hinterland.

53. Although the lecture programme seems to be revised down the years the broad outline of topics and their order remains relatively consistent (*Lectures*). Richard Sher (1985: 177) and John Robertson (1985: 91) have both made the case for Hutcheson's influence on Ferguson through the development of a Christian Stoicism that characterises the ideology of the Moderates. Jack Hill (2017: 21) has recently

questioned how appropriate this reading is in the case of Ferguson given the near total absence of explicitly Christian arguments from his discussions of religion.

54. Though he does return to the language of moral sense in the *Principles* (2: 133) where he cites Kames on moral sense.

55. See *Principles* (2: 128). Ferguson adopts the almost standard position of the Scottish Enlightenment of admiring Newton and deprecating Descartes on the question of method (*Principles* 1: 116–17).

56. Ferguson explicitly cites Bacon as an inspiration (*Principles* 1: 2) and cites Newton's principles of reasoning and empiricism with approval (*Principles* 2: 16, 118; *Black* 108–9). For the influence of Buffon see *Institutes* (13, 18–19) and *Principles* (2: 130).

57. David Kettler (2008: 87) points out the difficulty of trying to provide a consistent reading of Ferguson from the books based on his lectures, the danger being that he ends up looking like a 'mere pedagogical pendant to Thomas Reid'. See also Wood (2015a).

58. Throughout his career Ferguson reaches for the Reidian language of active powers and an active mind in his discussion of the Will (*Institutes* 119; *Manuscripts* 196).

59. See also *Principles* (1: 161).

60. Discussions of the relationship between Hume and Ferguson often dwell on Hume's dismissive judgement of the *Essay* – for a discussion of which see David Raynor (2009), Vincenzo Merolle (2009) and James Harris and Mikko Tolonen (2015: 173). The main conclusion seems to be that Hume disliked the content on grounds of its primitivism and anti-commercial message, as well as the style and form of the *Essay*.

61. A point he returns to in the unpublished essay on the Intellectual Powers (*Manuscripts* 262) 'Sceptics pretend to doubt: but they Act the Believer and do not mistake the purpose which things in Nature are fitted to Serve.' In a letter to Henry MacKenzie discussing Ossian, Ferguson argues that Hume's scepticism about the authenticity of the poems was a feature of his more general scepticism (*Correspondence* 2: 405). The charge here is that the sceptic always wants more evidence than necessary to convince most people. David Kettler (2005: 159) makes the interesting observation that 'for all his objections to Hume's method, he never departed very widely from Hume's conclusions.'

62. Ferguson references Hutcheson in a number of places in his later writings. In the *Principles* (2: 16) he draws on Hutcheson's argument on malice and on the idea of benevolence as the basis of moral

law (2: 111). The unpublished manuscripts contain discussions of Hutcheson's aesthetics (*Manuscripts* 56–7, 224).

63. There are a number of other minor engagements with Hume through Ferguson's work. In the *Institutes* (23) and the *Essay* (136) he cites Hume on the populousness of ancient nations. In the *Essay* (241) he expresses disagreement with Hume's position on luxury while in the *Principles* (2: 232) he both agrees with Hume's description of the origin of government in force and attacks his argument that justice is an artificial virtue (2: 192).

64. As with discussions of Hume and Ferguson's relationship, many discussions of Smith and Ferguson's relationship dwell on the supposed falling out between the pair over Smith's accusation of plagiarism, a dispute apparently only resolved when Smith fell ill shortly before his death. Smith seems to have accused Ferguson of borrowing some of his views on political economy, and given how close their views are on the matter it is understandable. Ferguson defended himself saying that they had both gotten these ideas from the same French writer. For a discussion of the feud see Hamowy (1968) and Weinstein (2009: 90).

65. Ferguson makes a number of references to Smith's economic writings from the *Institutes* (144) and *Essay* (140) to the late *Manuscripts* (143, 149). Ferguson did write to Smith following the publication of the *Wealth of Nations* in 1776 saying that he is recommending it to his students and including the humorous pointed comment that: 'You have provoked, it is true, the church, the universities, and the merchants, against all of whom I am willing to take your part; but you have likewise provoked the militia, and there I must be against you' (*Correspondence* 1: 41). This passage might be taken as evidence for the habit of treating Ferguson as opposing Smith and lining up with republican sceptics about commerce. But look at what he actually says: Ferguson agrees with Smith's views on church, university and merchants and raises only the militia, which Smith himself accepts, even given the support for a professional army in Book V of the *Wealth of Nations*.

66. Istvan Hont (2015: 29) points out that Ferguson's criticism of Smith on this point is essentially the same as that of Reid and Kames, though the similarity between the two positions does not mean that they were not arrived at independently.

67. Jane Rendall (1978: 149) sees this as the major bone of contention between Ferguson and both Hume and Smith.

2

Moral Science

... but notorious facts are foundation enough, upon which we may
safely erect the fabric of moral science, so far as it is of any importance
to mankind. (*Principles* 1: 155)

Ferguson's assessment of his own method appears at the start of the
Principles where he acknowledges that the work displays both 'a
continual effort to state the argument' and an attempt to 'arrange
the matter in question' that are undertaken in the light of a realisation that 'method is the principal aid he can give' (*Principles* 1: 1).[1]
What we need to be clear about is what, precisely, was Ferguson's
method? In the previous chapter we discussed some of the major
interpretations of Ferguson's thinking and the influence of a range
of thinkers on his thought.

It is often said that you know a man by the company he keeps
– and this is certainly true of Adam Ferguson: the influence of
the conversations and shared concerns of other members of the
Scottish Enlightenment is clear, the deep admiration for Cicero
and Marcus Aurelius likewise obvious, the open praise for
Montesquieu is marked. But it is also true that you know a man
by his enemies, and in this case that may provide us with an even
more useful way into Ferguson's thought. If we understand who
he disagreed with and why he disagreed with them, we begin to
see the shape of what he hoped to achieve in outlining his method.

Throughout his work Ferguson sought to rebut and avoid a
series of what we might call philosophical vices, and understanding what he sought to avoid helps us to understand why he frames
his theory as he does.[2] The philosophical vices arise from a faulty
methodology that Ferguson hopes to avoid in his own thinking.
Each of these methodological errors can be traced back to the
ubiquitous human desire to explain the world. When Ferguson

discusses the origin of superstition in the *Essay* he argues that the urge for explanation can prompt us along false paths of knowledge as well as true.

> In what depends on the known or the regular course of nature, the mind trusts itself; but in strange and uncommon situations it is the dupe of its own perplexity, and, instead of relying on its prudence or courage, has recourse to divination, and a variety of observances, that, for being irrational, are always more revered. (*Essay* 89)

In our perplexity and our desire to dispel it we can be duped by false explanations. From his earliest to his latest writings he persistently recognises three broad types of philosophical error: philosophers are 'the Dupes of Language and think we have made a discovery when we have changed the meaning in which we employ our words' (*Manuscripts* 243); they are 'sometimes the dupes of their own abstractions, and consider those things as separate in nature which are only separate in thought' (*Institutes* 65); and they are 'the dupes of a subtilty, which promises to supply every defect of our knowledge, and, by filling up a few blanks in the story of nature, pretends to conduct our apprehension nearer to the source of existence' (*Essay* 12). Each of these errors has a number of manifestations and, though they are linked in Ferguson's account, they are also distinct and can be seen to varying extents in Ferguson's criticism of his contemporaries.

Dupes of Our Own Language

One of Ferguson's chief bugbears is inattention to language and terminology. This can be a result of carelessness in the 'loose application of words' (*Principles* 2: 186), or it can be the result of a deliberate attempt to exploit rhetoric. He levels the charge of loose use of terminology against Hutcheson and Hume suggesting that their use of the term utility obscures important distinctions between pleasure and happiness.[3] Any systematic attempt at philosophy must be absolutely clear in its terminology, but it should not become obsessed with language. There is a danger that philosophical discussions can leave the substance of the matter behind and become bogged down in discussions of words.

If Hume and Hutcheson are guilty of carelessness, the charge against Rousseau and Richard Price is altogether more serious.

Here the charge is that a misapplication of terminology is deliberately being used to defend a favoured position. In the *Essay* this accusation takes the form of his attack on those who seek to privilege their position by identifying a particular form of behaviour as 'natural' (chiefly Rousseau's account of the state of nature).[4] We see a similar charge being made in Ferguson's pamphlet responding to Dr Price. The main thrust of Ferguson's argument here is that Price has misunderstood and misapplied the term liberty in his defence of the American colonists. Price has a particular agenda and as a result his use of the term liberty is loaded. As Ferguson puts it: 'The Doctor, in every step of his argument, is somewhat hurried by his own definition' (*Price* 8). The points at which Price's argument becomes strained are precisely those where he elides different meanings of liberty in a 'collision of words' (*Price* 6). The chief such elision is that between civil liberty and national independence where the whole of Price's argument rests on conflating different senses of the term liberty.[5]

Rather than analytical clarity, Price defines liberty in a way that suits the conclusion he wants to reach: like Rousseau's description of the state of nature it is more rhetoric than philosophy. The accusation then is that such thinkers have mistaken 'the obtrusion of a mere innovation in language for a discovery in science' (*Essay* 19) and that in doing so they sacrifice accuracy of analysis for 'cleverness of system'. A still more serious version of this criticism is directed at Bernard Mandeville. Mandeville's entire definition of virtue and vice are an abuse of language. This is a persistent criticism of Mandeville throughout Ferguson's works.

Thus in the *Institutes* Mandeville is an example of a linguistic error: 'from inattention to propriety of language' (*Institutes* 103). But it also arises from a deliberate use of controversial language to create the literary effect of paradox. Mandeville, according to Ferguson, knows very well what he is doing.[6] But the paradox, so Ferguson thinks, itself reveals the solidity of the distinction of virtue and vice. Ferguson's point is that the very absurdity of the Mandevillian proposition confirms to us the reality of moral distinctions. This, according to Ferguson, is demonstrated by the fact that 'expressions of praise and blame in every language . . . show, that the distinction of moral good and evil is real, and universally acknowledged' (*Institutes* 108). For Ferguson what exists in every language must have reference to something real and Mandeville's effect is only clever and funny if it subverts our natural view.

Taken as a philosophical paradox and not a linguistic trick for literary effect it is, in Ferguson's view, absurd.[7]

There are several other manifestations of the dupes of language error that crop up through Ferguson's writings. Philosophers who become the dupes of language can do so for a number of inno-cent reasons. One such arises from the confusion of metaphori-cal imagery for reality. Ferguson describes this danger through the use of metaphor in science. Metaphor is 'illusory in science' (*Institutes* 8) and leads us to mistake the images we use to illus-trate our arguments for facts. In the *Principles* Ferguson argues that identifying this vice in the work of Hobbes and Locke (and by implication Hume) is Reid's great contribution to philosophy.[8] Following Reid we must endeavour '. . . to state the facts, of which we are conscious, not in figurative language, but in terms which are proper to the subject' (*Principles* 1: 75; see also *Manuscripts* 175; *Correspondence* 1: 71; *Institutes* 86–7).[9]

For Ferguson philosophy must be undertaken in plain and accu-rate prose freed from literary allusion and metaphor. These literary effects can only lead to confusion and promulgate unclear argu-ment and thought. Ferguson is also aware of the difficulty of trans-lation between languages. As with his concerns over the danger of crude ethnocentric judgement (see below), he is keen to avoid the speakers of different languages talking past each other. This pro-vides us with one of the most difficult of the tasks that he expects from moral philosophy: he believes that there is an objective moral order, but worries that the conceptual language developed in dif-ferent cultures leads them to approach this moral truth in different ways. Moral philosophers must proceed by identifying and clearly stating the terminology that they are using and doing so in a way that would avoid errors of translation between cultures. Accurate translation will then allow us to identify the common underlying moral principle. Digging down through differences of expression we will be able to find 'the essential distinction of moral right and wrong' (*Principles* 2: 145). The difficulty of translation leads to another linguistic problem for moral philosophy, the problem of interpretation. One of the tasks that Ferguson hopes can be achieved by his moral science is to identify cases where there is an apparent diversity of opinion about moral actions. His belief is that after proper investigation seeming differences will turn out to be different expressions of an underlying universal moral attitude of mind. Thus the manifestation of a virtuous mindset in customs may differ between cultures, but the moral attitude will, in principle, be found to be the same.

Ferguson's belief is that moral science will allow us to abstract from local forms and observances and adopt a universal view of humanity. And so a moral philosophy based on this careful enquiry will allow us the opportunity to explore the underlying moral attitudes that are the proper material for moral philosophy. There is more than a little irony in this as Ferguson himself is hardly the most consistent writer in his use of language.[10] To be fair to him, that impression often arises from the fact that he uses slightly different terminology in different books, while maintaining consistency within each volume.

Dupes of Our Own Abstraction

Perhaps the clearest example of Ferguson's second philosophical vice can be found in his well-known criticism of the state of nature in Part 1 of the *Essay*.[11] Ferguson's particular target here is Rousseau. The accusation is that Rousseau has replaced realistic history with a biased account of natural man which serves to support his favoured system. This vice leads us to become dupes of our own abstractions and to confuse a theoretical abstraction for a fact. This 'substitution of fancy for reality' (*Principles* 1: 279) has been the greatest barrier to success in science.

Rousseau's vice was one of excessive imagination and abstraction.[12] He departs from the evidence of moral science, that all humans have always been sociable, and in his description of the state of nature he selects 'one or a few particulars on which to establish a theory' (*Essay* 8). A similar point lies behind Ferguson's criticism of great legislator explanations of political and legal change.[13] The desire to account for a socially generated phenomenon leads us to grasp after familiar models of explanation. If a system of law exists, then one mind, a Solon or Lycurgus, must have brought it into being. As we will see below Ferguson's approach to moral science involves a radical departure from this view.

What Ferguson has in mind in such cases is not simply that the abstraction departs from what is warranted by the evidence, but also that the language of abstract theory differs from the language in which we engage in moral judgement. If philosophers begin to confuse the theoretical use of language developed as part of moral science for the language used for moral decision-making they will begin to develop arguments which bear little relation to the actual act of judgement. In a nicely turned phrase he refers to this as us owing 'our perplexity more to the subtilties of the speculative, than to any uncertainty in the feelings of the heart' (*Essay* 64). When the conclusions of philosophy are unrecognisable to those who hold the actual moral beliefs under examination, then philosophy has become detached from its original purpose. Ferguson is clear that abstraction is necessary and central to philosophical thought, but it must be undertaken with an awareness that we are abstracting from reality. One danger that arises is that we tend to forget that what we are considering in isolation is in fact connected to a range of other phenomena. Abstractions in theory are not to be mistaken for facts as they will lead to an oversimplified understanding of the phenomena which detaches it from the complex circumstances in which it is to be found.[14]

Several manifestations of this vice arise from Ferguson's commitment to empiricism and doubts about the efficacy of a priori argument. For example, when he outlines the subject matter of philosophy of mind he is clear that the subject must focus its attention on what is commonly known of the phenomenon in question. Adopting a similar position to Reid he cashes this out through a demand that we recognise the limits of what is observable, and hence can serve as the basis of scientific generalisation. Ferguson is, quite simply, not interested in metaphysics.[15] Science has only begun to advance in the modern era, and Ferguson's commitment to his version of empiricism looms large in his assessment of earlier philosophy. While he may admire and agree with many arguments from the Stoics, Aristotle and others, he is clear that their method, their way of doing philosophy, is mistaken.

Dupes of Our Own Subtlity

Ferguson's third group of philosophical errors in effect explains the tendency to the first two types of error. As we have seen excessive commitment to the method of abstraction and inattention (deliberate or accidental) to language produce philosophical errors. These errors, in Ferguson's view are peculiar to philosophers because of what drives them to philosophy in the first place. The desire to manipulate language, or to focus on abstractions, arises from the desire to explain, to account for the world. If philosophers are not careful they can become prey to another vice: the desire to fit reality to their theories. This desire is partly an effect of the commitment to system, but it is also, tellingly, an expression of a desire for fame that philosophers seek to achieve through the novelty of their positions and by demolishing existing beliefs. The accusation is clearly apparent in the discussion of Mandeville that we noted above, but it is a charge that he also levels at Hobbes:

> To assume principles, or to adopt conclusions in direct contradiction to such obvious truths may indeed have the merit of novelty, or seem to proceed from profound observation, but is certainly in a much higher degree absurd than the repetition of any truth, however obvious and previously known. (*Principles* 2: 193)

This sort of philosopher is a show off, who would rather cause a stir than provide a small, but real, accession to human knowledge. There is an interesting and related manifestation of this vice: pretentiousness arises when philosophers take an unwarrantedly high view of themselves and of the place of philosophy in human life. It can lead to a sort of scholarly arrogance where philosophers tend to denigrate the work of practical men, as though philosophy were the only good and the sole source of status. The vice of subtlety can make itself apparent in the character of philosophers. But it also leads to a series of intellectual errors. Perhaps the chief of these arises from a combination of the vices of language and abstraction.

Philosophical confusions often arise because the philosopher seeks to extend their argument beyond what may be supported by the evidence. This tendency seems to arise from the very nature of the urge to engage in philosophical thinking. We want to understand the world and we come, if we are not careful, to mistake the patterns of thought that we have developed to explain a particular phenomenon as holding across the whole system of nature. This urge to system is ubiquitous:

> Men are often in haste to conceive the system, without attending to the parts of which it is formed; and apply the law without comparing its power with the measure of effect. The passion by which they are urged is busy in every breast; and the ordinary race of men in every nation and in every age, are greatly advanced in the gratification of it. The merest savage has conceived a scheme of nature upon which he acts; and, when new phenomena occur, he endeavours to refer them to

some law or predicament of being already known to himself; or if this be impracticable, he imagines some new principle better fitted to serve the purpose. (*Principles* 1: 278–9)

In some cases this leads thinkers to warp the truth to fit a system, an accusation that Ferguson defends himself against at the beginning of the *Principles* with reference to Stoicism. In other cases it leads them to excessive simplification: forcing 'the attributes of human nature, under single appellations, however comprehensive or general' (*Principles* 2: 40). There are two ways in which this manifests itself. The first involves an error in method where philosophers who are committed to a particular system conceive of consistency with the tenets of the system as an indication of truth. This involves mistaking our habit of thinking for evidence of truth. In terms of scientific thought the most obvious example of this is mistaking hypothesis for fact. The classic case of this for Ferguson was Descartes's vortices. Descartes's error was the result of a faulty methodology and an ambition to explain which took him beyond what the evidence would support.[16]

The second manifestation of this vice appears in Ferguson's criticism of the ancient and medieval schools. Schools commit themselves to particular systems of thought to the exclusion of others. Thus the range of possible explanations is constrained to those which fit with the existing assumptions of the school. This leads in turn to two propensities: the first is an excessive attention to the minutiae of the existing set of definitions and distinctions that prevail in the school. It was this that hampered the development of the scientific method (see below). The schools would 'assume the importance of wisdom in mere words and technical forms of expression' (*Principles* 2: 401–2). This sort of thinking is anathema to Ferguson: it 'were piteous indeed, to carry nothing with us hence into the world, but formal pretensions and technical terms' (*Principles* 1: 402). Ferguson's conception of the role of philosophy is, as we will see below, that it should be a practical, accessible and overall a useful activity. Philosophy is about explaining the real world and the further it departs from that into intellectual navel gazing, the less it fulfils its function. The ancient schools increasingly failed to provide a useful philosophy and obsessed over form, ready to value themselves more on their profession of faith than on the value of their arguments.

It is this sect-like feature that invites another error: a tendency to extremism. Rather than seek genuine accessions to knowledge the sectarians tended to try to outbid each other by reinforcing and extending the principles of the school. This leads to an increasing extremism in the beliefs of the school as they become more and more detached from reality and trapped within the system of the school. Ferguson gives an example of this in his discussion of Stoicism and Epicureanism. He notes that both schools went too far when their arguments departed from what was evident to 'good sense' (*Principles* 2: 68–9). What Ferguson is suggesting is that the schools, in trying to introduce new ideas, in trying to provide a consistent system, have extended their principles beyond what evidence will warrant.

Ferguson's philosophical vices are drawn from his reading of ancient and modern philosophy and his criticism of major contemporaries (such as Hume, Smith, Price, Rousseau and, crucially, Mandeville) involves some combination of these general methodological mistakes. As we will see Ferguson's own conception of moral philosophy and its task is developed in response to these failures. It takes the form of insisting upon the development of a realistic empirically founded account of human nature, and leads to a realisable notion of virtue. In order to promote this notion of virtue among his students and to avoid the errors of established philosophy he develops an interest in the accurate use of moral terminology to encourage clarity of thought.

Science

We can now begin to examine the outline of Ferguson's understanding of what is needed for the accurate study of morality. There are three main elements to this: first, that care and attention must be devoted to the use of language, especially to clarity of definition; second, that what is described is grounded in the evidence of observation rather than abstractions; and third, that we are suitably modest about what we are likely to be able to achieve from our system of thought.

In pursuit of the first of these Ferguson acknowledges that the ancient philosophers' pursuit of a single principle of morality, a moral truth, was intended to create a consistent system of thought and a consistent language for thinking about morality. However, the ancients were often led astray by this methodology. They came to develop an excessive focus on terminology and as a result their moral philosophy became too abstract and unrealistic. Ferguson hopes that his commitment to empirically based moral science will allow him to avoid this error.[17] Moral philosophy, by its nature, is aimed at what humans ought to be not what they are. But to avoid utopianism it must be based on knowledge of human nature. Ferguson thinks that moral philosophy can identify moral ideals but that these ideals are not something which can ever be realised in practice. The perfection identified by moral philosophy must be perfection for humans, and even then we must be aware that it will never be reached. Ferguson's thought is characterised by a distinction between the identification and clear definition of aspects of moral judgement and their application and implication in particular conditions and circumstances. Virtue and moral law can be described, but the content of virtuous action and the application of moral law in a given context is harder to determine.

We should take care that we use language to identify and distinguish different moral phenomena so that our argument does not, like that of Price, trade on ambiguous use of the same term to apply to different moral phenomena. On the other hand the conduct of philosophy must also be aware that the way we use language may lead us to use different words to describe different aspects of the same moral phenomena: 'These articles we have found to differ chiefly in words, but in matter and substance to be nearly the same. The different appellations in question have a reference to different aspects, under which the subject may be considered' (*Principles* 2: 108).

Although it might seem obvious to state this as the basis of an approach to moral philosophy, it is important to note that Ferguson's recommendation of the method is based on both his separate justification of moral science and his identification of the errors of his contemporaries. The rejection of ancient and more especially scholastic philosophy by early modern thinkers was, in Ferguson's view, necessary, but it risked throwing the baby out with the bathwater. In the late *Essay on the Principle of Moral Estimation* Ferguson has 'Clerk' make this point at the end of dialogue: 'We are apt to laugh now at the old Distinctions, Divisions, and Definitions of the Schools: but it were well sometimes to mind them' (*Manuscripts* 214). Rather than a rejection of the definitional approach to moral philosophy what was required was a combination of this approach with a form of empirically grounded moral realism. An accurate and a useful moral philosophy demands care that we not become bogged down in linguistic formulae, but also that we keep our thinking aimed at observable phenomena.

Ferguson was alive to the criticism of moral philosophy on the basis that it was unrealistic. Words are important, but the vice of the scholastic was to mistake their linguistic debates for substantive moral discussions. By returning to basics and combining rigorous definition and argumentation with the evidence of observation we will be in a position to generate a moral philosophy which is both accurate and useful. The precepts of moral philosophy will avoid the charge of sterility only if related to human nature and human practice.

> Before we can ascertain rules of morality fitted to any particular nature, the fact relating to that nature should be known. Before we can ascertain rules of morality for mankind, the history of man's nature, his dispositions, his specific enjoyments and sufferings, his condition and future prospects, should be known. (*Institutes* 9–10)[18]

Significantly this idea of a realisable, yet potentially never attainable, perfection is connected by Ferguson to the central concept to which he attributes the drive of human behaviour: Ambition.[19] We will explore this aspect of Ferguson's thought in more detail in Chapter 3. It is ambition that drives us to seek improvement, to move towards our partial conceptions of moral perfection, and this process requires both moral action and moral knowledge. Moral philosophy will build on the successful conclusions of moral science. It will conduct a normative exercise based on the descriptive exercise of moral science. Thus we will be able to separate out these two modes of enquiry which, though they are related, are to be conducted according to distinct methodologies. For moral philosophy, though grounded in the facts of moral science, is not limited by the facts about what people have believed about morality. We must discover 'independent of what men actually are' what is 'the greatest good to which they are competent' (*Principles* 1: 160). This will provide us with 'the true standard of estimation' (*Principles* 1: 291).

If we are imperfect but capable of improvement then the purpose of moral philosophy must be to facilitate moral education. Clear moral philosophy will allow us to identify error and to correct our own behaviour. This is an extension of Ferguson's general conception of learning: 'It is the tendency of experience to detect every false opinion, and, by this means, to narrow the scope of aberration and mistake' (*Principles* 1: 234). Knowledge of self and nature allows us to shape our own character in the pursuit of virtue. The ambition that drives moral behaviour includes by its nature a standard against which we measure or estimate ourselves. We are ambitious for better than we have at the moment and in morality we are ambitious to be better than we are at the moment. Ferguson thinks that this, almost by definition, means that we have something that we aim towards. We judge ourselves and others according to a standard of estimation which is, in itself, an idea of perfection or excellence. Moral philosophy is the discussion and identification of this normative ideal informed by observation of actual human behaviour and capabilities.

Moral Scientific Method

Ferguson begins his endeavour with a clear definition of science, 'the knowledge of general principles' (*Analysis* 3), and this is contrasted with history which is the narration of facts. He adopts a methodology that recognises the centrality of observation while accepting the difficulty of deliberate experimentation akin to that employed to such success in the natural sciences. The materials of moral science are to be found in the observation of social life as it is and as it has been lived. However, if undertaken as a factual narrative history of particular nations or periods, this would leave us stranded in near hopeless complexity. The very purpose of science is to seek abstraction and generalisations from comparison, to identify the main points of commonality in the complexity of the world.[20] A moral science must be capable of making generalisations or else it would provide no support to improved moral choice and would instead support a collapse into moral relativism. Ferguson is firm in his belief that laws of nature exist and can be discerned from the examination of history, the comparison of institutions and events, and the subsequent generalisation of common principles.

This science steps beyond the narration of history – which provides us with vital understanding of context – and the results of historical investigation become the material of the generalisations of moral sciences. As Ferguson would have it: 'The facts are presented not as discoveries, but as the data, from which to infer the judgements and conclusions of the second part, relating to the foundations of choice, or what man ought to wish for himself, for his country, and for mankind' (*Principles* 1: 10). In other words, the material of history allows us to draw 'scientific' generalisations about human nature and social life upon which we might better ground our moral actions. This, then, is the subject matter of moral science. We are to observe the world around us, to generalise from the data and form principles to guide moral behaviour.

Underlying Universalities

Ferguson's 'conjectural history' or sociological theory is based upon the identification of universal features of human behaviour from historical evidence followed by the examination of how these principles of human nature manifest themselves in particular societies. It is the search for generalisations based upon similar forms of behaviour observed across space and time. Perhaps most famously here it involves the comparison of accounts acquired from classical history with the accounts of travellers among the Amerinds such as Lafitau. Furthering his claim to recognition as one of the fathers of sociology, Ferguson makes an early use of the concepts of 'function' (*Essay* 49, 83; *Rome* 29; *Principles* 1: 12) and 'superstructure' (*Principles* 1: vii; *Essay* 159). While he wishes to understand the function of human institutions in relation to the laws of nature, he also displays a startling modernity when he recognises that these institutions are a superstructure built on the foundations of human nature. In other words, social diversity across cultures and through time is a product of superstructural difference. The underlying universalities of human nature and the discernible laws of nature underwrite all human experience.[21] If Ferguson's moral science is concerned with identifying the 'universal qualities of our nature' (*Essay* 16) that can be traced through the diversity of human societies, we may gain some traction for understanding his idea of moral science by taking a look at a list of these universals.

A list of features of human behaviour that Ferguson regards as universal includes:

- love and the institution of marriage (*Principles* 1: 28);
- the urge to propagate (*Essay* 16);
- the love of children (*Principles* 1: 29);

- the love of tribe or clan (*Principles* 1: 31);
- language (*Principles* 1: 42), speech (*Institutes* 46) and a 'natural language of sentiment' (*Institutes* 57) in the tone of voice;
- sociability (*Essay* 59);
- belief in testimony and perception (*Principles* 1: 83);
- religion (*Principles* 1: 164, 166, 175; *Institutes* 121–3);
- belief that fear and malice are always bad and benevolence and fortitude always good (*Principles* 1: 224);
- the physical sensation of pleasure and pain (*Institutes* 51);
- that 'Man is formed for an artist' (*Principles* 1: 299) and 'disposed to innovate on every practice' (*Principles* 1: 122);
- that man is 'active' (*Principles* 2: 56), requires exercise (*Essay* 48) and desires it (*Essay* 52);
- sport (*Essay* 92–3);
- moral judgement (*Essay* 37);
- the urge to persecute (*Principles* 2: 59);
- self-preservation (*Essay*: 16);
- right of self-defence (*Principles* 2: 180);
- that no one is entitled to molest his neighbour (*Principles* 2: 205);
- the 'disposition to oblige' which underlies different forms of manners (*Principles* 2: 376); and
- rank (*Principles* 1: 259).

There are also a series of concepts that follow inevitably from the development of human thought itself. For example he argues that: 'Some predicaments have their generic names in every language, have been universally admitted, and are coeval with human thought.' Examples of these include 'substance, quality, quantity, number, perfection, defect, good, evil, time, place etc.' (*Institutes* 89). Ferguson's account of language helps illustrate what he has in mind here. Language and society are 'coeval with the species of man' (*Principles* 1: 45): wherever we look in the historical record humans are social and have language. This allows Ferguson to assume that there are certain universal functions that exist in every human society.[22] As will be obvious from this list of underlying universals, Ferguson is committed to a position close to that of Hume, Smith, Reid and the other Scots: the identification of a series of universals that is sufficient for us to build a system.

In addition to the universal aspects that derive from human nature there is also a series of universals that follow from these facts in particular combination with the fact of society. Humans are moral and political as a result of their nature and there are, for Ferguson, certain truths that follow from that for all societies. As he puts it in the *Institutes*:

> But there being some circumstances common in the situation and disposition of all mankind; such as, their being united in society, and concerned in what relates to their fellow creatures; men universally admire qualities which fit the individual to promote the good of mankind; as, wisdom, justice, courage, and temperance. (*Institutes* 39)

For Ferguson the fact that we are social leads to the universal development of benevolence as a moral value. Similarly, when humans come to cooperate in groups there are certain functions that arise from the very nature of communal life. This isn't a particularly sophisticated argument, but it is, nonetheless, how Ferguson believes he can generate an approach to morality grounded in empirical observations of how humans have behaved and, crucially, what they have believed. Before exploring this a little further we should pause to consider the nature of the underlying universals that form such a crucial step in Ferguson's approach. Perhaps the clearest way to do this is by looking at the relationship between the key elements of Ferguson's version of conjectural history.

The first observation to make is that Ferguson's interest lies in explaining diversity through the adaptation of a universal human nature to circumstances, with the added layer that social life itself generates universal situations which each society must develop some way to deal with. This leads him to reject the idea of a sort of diffusion of human culture.

> This is a work which every separate nation or tribe appears to have performed for itself. And what, in one form or other, is universal to mankind, cannot have been the invention of one or a few: We cannot suppose one nation, or race of men, to have learned from another that in which all the separate races of men differ from one another; nor can we suppose what is indefinitely varied, in the practice of every separate horde, to have been the copy of a single invention. (*Principles* 1: 42)

So each society will, somewhere in its practices and beliefs, display some version of the universals. When we come to study them it is precisely this which should first attract our attention.

The universal characteristics, in the mean time, to which we have now referred, must, when we would treat of any part of history, constitute the first subject of our attention; and they require, not only to be enumerated, but to be distinctly considered. (*Essay* 17)

Using moral science to identify the universal characteristics engages us in looking, not for identical behaviours, but for the behaviours that each society has developed with relation to the universal. This obviously connects to the strong theme in Ferguson's discussion of conjectural history that relates to the need for accurate evidence. Indeed, the entire point is to avoid relying on conjecture at all. The moral scientist must be cautious of evidence and seek corroboration.[23] Their observations must be confirmed by the records of history and observation of the variety of different forms of society that exist in the present time. Comparing evidence from history of how our ancestors lived with the evidence drawn from travellers' descriptions of savage societies (suitably corroborated by more than one source) will allow us to identify the universals which in turn allows us to confirm their reality and at the same time form a framework for our thought.[24]

As is well established the aim here is twofold. It is to use the observation of contemporary savages to understand the deep history of our own society. But it is also to generalise and to identify types of society to help us better understand the phenomenon itself. It is both a genealogy of our own conceptions and institutions, but also a natural history or classification of social life itself. The task of the moral scientist is, at base, comparative. But it is not restricted to the evidence of history or of observation of contemporary societies. Ferguson adds two additional sources of evidence. The first of these is introspection. Our own recognition of the way in which we think, feel and act is itself a body of evidence, though, as we have seen, this evidence also needs to be handled with care lest we take the evidence of our own mind, formed as it is in our own society, for definitive evidence. Another source of evidence appears in a couple of places in Ferguson's writings. This is the idea of a thought experiment. Perhaps the most detailed of these appears in the *Essay* (10) where he discusses the idea of a colony planted with children as a way of thinking about what sorts of functions such a society would have to answer. Now this does seem to come close to the sort of fiction that he accuses Rousseau of maintaining, but crucially the point for Ferguson here is that the abstract exercise is then compared to generalisations from the empirical record for confirmation. The confirmation is not argument or rhetorical flourish, it is a reinforcement of the comparative approach.

Diversity and Universality

Ferguson clearly intends his moral science to provide a means through which to explore the universalities that lie behind the fact that 'men are greatly diversified' (*Principles* 1: 231) and is well aware that the particular manifestation of human nature or the law of nature is shaped by the circumstances in which a nation finds itself. However, this does not render generalisation, and hence moral science, impossible. Instead it provides us with another subject for moral science and we are led to trace 'the imperceptible circumstances by which they are led to have different customs' (*Essay* 65). The interaction of universal modes of human behaviour with the particular circumstances of each nation both explains diversity and allows yet more historical material for comparisons through which to refine the principles of human nature. Ferguson's opposition to theories of the state of nature and his assertion that all conditions are equally natural to man is an extension of this attitude that seeks to account for diversity.

For Ferguson one of the most significant underlying universalities is his belief that all human minds operate in a like manner. Human minds are systems of generalisation from experience.[25] Differences between individuals and cultures are not the product of a difference of kind, but are instead the result of different socialised experiences. Human minds operate in the same manner: it is the content of acquired classification systems that leads to diversity.

There is one area where Ferguson's commitment to universalism does come into question. His engagement with Montesquieu leads him to take seriously the former's claims about a direct physiological effect of climate on behaviour.[26] In a long discussion in the *Essay* (106–15) Ferguson concedes that there appears to be evidence for the popular generalisations about climate. Climate then seems to have an effect, but Ferguson quickly qualifies this by noting that we are unlikely to be able to explore this effect until we have better medical knowledge. Such speculations are unreliable. Instead, we can point to moral rather that physical causes that are observable and allow us to provide accounts of the phenomena at hand. It is also worth noting that this argument is largely absent from the rest of Ferguson's work where he instead focuses on the moral scientific rather than physiological account.[27] By the time of the *Principles* Ferguson is apparently uninterested in notions of climate and race: 'We have not any sufficient reason to believe that men, of remote ages and nations, differ from one another otherwise than by habits acquired in a different manner of living' (*Principles* 1: 221).

Ferguson, like Reid, takes the universality of language as evidence for this assertion. Languages differ, but the recurrence of certain universal aspects of human experience leads to a startling uniformity in the kinds of concept that occur in all languages. Of particular interest here is Ferguson's development of a 'common-sense' style argument with regard to the universality of moral distinctions. He argues that the distinction between good and evil is 'universally acknowledged' (*Institutes* 108) and as a result we can regard morality as a universal attribute of human behaviour. Ferguson is able to make this move because he bases the impetus to moral behaviour in the passions. Despite external differences of form or object all humans are driven to pursue certain basic passionate desires. As he would have it: 'They engage in different pursuits, or acquiesce in different conditions; but act from passions nearly the same' (*Essay* 51). The identification of these passions and the observation of the diversity of their manifestation provide a dataset for Ferguson's moral science. For example, Ferguson regards it as a universal principle of human moral behaviour that benevolence and courage are regarded as pleasant while malice and cowardice are regarded as painful. Thus benevolence and courage are regarded as morally good, while malice and cowardice are regarded as evil. While specific cultures may differ over what actions constitute benevolence, courage, malice and cowardice, Ferguson believes that the concepts themselves are universal.

Moral distinctions are real and the evidence for this is to be found in 'expressions of praise and blame in every language' (*Institutes* 108). If human beings are morally judgemental creatures whose languages speak to the existence of some basic conceptual and evaluative universalities, then we have the nascent basis for a science of morals that generalises regarding these concepts. Ferguson also believes that there are 'some circumstances common in the situation and disposition of all mankind' (*Institutes* 39). As a result there will be certain universally experienced circumstances about which different social groups form moral judgements.

Before moving on to examine some of these we should pause here and say a little about another two underlying universalities of human nature that are being invoked in this form of argument. The first of these is habit. Ferguson regards habit as a natural propensity of human nature. Individuals become habituated to circumstances in which they repeatedly find themselves and this habituation extends to patterns of behaviour. Thus external circumstances and habit affect the manifestations of the universal aspects of human behaviour. As external circumstances differ to a considerable degree we find humanity diversified through the 'principle of ductility or pliancy' (*Principles* 1: 232) that allows them to adapt to their surroundings. However, Ferguson is keen to assert that this diversity does not preclude scientific generalisation nor does it imply moral relativism. His first response to this is once again to invoke the supposed universalities of human behaviour that lie behind different cultural manifestations. As he would have it:

> It is well known that external expressions, whether of moral sentiment, or devotion, in the manners or religious observances of men, are, like the words of their language, mere arbitrary signs, which custom accordingly may alter: But the sentiments themselves, whether of benevolence towards men, or devotion to God, retain their distinctive quality under all the variations of external expression. (*Principles* 1: 223)

Moreover, Ferguson invokes a second underlying universality of human behaviour to bolster the potential for generalisations through moral science. Ferguson's commitment to the 'fact' of natural sociability allows him to stress the importance of the fact that groups of humans form conventional forms of interaction – for example languages – that allow group coherence. Diversity of manners occurs between groups of individuals and not between all individuals (a point underlining Ferguson's interest in nations – see Chapter 6).

Human Nature

Ferguson's development of a moral science is grounded in the identification of principles of human nature and the subsequent examination of the practices that result from the interaction of these principles with the diverse circumstances in which different social groups find themselves. Underlying this approach is the recourse to pneumatology. Ferguson's chair at Edinburgh was that of Professor of Pneumatics and Moral Philosophy and he sought to bring the two together in his theory of human nature. In Ferguson's hands pneumatology was understood as 'the description and natural history of mind' (*Principles* 1: 78). In his view a theory of human nature was an essential precondition of the moral science that would allow the proper development of moral philosophy, and this theory of human nature itself must be grounded in a science of the human mind. The development of human mental capacity can be traced from the concrete immediacy of instinctual biogenic drives such as hunger and the procreative drive that characterise the 'savage' to the increasing abstraction and complexity of rational, scientific 'civilised' man. This is not an expression of the naive progressivism that marked some enlightenment thought. The 'principles of progression in human nature' (*Principles* 1: 131) do not detract from the fact that the basic operating system of the human mind applies universally.[28]

At this point Ferguson appears no different from other enlightenment thinkers who sought to anatomise human nature the better to understand the results of human interaction. However, he clearly wants to set himself apart from what he regarded as crude attempts at identifying the dominant principles of human psychology. He doubts that human nature can be reduced to any one principle of explanation no matter how much past thinkers would desire such a deed to be possible. To avoid this error Ferguson wants to apply the strict principles of evidence from observation. As a result he believes that 'all actions of men are equally the result of their nature' (*Essay* 15) and all conditions in which humans are found are equally states of nature. Those who would decry a form of behaviour as being 'unnatural' are guilty of regarding the 'general and prevailing sense or practice of mankind' (*Principles* 1: 15) as an eternal standard not just of moral approbation, but also of the descriptive characteristics of the human mind.

Given our present focus on Ferguson's moral science there are two principles of human nature that are of immediate interest. The first is the idea that the development of science is merely an unfolding of the basic operation of the human mind as a system of classification from experience. The development of the deliberate pursuit of science is an expression of a principle of human nature that is the very basis of consciousness. Science is an expression of human nature. Secondly, drawing on his observation of universal instinctual drives that mankind share with animals, Ferguson homes in on sociability as a principle of human nature with enormous explanatory potential. He regards this 'Principle of Society in human nature' (*Principles* 1: 26) as so obvious an observation as not even worth arguing over.[29] Thus the 'fact' of human sociability and its manifestation in language and communication are to be regarded in the same way as wings are regarded as part of the essential description of birds in natural science.[30] Indeed, there is a biogenic origin for sociability arising from the conditions of human childrearing and the 'natural' development of family bonds and affection that arise from this process. Sociability, then, is an underlying universal of human behaviour and can be seen in a variety of manifestations throughout human history. Or as Ferguson would put it: 'The associating principle is combined with a variety of considerations and circumstances, which lead mankind to vary their forms indefinitely' (*Principles* 1: 24).

Ethnocentrism

Ferguson's consideration of the relationship between universal aspects of human nature and the diverse form that they take in different societies leads him to consider what modern sociologists call the problem of ethnocentrism. The argument flows naturally from his criticism of Rousseau's state of nature through the argument that all human behaviour is 'natural'. While he rejects Rousseau's method from the *Discourse on the Origin of Inequality* on the grounds that its abstraction presents a meaninglessly biased account of natural man based on the arbitrary selection of favoured principles that are then ascribed to a natural condition, he does take Rousseau's criticism of Locke and Hobbes on board. He notes: 'We are ourselves the supposed standards of politeness and civilisation; and where our own features do not appear, we apprehend, that there is nothing which deserves to be known' (*Essay* 75). This partiality for current modes of behaviour is a feature of all human groups in all ages. When asked what constitutes human happiness men 'pronounce in favour of their own condition' (*Principles* 1: 248) and the language of cultural comparison is steeped in condescension and dismissal.

According to Ferguson this is the viewpoint of the 'vulgar' (*Institutes* 184) able only to understand the manners of their own country and incapable of adapting to strange customs.[31] There is a subtext to Ferguson's argument here, and that is that he does not believe that this tendency completely discredits the idea of a moral science. Ferguson believes that while 'the opinion of one country is not the rule or standard by which to judge of the manner of another' (*Institutes* 184–5), there remains the possibility of a universalised viewpoint that would allow the construction of a viable moral science. It is this project that Ferguson himself pursues as he seeks underlying universalities of human social life that will allow him to construct some cross-cultural notions of civilisation and barbarism.

One issue that Ferguson does wrestle with is the comparative status of the cultures of Greece and Rome. Ferguson accepts that these ancient cultures do indeed represent civilisations – just as he accepts that in some cases the manners of the Amerinds are more refined than those of Europeans (*Essay* 86). However, he also notes that even at the height of their achievements the modern sense of the term barbarian could easily be applied to them (*Essay* 184). Even the 'highest measures of civilisation' (*Essay* 89) did not prevent the Greeks and Romans from a widespread belief in superstition and acceptance of barbaric practices such as infanticide. For all of Ferguson's admiration of the ancient world he does not wish himself to have been born into it. Indeed, he traces the modern admiration of classical civilisation to the recognition of its literary achievements. We are so dazzled by the records of literature left to us that we excuse the barbarity of some of the deeds described in them. To highlight this point Ferguson indulges in an extended digression, after the fashion of Herodotus, where he imagines the reaction of a modern returned to everyday life in ancient Greece. His point here is to reinforce the idea that Greek civilisation ought not to be judged by present standards, while at the same time acknowledging that some of the everyday practices of the Greeks may indeed violate the 'neutral' criteria of a civilised nation.

In order to get around our partiality for our own culture and our admiration for the achievements of others we must adopt a rigorous attitude of stripping away inessential concerns. Certain aspects of a culture are not essential to the proper understanding of its operation. Thus such matters as fashion and clothing can vary from place to place and time to time, but they are not the proper subject matter of social science as they represent the ephemeral and non-essential aspects of culture. Having stripped away the superficial differences that set nations and ages apart Ferguson is still left with the problem of the great 'diversities of manners' (*Institutes* 184). For the Fergusonian moral scientist, purged of national pride and intent on universalisable standards, these diverse manners become the source of comparative material. For example, Ferguson compares the attitudes of the elderly to death. He notes that the Eskimo expects his children to kill him when he reaches a certain age, while the European widow expects to be provided for and the Hindu widow to be burnt on her husband's funeral pyre (*Institutes* 182). The problem of interpretation for the moral scientist (and historian) is the difficulty of comprehending 'the conceptions and sentiments of the age in which they were composed' (*Essay* 76–7).

There is a real problem for a historian in a 'learned and polished age' who seeks to 'connect the story of illiterate ages with transactions of a later date' and this difficulty is that of attempting 'to convey a just apprehension of what mankind were in situations so different'. The central problem here is one of vocabulary. How can one express the beliefs of another culture in the 'names' of 'a new state of society' (*Essay* 79). The answer to this for Ferguson is a return to the idea that there is a set of universal concepts that can be applied to humans in whatever society they are found. The moral scientist can then use these to cut through superficial differences and problems of interpretation in order to access the 'raw' material of the society.

One example of this approach is Ferguson's consideration of religion. Ferguson was of the opinion, along with fellow Scots such as Thomas Reid and Lord Kames, that belief in God is a universal attribute of human behaviour. While forms of religious belief differ the evidence of history suggests that all cultures possess a concept of the divine. Ferguson traces two possible conclusions: (1) belief in God is a feature of human nature; or (2) belief in God is the product of circumstances that occur in every age and place (*Institutes* 123). There is a great diversity of religious beliefs and this diversity would seem to preclude generalisations, but the social function of religion and the aspects of human nature that predispose us to it can be identified and their presence confirmed with a sufficient degree of familiarity to warrant confidence in a natural history of religion. However, Ferguson is clear that the religious beliefs of most cultures are riddled with superstitious nonsense. The superstitions of the Amerinds are 'grovelling and mean' (*Essay* 89), but they can be explained by scientific enquiry. The immediacy of savage life tends to produce ritualised religious practices that are similar across cultures because they deal with similar experiences of the inexplicable.

> When we have considered the superstitions of one people, we find little variety in those of another. They are but a repetition of similar weaknesses and absurdities, derived from a common source, a perplexed apprehension of invisible agents, that are supposed to guide all precarious events to which human foresight cannot extend. (*Essay* 89)

As we have seen Ferguson rejects the idea that the standards of one culture can be used to judge another. In ordinary life we are inclined to trespass on this principle, but in moral science we must maintain a strict adherence to universalised principles. However, Ferguson is clear that this tolerance or, in the case of moral science, 'latitude of judgement' (*Principles* 2: 152) has a limit beyond which it 'cannot be safely carried' (*Principles* 2: 152). This limit, according to Ferguson, lies at the point where customs reject 'what is evidently salutary' or prefer what is 'pernicious' (*Principles* 2: 152–3). In other words the generalised evidence of moral science can provide us with the material to judge a cultural practice by a universal standard of science freed from the possible accusation of ethnocentrism. We'll return to this point in Chapters 5 and 6.

Ferguson, like Thucydides before him, saw clearly that if we are to understand our own civilisation we must study the behaviour of those whom we regard as savages, because our own culture had developed from a similar form of society. Moral scientists must 'divest themselves of prejudice' (*Principles* 1: 248) and seek 'fixed principles to which we may recur' (*Principles* 1: 249) for judgement and comparison. These principles are the underlying universalities of human nature, those aspects of human behaviour that can be traced throughout history. It is possible to compare cultures and their institutions in a meaningful manner; moreover, it is possible to make judgements of preference between them based on the universal aspects of human nature. As Ferguson notes: 'When, under one species of establishment, we observe the persons and possessions of men to be secure, and their genius to prosper; under another, prevalent disorder, insult, wrong, with a continual degradation or suppression of all the talents of men, we cannot be at a loss on which to bestow preference' (*Principles* 2: 499). From this we can conclude that the knowledge produced by moral science can provide meaningful universally applicable generalisations that will help guide our moral and political action.

Human Universals: Sociability

As we noted above, Ferguson's conception of human nature includes a 'disposition to society' (*Principles* 1: 48) that leads him to reject state of nature theories and to assert that 'To be in society is the physical state of the species, not the moral distinction of any particular man' (*Principles* 1: 24). This sociability is an underlying universality of human existence that is supported by all the evidence of history, and even the occurrence of isolated cases of 'wild men' or feral children cannot be held to invalidate it. As a result, the principle forms part of the basis for the consideration of universal aspects of existence.[32]

To attempt to understand social interaction through the metaphor of contract and choice is to fundamentally misunderstand the nature of social bonds. Man, according to Ferguson, 'is born in society, and, while unconscious of benefit or wrong, is anxiously preserved in his state' (*Principles* 1: 30). This seems to be a very strongly stated position: human beings are social before they are rational or moral.[33] As if to underline the idea that it is not calculated self-interest that first attaches us to society, Ferguson suggests that society is also the source of 'almost the whole of his rational character' (*Essay* 23). As a result society is unlikely to have been the product of a calculation of interest if it pre-exists human rationality. Ferguson further underlines the vital importance of sociability to the understanding of human behaviour by noting the connection between happiness and society. Human beings left isolated are miserable and seize the first opportunity for human contact. Friendship, conviviality and interaction with others are the sources of real pleasure to humans everywhere and our happiness depends on us exercising our role as a member of a community. As a result we regard the sociable and friendly as admirable. Man is 'formed for society, and is excellent in the degree in which he possesses the qualifications of an associate and a friend' (*Principles* 2: 41). Ferguson admits that other, less admirable, forms of human interaction such as envy and malice are nonetheless outgrowths of our sociable nature, but he takes this as a reinforcement of the fact that morality is social rather than evidence of the corrupting effect of society suggested by Rousseau.

Our attachment to society cannot be explained by the instinctive, animal principle of herding, nor can it be reduced to calculations of interest; instead, connection to others is an emotional constant of human nature.[34] Ferguson believes that the decisive argument against theories that ground sociality in a principle of interest is provided by our willingness to fight in war (a point we will return to in Chapter 6). Instead society has its origins in biology: the emotional links between a child and its parents form the basis of human sociality. The nature of human childrearing necessitates a prolonged contact between the helpless child and its parents and this nurturing period fosters emotional bonds that persist throughout the lives of individuals. Ferguson is clear that this bond cannot be explained in terms of interest because it is characterised as a disposition or affection – and affection is an other-regarding mode of behaviour. The origins of the family, and hence of human society, lie in an emotional reaction to the realities of human reproduction. The bond of familial affection is established through the idea that 'instinctive attachments grow into habit' (*Principles* 1: 30).

What we also see here is the identification of another universal pattern of human behaviour: the family. Ferguson has drawn on his explanation of the universally observed sociality of humanity to further observe the universality of an institutional form of kin relationship grounded in familial affection. Ferguson's observation of the universality of families does not involve the demand that such association take a universally similar form (say nuclear as opposed to extended), nor do cases of child abandonment negate the claim to universality. The reason for this again lies in the evidence of history – all historical and contemporary evidence displays that some form of family unit is a feature of all known societies.

The question now becomes one of how these familial groupings are extended into larger social associations, how we 'pass over the bounds of personal acquaintance or personal relation' (*Principles* 2: 293). Ferguson notes that the 'name of society may be given to a mere family, a tribe, a select company of friends, and to a nation or an empire' (*Principles* 1: 25). The difference between these forms of society, according to Ferguson, is not the numbers of individuals involved, but rather the principles of association. In order to understand the move from family to nation we must understand the steps involved in generating the larger association. Families grow and become extended through kinship association as they provide the secure conditions for the natural pursuit of procreation. The bond of association in these small groups is that of 'affection' and 'choice' (*Institutes* 21) as parental affection becomes habitual and familiarity builds extended kin relationships.

The next step in Ferguson's analysis involves the advent of larger associations of locality, region and nation. He accounts for these, in a similar manner to Hume, as arising from 'necessity' and the 'authority of leaders' (*Institutes* 21). There is a gradual rise of chiefs and the generation of bonds of common defence in the face of external threats. This represents the effective start of non-kin-based social associations and as such is the origin of civil society. As Ferguson would put it: 'Without the rivalship of nations, and the practice of war, civil society itself could scarcely have found an object, or a form. Mankind might have traded without any formal convention, but they cannot be safe without a national concert' (*Essay* 28). Great nations arise from confederacies for mutual defence between pre-existing groups bound by sentiment.[35]

What we can appreciate from all of this is that Ferguson's understanding of human sociality is far subtler than might first be expected. In the first place, though sociability is universal, the object of that bond is not the whole of humanity, but rather a particular group the origins of which lie in oppositions between groups. Our sociability does not manifest itself as a love of all mankind. Instead it unfolds through affiliation with particular groups who are opposed to each other. The origin of extended human societies is mutual antipathy. Ferguson pays particular attention to the concept of a nation and its unifying bond of national spirit. While he does, in places, accept the legalistic definition of a nation as a corporate body of individuals and make use of corporeal metaphors, these approaches are incidental to his main concern with the nature of the interaction and bonds that constitute a nation.

Having identified sociability, the family and the nation as universal forms of human experience, Ferguson goes on to analyse another underlying universality of human nature that underpins the movement from family to extended group life. The affection that links parents to children is acquired through habit, and it is similarly the development of shared habits that marks the bond of nations. Ferguson defines a habit as 'the acquired relation of a person to the state in which he has repeatedly been' (*Principles* 1: 209). Habits are acquired through repetition 'without reflection or design' (*Principles* 1: 210) and manifest themselves in affection for the familiar. As such the basis of group bonds is an acquired habit of being in certain company and the conventional forms of association that arise within this company.

Ferguson considers the bonds of social life as expressions of conventions developed through habit into customs and traditions. He notes that the 'Great part of the civil conventions of men are constituted by the received customs of their society' (*Institutes* 207). Groups of humans accommodate themselves to each other and the circumstances in which they find themselves such that: 'Men form themselves into society and the Society reacts upon its members to an Effect that contributes more than any other circumstance to the Form which its members Assume and the Rank that they bear' (*Manuscripts* 83). Put another way, most human behaviour can be explained through the socialisation of individuals into the customary forms of behaviour that hold within the particular social group into which they are born. Socialised acceptance of group conventions arises in exactly the same manner as the bonds of affection are solidified between children and parents: through familiarity and habit.[36]

One consequence of this, and indeed one of the advantages of the process, is that it renders human behaviour relatively predictable. We can 'guess' how a certain person will respond given our familiarity with the patterns of behaviour of our group. Socialisation, like habit, has the unintended consequence of introducing stability of expectations into human life. Another advantage is that socialised customs extend stability of expectations beyond the experience of particular individuals. Our sociable nature leads us to 'credit' or trust the opinions of our fellow group members in a manner that encourages social cooperation. This credit becomes central to the extension of trading relations into an abstract idea of contract.

Socialised individuals acquire 'rules' of acceptable or, to be more accurate, 'expected' behaviour from their interaction with their peers. It is these rules that represent the basis of civil association. As a consequence of this, group membership becomes not just a matter of having been born into a particular group, but of conforming to the standard forms of behaviour developed by that group. In each group socially acceptable behaviour becomes informally codified into the rules of propriety or manners: 'There is a rule of propriety, which, though it may be different in different instances, is to each the canon of estimation, and the principle from which they are to judge' (*Principles* 2: 150).

Contagion

The generation of shared conventions of behaviour and their transmission through the socialisation produced by natural sociability lie at the heart of Ferguson's understanding of the unity of social groups. The bonds of affection that attach us to other members of the group are heightened by appreciation of shared beliefs and practices. As Ferguson would have it: 'The influence of prevailing opinions and examples, arises from the social nature of man; and is one condition by which men are fitted to act in companies and societies' (*Institutes* 238). Natural sociability, combined with the propensity for habit formation, in group interaction produces 'a general conformity of thought' (*Principles* 1: 135), analysed by Ferguson through the idea of a 'contagion' (*Essay* 156). The idea is that social interaction itself produces spontaneous regularities of behaviour that constitute part of the group bond. Crucially these contagions provide a basis for shared belief that is independent of institutions. Societies are subject to contagions of manners and beliefs that spread through the body of the people without the conscious intervention of any particular individual. This, of course, forms the crux of Ferguson's argument against the accuracy of great legislator theories and his assertion that institutions are the result of the unintended consequences of the interaction of individuals with the circumstances in which they find themselves.

What is particularly interesting about Ferguson's approach here is his recognition that such an analysis of group behaviour does not lead to the view that mankind are hopelessly conservative and unwilling to accept change to establish forms of behaviour. This is because his theory of contagion is linked to a clear appreciation of the nature of crowd behaviour and its reaction to circumstances. Ferguson's contention that we are 'submissive to government, or docile to religion' is explained by contagion, but he also points out that we 'are no less vehement reformers of religion, and revolutionaries in government, when the current of opinion has turned against former establishments, than we were zealous abettors while the current continued to set in a different direction' (*Principles* 1: 135). Ferguson refers to this phenomenon as a 'contagion of sentiment' (*Principles* 2: 123) and cites as an example the idea that laughter is contagious. Laughter can spread through the members of a group even where some of its members are unaware of the original source of the mirth. This is important for Ferguson because it demonstrates that contagions do not depend on a rational apprehension of the origin of the practice or opinion. Contagions operate on crowds through emotion and not reason. Panic spreads through a large assembly by 'contagion' (*Principles* 1: 137) driven through feeling and rumour. As he puts it: 'Passions are thus communicated from one person to another by contagion, without any communication of thought, or knowledge of the cause; and the person, to whom a passion is so communicated, may mistake for the object of it some trifling incident or circumstance, which happens to accompany the emotion' (*Principles* 1: 143).

In its extreme form this sort of contagion can produce baseless group hysteria that threatens social order by sweeping individuals into an emotional frenzy that has more to do with their position in a group than any event that impinges on them as individuals. The danger of this in social and political life is apparent. At several points Ferguson applies the contagion theory to popular assemblies in a manner that suggests he sees 'numerous assemblies' as prone to emotional contagion that overwhelms considered opinion and turns the people into a mob. Although all humans are susceptible to this side effect of sociality, the common or vulgar are particularly prone to the mob mentality that is an extreme manifestation of the way common practices spread among a social group.

Ferguson is clear that the process of social contagion is the original form of coordination among extended groups of humans. Its influence on groups of humans is such that the only people capable of avoiding 'infection' are those with a particularly strong will and a sense that the general opinion is misplaced. Such individuals will generally go along with the crowd unless they conceive it as being mistaken. There are, however, two other types of individual who are an exception to the contagion of society. The first of these are the rare freethinkers, individuals who question all assumptions in a Socratic quest for truth before conformity, and the second are the deliberate contrarians, those who regard the possession of eccentric opinions as a badge of fame or merit. Neither of these are in a position to respond to the danger of an inflamed mob. But, as we will see below, Ferguson did think that a reliable gentleman class would have a role in managing such situations.

He observes that the origin of government and authority within groups is to be understood through the spread of opinion among the group.

> Involved in the resolutions of our company, we move with the croud before we have determined the rule by which its will is collected. We follow a leader, before we have settled the ground of his pretensions, or adjusted the form of his election: and it is not till after mankind have committed many errors in the capacities of magistrate and subject, that they think of making government itself a subject of rules. (*Essay* 64)[37]

The development of behaviour patterns shared among groups of humans facilitates social interaction by stabilising expectations and providing the shared experiences and attitudes that are recognised as binding the group together. Ferguson then extends this analysis into a discussion of the implications of such shared attitudes for individuals and nations. It's worth examining this in some detail as it has considerable ramifications for Ferguson's understanding of a civil society.

Ferguson begins the passage in the *Principles* by arguing that social cohesion requires that we conform to social norms on matters of 'small moment' such as 'the ordinary constituents of good or ill manners; the proprieties of language and dress; the routine of hours for meals, for business, or play; the place of distinction in company.' The benefits that we acquire from establishing common patterns of behaviour exceeds the 'reason' for any one such form. These shared practices are an important part of what constitutes group membership and the act of sharing them constitutes, in an important sense, the 'band' of society. So the 'authority of prevailing opinions makes at least one bond of society' (*Principles* 1: 218), and in matters of minor civility this enforces itself through social interaction.

Where Ferguson goes next with this is interesting for a number of reasons. First, he makes a distinction between matters of small moment and more serious moral matters; second, he does not suggest a difference in kind between small moment and more serious matters – the difference is in the subject and in the enforcement mechanism. As he puts it:

> The volume of nature is open for the information of mankind. If, in matters of importance, the sagacious are well informed, they may lead the opinions of others: And it is beneficently provided, that opinions once formed, and continued into habit, should give to human affairs, in every country, and in every age, a certain stability or regularity, to which every person, in the choice of his own conduct, may accommodate himself.
>
> As uniformity, or the coincidence of many, in a particular way of thinking, proceeds from communication, and is preserved by habit, it were absurd to employ any other method, to obtain or preserve unanimity. The use of force in particular, to dictate opinion, is preposterous and ineffectual: It tends to give importance to triffles, to awaken suspicions of a design to tyrannize, and arms the mind with obstinacy or enthusiasm, to retain what was slightly adopted, to reject what is violently offered, and what, if the mind were left to itself, would be easily changed for any other apprehension of things that is more prevailing or common. (*Principles* 1: 218–19)

This long quotation is central to what will follow in the rest of this book. Not only does it outline the theory of society that forms the core of his moral science, but it also indicates the underlying purpose of that science. Ferguson's entire system of thought is geared towards the identification of a moral code that would form the basis of the education of a class of gentlemen who will direct society and ensure its smooth operation.

Conclusion

We can see from the discussion above that Ferguson wishes to draw a distinction between conformity in unimportant matters of social cohesion and a responsibility to defend what is morally right in more serious matters. However, this does not lead him into making a qualitative distinction about the way the more serious moral beliefs originate or spread through society. He notes that our sentiments of justice and right or wrong 'are greatly enhanced by the sympathy and contagion of social nature' (*Principles* 1: 268). The 'communication of numbers' (*Principles* 1: 268) plays a vital role in the generation and spread of a conception of morality among a social group. It becomes clear that this fact need not be a positive feature of social life. For example, Ferguson repeatedly refers to how there can be contagions of immorality that spread through social groups as a corruption. Examples of this include the 'contagion of baseness' (*Principles* 1: 149) brought about by the excessive admiration of wealth, the 'contagion of mercenary manners' that arose at Carthage (*Rome* 36); the 'contagion of mean and degrading examples' (*Rome* 477) set by the successors to Augustus and the 'contagion of military arrogance' (*Rome* 479) that spread from the Praetorians to the legions as the Empire became prey to its armies.

Like many other aspects of human behaviour moral sentiments are 'kindled' (*Principles* 1: 268–9) in society and spread by contagion. Individuals become socialised into the prevailing manners and beliefs of their nation and become habituated to certain understandings of right and wrong. Their shared experience of these conventions acts as a badge of their membership of the group. As we noted above such conformity is perfectly acceptable in 'matters indifferent' (*Institutes* 186) but 'in matters of Importance, we ought to chuse what is for the good of mankind, in opposition to opinion and custom' (*Institutes* 186). It is here that the study of moral science comes into its own. Moral science has 'a perpetual reference to society' (*Principles* 1: 269) because society is the location in which morality comes into existence and contagion through sociability is how it spreads through a group. In Ferguson's view this is not the same thing as saying that whatever a society regards as morally right is necessarily so. Ferguson is not a relativist. Before proceeding to consider the role of moral science in determining the content of morality we should pause to consider what Ferguson says about the actual operation of morality within social groups.

We have seen how Ferguson approaches the spread of belief patterns through socialisation, habit and contagion, but this tells us little about the individual experience of moral behaviour. What will become clear is that there are two key principles in play in Ferguson's analysis: choice and judgement. Both choice and judgement are intimately linked to natural sociability. Ferguson observes that 'It is part of the social nature of man, to desire praise, and to shun blame' (*Institutes* 239). Humans constantly judge the actions of their peers and are aware that they are, in turn, subject to judgement by them. Humanity 'distinguishes characters by epithets of praise or blame' (*Analysis* 10). Humans are active creatures and their actions become the subject of moral assessment. In this sense we judge others and assign them responsibility for their freely chosen actions. Every time we pass judgement on others we are tacitly acknowledging the reality of morality. Morality is the natural consequence of human group life: we are moral because we are sociable.

Moreover, because Ferguson conducts his discussion of the origins of morality in terms of the affection for group membership and praise/blame he highlights the central role played in moral judgement by feelings of right and wrong. His recourse to this idea is a response to those moralists who had sought to reduce morality to a simple principle or set of principles that can assess all actions in all circumstances. He argues: 'It may be difficult, however, to enumerate the motives of all the censures and commendations which are applied to the actions of men. Even while we moralize, every disposition of the human mind may have its share in forming the judgement, and in prompting the tongue' (*Essay* 39). This passage is followed immediately by one in which Ferguson admits that specific acts of judgement need not represent 'moral' judgements – they may, for example, express envy, jealousy and so on – and that as a result it may often be the case that one individual will censure another for immorality while the censor's actual motive is far less noble.

However, when we do undertake moral judgement we tend to conduct the process in terms of a reflection of an external action upon the character of the individual. We appear to possess a scale of merit and demerit upon which we range those whom we meet. This scale is sensitive to context and displays a subtlety of judgement. For example, Ferguson observes that our generalised principles of right and wrong can make distinctions of circumstance. Ferguson traces the content of these standards or generalisations about moral behaviour to the conventions and practices of the social group. As he would have it:

> The great distinction of right and wrong, of virtue and vice, on which men experience such extremes of complacence or indignation, of esteem or contempt, is formed on the dictates of a social disposition, which receives, with favour and love, what constitutes the good of mankind, or rejects, with disapprobation and abhorrence, what is of a contrary nature. (*Principles* 1: 35)

Individual moralising is guided by principles that have developed from human group life and as a result of this many of our moral generalisations have as their object the continuation of the group bond or, as it comes to be known, the public good. Our notions of right and wrong, of what is just and moral, are largely shaped by our socialisation into the practices of a group that has developed a tradition of behaviour that facilitates the existence of an extended society. In turn this sociability is grounded in affection for the familiar and for those who share the characteristics of the group with us.

Moral science, like all science, requires us to generalise from evidence. Once we have a body of evidence concerning human nature and how it responds to circumstances we are in a position to develop a comparative account of types of behaviour and types of institution and practice. Ferguson believes that this will provide him with a secure basis (the universals) to identify moral laws. The generalisations of the physical sciences possess their authority with references to matters of fact. But those of the moral science depend on the notion that they are 'obligatory' (*Institutes* 5). A moral law is an expression of what is 'good' and as such is the proper object of choice. This leads us to a relatively straightforward understanding of moral philosophy as 'the knowledge of what ought to be, or the application of rules that ought to determine the choice of voluntary agents' (*Institutes* 9).

If the enforcement mechanism is sociable judgement, then its subject matter is choice in a social context. Moral principles are abstract guidelines that help to direct human choices. Or as Ferguson puts it: 'A moral law of nature is equally general, though an expression not of a fact, but of what is good; and is addressed to the powers of estimation and choice' (*Principles* 1: 160). The moral law may be directed at the faculty of choice, but its determination lies in the examination of human nature and the record of human life. His project, in a sense, is the same as that of every political thinker from Aristotle, but Ferguson is working in a world where what counts as science has changed. This moral science itself is based on a generalisation. We do not look back into history and identify a golden age of morally perfect individuals that will act as a standard for our emulation, nor do we privilege the beliefs and practices of our own society. Instead, Ferguson calls on us to examine the evidence of history and seek the universal patterns of behaviour that we find there. As he argues: 'We endeavour to understand what he ought to be; without being limited, in our conception, to the measure of attainment or failure, exhibited in the case of any particular person or society of men' (*Principles* 1: 2). It is in pursuing this that we move from the empirical basis of moral science to the normative prescriptions of moral philosophy.

Notes

1. Andrew Skinner (1967b) sees this aspect of Ferguson's thought as an example of the widespread Scottish Enlightenment concern with the methodology of natural history.

2. Lehman (1930: 170–1) notes the presence of these attacks on philosophical vices and compares them to the 'Idola' of Bacon. Lehman's list is repetitive and rambling, and while it identifies many of the points that will be covered in this chapter, it makes no attempt to relate these errors to each other or to the overall shape of Ferguson's methodology.

3. Ferguson returns to the point in the discussion of happiness in the late essays where he cautions against substituting pleasure and pain for good and evil – it may not lead to 'discernment of particulars' – 'but in the application endangers the oversight of differences the most important in the application of Words' (*Manuscripts* 106).

4. Ferguson criticises Rousseau's account of the state of nature in a number of places throughout his work. See, for example, *Principles* (1: 55), *Principles* (2: 218, 339), *Essay* (12, 3).

5. It is also worth pausing at this point to indicate an additional feature of the vice of language that is apparent in Price's argument. Ferguson wants to make a distinction between an idealised sense of liberty and a practically attainable notion of liberty and so comparing the British constitution with some imaginary ideal is an error. This argumentative vice is used to rhetorical effect by Price, but for Ferguson it leads him to form unrealistic expectations. The choice is not between an ideal constitution of liberty and the imperfect British form, it is between the British form and some other practicable system of liberty which is as likely to be imperfect.

6. For Ferguson's criticism of Mandeville see *Institutes* (104), *Essay* (18–20, 36–8), *Manuscripts* (213, 250).

7. A point that Ferguson puts into the mouth of 'Hume' in *The Discourse on Moral Estimation* (Manuscripts: 231).

8. For Ferguson's criticism of Hobbes see *Principles* (1: 12, 68, 72–3) and *Principles* (2: 197, 215, 234, 237). The extended discussion

of Hobbes, Locke and the system of ideas appears at *Principles* (1: 73–4).

9. Ferguson offers similar observations on the mistaken use of mechanical analogy in discussing free will and determinism: 'Such substitutions of mechanical imagery, in this, as in many other instances, serve to mislead our conception' (*Principles* 1: 153).

10. A point noted by Kettler (2005: 240) and Hill (2006: 14).

11. Though it is worth noting that he had raised it as early as *Of Natural Philosophy* (2).

12. Bernstein (1978) argues that Ferguson underestimates the strength of Rousseau's argument in the *Discourse on the Origin of Inequality*. But this could not be further from the truth. In the background of all of Ferguson's work, but perhaps most obviously in the *Essay*, he is engaged in an analysis of precisely the forces of socialisation upon which Rousseau's argument depends. His point is that Rousseau's rhetorical tactic of highlighting socialisation through a contrast with a state of nature is methodologically unsound. Again, this misses the methodological point being made. Alexander Broadie (2001: 80–3; 2012: 184) has suggested that Ferguson is perhaps unduly harsh on Rousseau's use of a thought experiment and Höpfl (1978: 26) makes a similar point when he suggests that the Scots simply treat the first stage of their stadial schemes as the state of nature in much the same way as Rousseau does.

13. One likely source for Ferguson's views on excessive abstraction is Shaftesbury. For a discussion of Shaftesbury's influence on Hume in this connection see Harris (2015: 44–5).

14. See also '. . . is a mere abstraction, no where existing in nature; but convenient, like other abstractions, in the statement of a subject, as matter of discussion or argument' (*Principles* 1: 128).

15. Annette Meyer (2008: 140, 145) has noted that Ferguson's empiricism is combined with a near total disinterest in metaphysics. His attempts at formalisation and the identification of moral laws aid the project of moral judgement, but Ferguson has little interest in granting them any deeper metaphysical status. The complicated nature of the relationship between empirical and normative arguments in Ferguson's work has led David Allan to describe him as 'in no sense the purveyor of a descriptive science of society' and a 'shameless partisan for the cause of virtue' (Allan 2006: 21). It is one of the main contentions of this book that Allan is wrong in this, and that Ferguson is both a moralist and a descriptive moral scientist. Richard Sher takes a less extreme view and argues that Ferguson

'bound together his science of society and his ideology more tightly than did Hume – so tightly, in fact, that they frequently appear indistinguishable' (Sher 1985: 196). While this seems closer to the truth of Ferguson's intentions it suffers from the pejorative implications of the term ideology which suggest that Ferguson's political commitments shape his argument. See also Waszek (1986: 143).

16. See *Principles* (2: 118).

17. Christopher Berry (1997: 24) notes that the thinkers of the Scottish Enlightenment were empiricists in the basic sense of stressing facts and experience above theory. We have already observed Ferguson's lack of interest in metaphysical arguments and his dismissive attitude to Hume's scepticism, so to call him an empiricist is not to make any grander claim for his epistemology than to say that he stresses facts and evidence.

18. 'Reason and knowledge may hasten its effects; and for this purpose our feeble endeavours to erect the fabric of science, that they who resort to it may proceed on a just knowledge of their place and destination in the system of nature' (*Principles* 2: 104–5).

19. See Forbes (1967: 42).

20. See *Institutes* (61): 'Facts become remarkable by their reference to ourselves, or by their comparison, similitude, or contrast, with each other.'

21. For example, when Ferguson discusses the centrality of stable expectations arising from government and law as essential preconditions for the growth of civilisation he notes that: 'Mankind having laid the basis of safety, proceed to erect a superstructure suitable to their views' (*Essay* 180).

22. Ferguson returns to this idea when he comes to delineate the scope of political science in the *Principles*. Here he argues that commerce, science and politics are coeval – but for analytic purposes we can separate them out (*Principles* 1: 240).

23. See *Essay* (75) and *Principles* (1: 84). Both Sampson (1956: 93) and Heath (2009: 161) point out that the term conjecture is particularly inappropriate in describing Ferguson's method as it is based on a refusal to conjecture.

24. Ferguson's discussion here shows a quite sophisticated grasp of the issues with handling historical evidence. One indication of this is his lengthy discussion of the use of literature as evidence for the thoughts of a past society. Another is his argument about the transmission of mythical history where he argues that the survival of myths tells us as much about the ages who retell them as it does about the society

in which they originated: 'They are made to bear the stamp of the times through which they have passed in the form of tradition, not of the ages to which their pretended descriptions relate' (*Essay* 76).

25. Alexander Broadie (2001: 195) has observed that it is a shared view of the Scottish Enlightenment that we are 'by nature classificatory animals'.

26. Lehmann (1930: 188) and Sebastiani (2013: 42) point out that Ferguson follows Montesquieu on climate. While it is true that he takes the issues of climate more seriously than the other Scots (Berry 1974: 287–8), his position is ultimately 'equivocal' (Berry 1997: 83–4) or 'mitigated' (Sher 1994: 392) by his refusal to speculate on the nature of physiological impacts of climate.

27. Ferguson also briefly mentions race, citing Buffon (*Institutes* 18–19; *Analysis* 10), but assigns it no significant role in his moral science. Indeed, though he seems to admire the general idea of a natural history of man that he sees in Buffon, he is critical of details of his system and the way in which it connects humanity to the order of nature (*Principles* 2:130). Lehmann (1930: 95) suggests that while Ferguson recognises races as descriptive categories, he denies polygenesis or that race can affect the universality of human nature.

28. Ferguson argues that 'Human Nature is actually in motion' (*Institutes* 163–4) and that this motion can be 'retrograde' (*Rome* 481) as well as progressive. An impartial examination of the evidence of history will allow the identification of principles of behaviour that drive human action in all forms of society. As David Kettler (1977: 449) points out, this leads Ferguson to a conception of institutions and customs which sees them as in a constant state of gradual formation rather than confirmed and established.

29. A position he believes that he has established at the start of the *Essay* when he attacks Rousseau (Buchan 2005b: 10). Natural sociability is an idea pervasive in the thought of many of those who influenced Ferguson. Aristotle makes it central to his system, Cicero notes it, while Marcus Aurelius observed that: 'Social obligation then is the leading feature in the constitution of man' (1930: 187).

30. *Essay* (9).

31. David Allan (2006: 61) observes that the thinkers of the Scottish Enlightenment never fully faced up to the cultural relativism suggested by their method. Similarly Lisa Hill (2006: 59) has suggested that Ferguson never fully frees himself from his Western outlook. She also argues that Ferguson's faith in the existence of human universals is grounded in a 'Providentialist functionalism' (Hill 2006:

102), but it is not clear in what sense, given Ferguson's empirical method for identifying the universals and his relative disinterest in metaphysics, providence is any more active in Ferguson than it is in the other thinkers of the Scottish Enlightenment with their multiple references to Nature. Ferguson was not troubled by the spectre of cultural relativism precisely because he believed that he had identified a methodology that denied it any substance. For further discussion see Smith (2013).

32. Ferguson's extended criticism of social contract theory as a 'mere fiction in theory' (*Institutes* 220) is repeated in the *Institutes* (219–25), the *Essay* (8–15, 73) and the *Principles* (1: 195–9; 2: 460).

33. Ferguson goes on to argue that we 'find a clear apprehension of right and wrong prior to convention' (*Principles* 2: 218) suggesting that moral judgement is coeval with human nature.

34. Waszek (1986: 155) suggests that Ferguson's account of sociability blends parental affection, gregariousness and feelings of attachment to account for the inducements to live in society.

35. It is worth noting here that Ferguson is, by way of an aside, identifying another early universal form of human interaction – trade. If uncertainty and fear of invasion lead to the formation of social bonds that develop into political states, this does not detract from the fact that trade was possible between tribal groupings before the rise of what we understand as the nation.

36. As Ferguson notes: 'Men are much affected by early impressions; and continue to take much of their characters from notions that they entertain, and the habits of thinking they have acquired' (*Principles* 2: 72), an observation that informs his educational theory (see Chapter 4).

37. This is particularly apparent in monarchies where the power of one man is dependent on the opinion of those who follow him: what Ferguson terms the 'contagion of monarchical manners' (*Essay* 126).

3

Moral Philosophy

As the study of human nature may refer to the actual state, or to the improveable capacity, of man, it is evident, that, the subjects being connected, we cannot proceed in the second, but upon the foundations which are laid in the first. Our knowledge of what any nature ought to be, must be derived from our knowledge of its faculties and powers; and the attainment to be aimed at must be of a kind which these faculties and powers are fitted to produce. (*Principles* 1: 5)

Having outlined the methodology adopted for Ferguson's moral science we can now move on to the normative aspect of his project. Lisa Hill (2006: 57) has observed that Ferguson's method represents a 'procedure simultaneously empirical and normative', which may indeed invite Hume's (1976: 469) criticism of moving between the two without acknowledging it. But as Hill points out, Ferguson rarely lets his moral prejudice 'interfere with the empirical evidence' (2006: 7). There is a very good reason for this: Ferguson's view was entirely clear and consistently made throughout his career – there can be no worthwhile philosophy without a descriptive and scientific grounding. The question that we must now address is that of how, exactly, Ferguson envisaged the link between the empirical and normative elements of his thought, or as Annette Meyer (2008: 139) describes it, between the empirical laws of nature and the moral laws of nature in Ferguson's thinking. One way into understanding this is to look at the consistently applied distinctions that Ferguson draws between the two modes of thinking. In the *Institutes* he describes how there are two types of laws of nature: physical and moral. The two types of law invite distinct, but related, modes of enquiry and their law-like status refers to different sources:

A physical law exists so far only as it is the fact.
A moral law exists in being obligatory. (*Institutes* 5)

The immediate use of physical laws is theory [in the language we are adopting, moral science].
The immediate use of moral laws is moral philosophy. (*Institutes* 6)

In the earliest versions of Ferguson's attempt to systematise the distinction between the empirical study of human nature and the normative moral philosophy built upon it he blends in the discipline of pneumatics. Thus in the *Analysis* (6) 'Human Nature treated Physically is in part the subject of Pneumatics' 'Treated Morally is the subject of Moral Phil', with pneumatics representing the link between the realm of spirit and that of the material. But even here Ferguson rejects the idea that the physical study of the human body can provide us with a locus for the study of human choice. He returns to the theme in the *Institutes* where he argues that: 'Pneumatics, or the physical history of mind, is the foundation of moral philosophy' (*Institutes* 10), but, crucially for Ferguson, it does not determine moral philosophy. The study of moral philosophy must know the operation of the human mind, but neither the physical study of the brain nor the philosophical analysis of the human mind are sufficient as anything other than the basis for the further exploration of moral philosophy.

One of the problems with identifying this central point of Ferguson's methodology is that in each of the three books based on his Edinburgh lectures he adopts a slightly different, and apparently contradictory terminology (ironically enough given his identification of the 'vice' of inattention to language). The point to bear in mind is that within each book Ferguson is consistent in his use of terminology, and across the three books the methodology remains broadly the same. For the sake of clarity, the analysis that follows will continue to describe the empirical comparative examination of universal elements of human experience as moral science, while reserving the name moral philosophy for the normative exercise of constructing a theory of how we ought to live. Ferguson himself notes the two distinct aspects of his method, but he refers to them both as science or philosophy indiscriminately, and using distinct terms for each aspect allows us to get a better sense of the exact relationship between the two.

Moral philosophy is 'the knowledge of what ought to be, or the application of rules that ought to determine the choice of voluntary agents' (*Institutes* 9). The crucial step for Ferguson, and one which places him squarely in the tradition of thinking running from Aristotle to the natural lawyers of the sixteenth century and, perhaps most importantly, to Francis Hutcheson's pedagogy, is the view that: 'Before we can ascertain rules of morality fitted to any particular nature, the fact relating to that nature should be known' (*Institutes* 9). Moral philosophy must be moral philosophy for the type of beings that humans actually turn out to be, and the only secure basis for this (as Hume was to observe) is observation and experiment. Notice the order of priority here: moral science precedes moral philosophy. Moral philosophers in the past have proceeded too hastily to the normative project before they have provided a solid basis in the observation and analysis of human nature. It is only once the nature of humanity has been studied that we will be in a place to identify the principles which ought to guide their behaviour. Consequently, it is only a scientific study of human nature that can begin the project of moral philosophy as a normative guide to how we ought to live.

As we saw in Chapter 2, Ferguson believed that it was a universally observed fact concerning human nature that humans exercise 'censorial inspection' so it becomes the task of moral philosophy to guide that judgement in line with the natural laws generalised from the study of human nature. To do this humanity must be understood as part of a wider system of nature and it is only then that Ferguson makes the key step which he regards as the lynchpin of the relationship between the theory of human nature and the normative system of moral philosophy. That step, like that made by Aristotle, is the observation that humans are sociable.

If the first volume of the *Principles* is supposed to provide us with the 'theory' of human nature grounded in observation, then the second volume is intended to generalise from that to provide a normative system of moral philosophy for the type of creature described in the first book. The two books are related, but the aim of each is distinct: 'The facts are presented not as discoveries, but as the data from which to infer the judgements and conclusions of the second part' (*Principles* 1: 10). Later in the *Principles* he reiterates the point:

We have thus, in pursuance of the method proposed at the outset of this work, attempted to state the actual distinction of man in the system of nature; his powers of discernment and choice; his pursuits and attainments, the progress he is fitted to make, and of which the direction and effect for the present is committed to himself; but which the final termination is, we trust, far removed from his own view. (*Principles* 2: 400)[1]

The Fact of Morality

So we start with a basic datum: human beings are censorial: 'He distinguishes characters by epithets of praise or blame. He loves or hates, he admires or contemns' (*Analysis* 10). The exercise of moral estimation is a 'fact' which can be observed and confirmed by the study of human history. Put bluntly: 'There never was a people who did not perceive and apply the distinctions of right and wrong' (*Principles* 1: 159; see also *Principles* 2: 2). The study of this phenomenon proceeds by building on the observation of how humans have behaved and the observation of the sort of problems they face in the course of life. The moral philosophy that Ferguson hopes to build is one that will provide a guide to practical judgement. We can then study the sort of things that, in general, make our lives go better: 'Our information is to be collected from his experience of what is agreeable or disagreeable to him, and the result will amount to a choice of that, on which he is chiefly to rely for his happiness, and caution against that, of which he is chiefly to beware as leading to injury' (*Principles* 2: 3). The examples which he intends to use as the basis for both this study and for the pedagogy that will be built upon it are those which are accessible to 'ordinary men' (*Principles* 2: 71).[2] A system of moral philosophy which is not recognisable to the sort of moral creatures that it purports to speak to will, in Ferguson's account, be next to useless.

So wherever moral philosophy takes us, it must take us there from the facts of the situation, whatever problems we come across we must submit them to 'the tribunal of fact and experience' (*Principles* 2: 78–9). More polemically put, when we are offered a vision of human happiness conjured up by philosophy and one which exists in actual life: 'Let the fact therefore decide!' (*Principles* 2: 79). Humanity's nature as a moral creature is an 'ultimate fact' (*Principles* 2: 128) and as such can act like the principles of gravity – as the basis of an explanatory system.[3] The laws of Ferguson's moral philosophy, like Newton's Laws, provide us with the efficient causes of the moral universe, even if they cannot themselves be understood as anything other than generalisations draw from observation. This level of uniformity allows them to serve as 'Principles of science' even though it may be in 'no way susceptible of explanation or proof' (Principles 2: 128).

Ferguson's approach to normative moral philosophy is based on the idea that moral judgement is both real and universal. Human beings possess and exercise 'censorial powers' and engage in 'censorial inspection' (Principles 2: 22). This is part of our intelligent nature and is realised in judgements of characters and actions. The distinctions of good and evil and the preference for the former are universally observed in human history. For Ferguson this fact about human beings is sufficient to dispel the sceptic's doubts about morality. It is important to note that this is an empirical argument for Ferguson. The conceptual possibility of a human society without morality is a philosopher's abstraction which may be dismissed out of hand as describing some society unknown in human history. As he states in the Institutes:

> Men, fond of paradox, have questioned the reality of moral distinctions: but expressions of praise and blame in every language, the importance of mens actions to mankind, the opposite nature of dispositions that form the characters of men, the most vehement sentiments of the human heart, which refer to this subject, – show, that the distinction of moral good and evil is real, and universally acknowledged. (Institutes 108)

This is a line of argument that recurs throughout Ferguson's works and forms a key plank of his methodology. As we saw above, in his attack on Mandeville he follows Hutcheson and rests his analysis on the fact that the paradox only appears as such because it trades on the universality of moral judgement. Mandeville is only amusing, and challenging because he subverts the content of morality while passing moral judgement. The underlying fact of moral judgement should not be lost in the variety of disagreements about the content of morality. Moreover, disagreements about moral theory 'do not amount to any degree of uncertainty in the fact' (Principles 2: 127) that morality is real.

Indeed, Ferguson argues that the appearance of diversity in moral matters refers to the content of morality rather than the phenomenon itself. All humans exercise moral judgement and there are certain basic moral attitudes which are always present even though their object and content may differ. As he puts it:

> The distinction of right and wrong is coeval with human nature: It is perceived without instruction, in acts of fidelity and beneficence, or of perfidy and malice. These are the topics of praise and blame, in every nation and in every age. That, indeed, which in one instance is considered a benefit, in another instance is considered as harm or detriment. (*Principles* 1: 300)

Ferguson takes this as the basis for his answer to a number of philosophical issues. Perhaps the easiest way to understand this is to see how he squares the 'fact' of different moral beliefs with the universality of the phenomenon of moral judgement. As we saw above, diversity of habit and belief can be explained by context. But the universality of human nature and the universality of the urge to 'censorial inspection' are also supported by the evidence of history. As a result we are left with the two tasks of producing a moral science which explains the reality of human moral life as it is and has been lived, and a moral philosophy which will allow us to improve on our current beliefs and practices and approach the truth about morality.

This is a task for the educated. While the great bulk of people can be trusted to follow their habitual path in judging others, the educated 'few' (*Principles* 1: 306) are left with the task of 'improving' moral beliefs and disseminating them through society. So Ferguson draws a close connection between the fact of human diversity and the task of moral philosophy. Differences in belief and behaviour should not be casually dismissed in the search for a single moral belief system. Instead they form part of the material for the moral scientist and the moral philosopher.

This allows Ferguson to set out a number of clear tasks for his project. He lists these in the *Institutes* (109) as the four parts of the study of moral approbation:

1. What do men, for the most part, approve or blame?
2. By what principle, or consideration, are they directed, in particular cases, to bestow their approbations or censures?
3. What is the proper subject of approbation or censure?
4. What is the rule or principle by which men ought to judge of moral characters?

The first two, using the terminology of the *Institutes*, are 'physical' and the second two are 'moral' – in our terms they are respectively the subject of moral science and moral philosophy. Stating them clearly and apart is quite deliberate.

The care with which Ferguson addresses this issue is significant. He wants to examine the relationship between moral philosophy and current moral beliefs with the further complication being that imperfect individuals fail to live up to the beliefs that prevail in society. But these factors should not lead us to abandon the project and question whether there is anything that we ought to esteem. Ferguson wants to be very clear that his factual study of existing moral beliefs is not going to lead to an argument from authority. Because something has been believed does not mean that it should be believed. Moral science and moral philosophy must come together in a critical analysis of moral experience. As he would have it: 'The fact, however well established, and however universal, does not preclude us from conceiving and chusing what is better' (*Institutes* 110). Our conception of what we ought to be is not limited to what we are and have been, but our morality must be a morality for human beings. To this end we must study their nature and the beliefs that they have had in order to understand what makes us tick on a moral level. Ferguson's point is that we must have a morality informed by what humans can achieve, but this does not limit us to what they have in fact believed or done in the past. In the following sections we will run through the main elements in Ferguson's moral philosophy, indicating as we go how he melds the empirical and normative elements of his argument and draws together the traditional languages of moral philosophy.

Ambition

Perhaps the central idea in Ferguson's moral philosophy is his notion of ambition. He flags it up in the introduction to *Principles* 1 (iii) as a core part of his analysis. The 'desire of something better than is possessed at present' (*Principles* 1: 202; see also *Principles* 1: 236) might at first glance be supposed to be a synonym for self-interest. But in Ferguson's hands this is quite markedly not the case. Ambition is 'universal to mankind' (*Principles* 2: 94) and suited to our nature. It is a propensity, a feature of human nature, which he defines in the *Analysis* as 'an original or acquired disposition of our nature, operating independent of reflection or design'

(*Analysis* 20). Ferguson's main interest in ambition is as a prompt to action. It is because we desire something better than we possess that we are 'prompted' to act (*Principles* 1: 208). If human beings were not constantly driven by ambition they would lack not just an object at which to aim, but also the impetus to activity itself which, as we will see, is a good in itself for Ferguson. As he puts it:

> If the desire of any thing better than the present should at any time cease to operate in his mind, he becomes listless and negligent, loses the advantages he had gained, whether of possession or skill, and declines in his fortune, till a sense of his own defects and his sufferings restore his industry. (*Principles* 1: 56)

The centrality of ambition is also interesting because Ferguson links it to the emotional experience of hope, or 'the expectation of some good that is future' (*Principles* 2: 11). This is the case in the sense that we hope for the object of our ambition and that our actions will secure it. But it is also true for Ferguson that we hope to be better people. In Ferguson's mind the urge for moral improvement is a form of ambition: the ambition to be a better person. This moral ambition is closely related to moral judgement, and to the assessment of excellence and defect.[4] We are subject to 'a radical principle of elevation or progression in the human mind, to which there is ever presented, as an object of desire, something higher and better than is possessed at present' (*Principles* 2: 32). Note the phrasing here, the object of desire is ever present. This desire for perfection, or more accurately for improvement, can never be satiated. This is exactly the same point that Ferguson makes about the material desires that drive commerce.[5] We want to be better and are constantly striving to be what we think human beings ought to be. Moreover, it is only because we perceive good/ evil and perfection/defect that we have a reason to act. To make a judgement that one set of affairs is preferable to another is an operation of the censorial faculty. It is a choice, and that choice involves a commitment to the view that one thing is to be preferred to another. Human ambition is by its very nature discriminating and evaluative.

Ferguson returns to ambition in his late unpublished *Manuscripts* and here the discussion is put in even more stark terms: 'Ambition or the desire of Elevation or Perfection is certainly among the Strongest or the most powerful [in] the human

Breast' (*Manuscripts* 80). In the *Manuscripts* the discussion takes the form of a Stoic inspired consideration of the nature of 'just Ambition' (*Manuscripts* 94), which is defined as the desire of absolute value rather than comparative value. And it is here that we see one of the tensions that arise from his concept of ambition come to the fore (see below on happiness). In the sense that human beings desire something better than they possess at present, they are always conducting a comparative judgement between their present situation and some hoped for improved condition, but in his attempt to tie ambition to morality as closely as possible Ferguson introduces the idea of an object of ambition that has ultimate value. The aim here seems to be to distinguish morality from other objects of human ambition, almost as though, having deployed the same concept of ambition to both moral and material concerns, he wanted to reintroduce a distinction of kind. There is no easy way to overcome this late, apparently contradictory, shift in his discussion of ambition.

It is worth pausing at this point to note that there is another implication of Ferguson's commitment to the central role of ambition. If there is 'an improveable nature in man' (*Principles* 2: 405) and he is driven by ambition, then he is destined not to be 'stationary' but 'Progressive' (*Principles* 1: 56). Ferguson links this to the fact of moral judgement. The fact that we perceive some phenomena as evil is a recognition that they should be otherwise. Recognising the wrong is a demand for it to be made right. As he puts it: 'Complaints of moral evil are the symptoms of a progressive or improving nature. A being that perceived no moral evil, or no defect, could have no principle of improvement' (*Institutes* 132).

Critics who read Ferguson as providing a teleological or perfectionist account of humanity have dwelt on this central element of his theory.[6] But they have also been forced, in so doing, to note that Ferguson does not provide us with a glimpse of the telos or ideal in anything other than the most hackneyed platitudes. Thus the 'passage or transition from defect to perfection is that which constitutes the felicity of a progressive nature' (*Principles* 1: 200); through our lives we move progressively towards moral perfection, never reaching it, but rather improving a step at a time, both in our understanding of our duty and in the exercise of our capacities. Life, for Ferguson, is a moral schoolroom in which we are sensible of the changes in our lives and habits and can be held responsible and judged for the choices that we make.

Perfectionism

There are two sides to this: that we are capable of perceiving moral perfection and that we are capable of choosing or willing it. For Ferguson these are both uniquely human characteristics that come together to explain how we are capable of moral judgement and of being the object of moral judgement. Man alone is capable of ideas of 'perfection and defect' (*Principles* 1: 236) and it is the 'object of human reason' (*Institutes* 163) to distinguish between them. In the *Institutes* this is characterised among Ferguson's laws of the Will, the third law stating that: 'Men naturally desire what constitutes excellence, and avoid what constitutes defect' (*Institutes* 94).

In regard to morality this involves us in a search for a conception of morally perfect behaviour. When philosophers talk of the good man, or the just society, or the beautiful work of art, they are conceiving an object that is idealised and perfect.

> If we are asked, therefore, what is the principle of moral approbation, we may answer, It is the *Idea of perfection* or excellence, which the intelligent and associated being forms to himself; and to which he refers in every sentiment of esteem or contempt, and in every expression of commendation or censure. (*Principles* 2: 134)

To pass censorial inspection on another person's behaviour involves holding their behaviour up to some notion of perfection and finding it wanting, and the same is true of censorial inspection of the self. But Ferguson is conscious that there is a third, intermediate, position which is more significant for moral judgement. 'Men conceive perfection, but are capable only of improvement. Their dispositions are various, and their forces unequal' (*Institutes* 162). Philosophy deals in ideals, and that is all very well, but men are imperfect and will never match those ideals. The danger then is that 'in our general account of perfection, we far exceed what human nature is fit to attain' (*Principles* 2: 401) and our philosophers would be 'absurd' should they suppose 'that men attain to anything above their strength' (*Institutes* 163). This indeed has been a common complaint against philosophers and one which Ferguson shares, but with a crucial caveat: 'Philosophers have been censured as recommending a perfection too high for human nature: Would it therefore be reasonable to recommend defects?' (*Institutes* 162). Perfection has a role as an aspiration, or perhaps

more accurately in Ferguson's terminology, as an object of ambition. Ambition has to do with improving our situation and in the
moral sphere this involves mending our behaviour in the pursuit
of moral improvement. In our judgement of others this should
always be undertaken with a sense of what might realistically be
expected of such imperfect creatures.

The human desire to 'better themselves' (*Institutes* 164) is
undertaken by men who are 'generally as far from the extreme
of perfect vice, as they are from that of perfect virtue' (*Institutes*
301), but who are nonetheless capable of improvement and, what
is more, who actively desire it. So thinking about what is perfect,
engaging in moral philosophy driven by moral ambition, is the
prompt to improve our behaviour. We can now see how Ferguson
links this activity to moral science. We choose in the light of our
'observation and experience' (*Principles* 2: 122). It allows us to
identify 'false opinion', to 'narrow the scope of aberration and
mistake' (*Principles* 1: 234) and to correct our views in the light
of 'the progress of experience and better information' (*Principles*
1: 302).

Humans are capable of 'indefinite advancement' (*Principles* 1:
183) because we are capable of choosing to direct our action to
our conception of morally perfect behaviour. As a result of this
commitment Ferguson has no truck with the idea that a failure to
choose to aim at moral improvement can be excused. Humans are
not perfect, but 'progress itself is congenial to the nature of man'
(*Principles* 1: 249), and a failure by an individual to direct his
ambition to such improvement is worthy of censure. This indeed is
one of the points of tension in his thinking as it seems to clash with
the idea of providence drawn from both Stoicism and Presbyterian
Christianity. How can Ferguson argue that ambition drives us to
activity and to want to become better people, to strain for that
beyond our current possession, and at the same time draw exten-
sively on passages from Stoic authors which appear to counsel
acceptance of one's position and fate in the pursuit of quietism or
a submission to predestination and a providential plan? We will
return to this theme in Chapter 4.

We now begin to see how the two aspects of Ferguson's project
come together. Moral science tells us what kind of being humans
are. This allows us to develop a moral philosophy of what they
ought to want, and this image of moral perfection creates the
incentive to improve that draws imperfect individuals to pursue or

to want the good. Ferguson's empirical basis and his acceptance of the imperfection of actual individuals distances his thought from what he regarded as the more naive of the enlightenment progressives. As he notes in a barbed comment directed at Richard Price: 'I observe, with some writers, to give high expectations of the great perfection to which human nature is tending' (*Price* 22). This is not to say that progress has not been made. For all Ferguson is willing to speak in admiration for savages, he regards it as an obvious evidence of moral progress that we are not the same as them. Indeed he implies that anyone who doubts the reality of moral progress need only compare a savage's behaviour with that of a civilised man.[7] Properly filtered for ethnocentrism the moral philosophy based on moral science allows proper comparison and the savages 'may serve as examples of a defect to be supplied in the progress of moral apprehension and manners' (*Principles* 1: 301).

But Ferguson is clear right from his earliest version of the theory in the *Analysis* that his account of moral experience is crucially also an account of moral learning: 'It is a privilege of the mind to contemplate itself; to chuse its inclinations and sentiments; to suppress what is evil, and cultivate what is good' (*Analysis* 23; see also 27). This capacity for choice is the basis for moral responsibility – it is what makes us capable of censorial inspection and also what makes us the subject of such inspection.

Action

Ferguson believed that human beings are active by nature and driven by ambition to improve their situation: 'this active and aspiring being' (*Principles* 1: 178) 'is by nature an artist, endowed with ingenuity, discernment, and will' (*Principles* 1: 200). He is 'disposed' to 'invent' and 'fabricate' (*Principles* 1: 285) in the realisation of 'active and progressive natures' (*Principles* 1: 297). He regards action as a basic feature of all animals which seems to be a biogenetic observation about the nature of animal life itself in Ferguson's account. But he moves swiftly from this animalistic, instinctive action to the higher animals who 'have pleasure also in the active exertion of their powers' (*Principles* 1: 14). Action itself is a source of happiness such that 'even labour is its own reward' (*Principles* 2: 13). This leads Ferguson to observe that human beings seek out arenas to exercise their mental and physical abilities: 'Nature seems to require that we seek for the interesting scenes of human life' (*Principles* 2: 329). It is here that Ferguson most clearly differentiates himself from the quietistic elements of Stoicism and in doing so he is mining a line of argument that is Ciceronian rather than Stoic. Cicero's 'exultation of spirit seen in times of danger' (Cicero 1913: 65) allows Ferguson to simultaneously distance himself from Epicureanism and Stoicism while offering his own account of activity as central to human life.

Happiness is active for Ferguson: it is not 'that state of repose, or that imaginary freedom from care' (*Essay* 51). The 'busy' (*Essay* 45) pursue an object but gain pleasure from the exercise of their faculties as they do so. As ambition provides the direction to human activity we find man 'fitted to accommodate himself; destined to be the artificer of his own fortune' (*Principles* 1: 52). Moreover he will enjoy himself as he does so. In addition to this Ferguson regards much ambition-driven activity to result in an improvement in the faculties which it challenges. The human mind is improved with exercise, as is the human character. Ferguson even takes this so far as to argue that the pursuit of a mistaken end can still produce improvements to our capacities. Intriguingly this opens up the possibility that even pursuit of mistaken goals can be morally improving. So wedded to this idea is Ferguson that he feels compelled to dissect the variety of human activities to stress the key role played by the notion of difficulties.

Mankind is first directed towards the satisfaction of their material needs. But: 'When his preservation is secured, the life he preserves still requires to be otherwise occupied' (*Principles* 2: 9). And here we see Ferguson make another interesting claim about human nature. He argues that human pursuits tend to become competitive. Once we are secure we 'fill up the blanks of a listless life' (*Essay* 58) through pastimes which exert our mental and physical capacities. This leads Ferguson to one of his most sociologically acute analyses, that of the role of sport in human life. Sport is both explained by and illustrates perfectly the human disposition to activity and the exertion of our capacities. This 'disposition to action' makes 'difficulties' attractive to us (*Essay* 47) and Ferguson repeatedly turns to sport to illustrate the idea that human beings are not, by nature, made for retirement and repose. Once subsistence is secure they begin to fill their leisure time with activities which are competitive and even dangerous.[8]

As willing as Ferguson is to recognise the role of sport as a medium for exercise he returns to the idea that some forms of activity are more worthwhile than others. The key feature in making this distinction appears to be the purposefulness of the activity. 'The greatest danger ... is that of neglecting business for the sake of mere amusement or pastime' (*Principles* 2: 388). The enjoyment of pastimes is not considered to be a real threat to purposive activity in Ferguson's view. This is because once we have experienced the real thrill that arises from action in difficult and serious circumstances we 'cannot stoop to employ' (*Principles* 1: 222) our powers on less serious matters. Sport is a diversion from boredom and listlessness, but it is no substitute for the real business of human life.

It is at this point that we begin to see Ferguson connect the concepts of ambition and activity together. Ambition directs us to improvement, action and exercise of our capacities is the natural source of pleasure to humans, and the result is that purposive action in pursuit of the objects of our ambition is characteristic of a healthy human life. Ferguson builds a number of important steps in his moral philosophy on this platform. Perhaps the most characteristic of these is that, in almost total contrast to Rousseau's account in the *Discourse on the Origin of Inequality*, ambition, competition and division are healthy features of social life which exist wherever we find humans.

Humans delight in difficulties and seek occasions of opposition and contest both among themselves and with other animals. Such situations are the test of human character and the school of human capacity: 'Whoever can keep possession of his mind and his faculties, in the midst of difficulty or danger, will find his fortitude and his ability for conduct increased by the mere repetition of trying occasions' (*Principles* 1: 229). Capacity and virtue are produced by exercise in difficult situations.[9] So we prefer business to pastimes, and business is also characterised by the seriousness of the purpose of the activity.

But again, these struggles must be meaningful. It is action towards improvement that matters and this is no more apparent than in the role played by the active pursuit of moral improvement in our activity. What this allows Ferguson to do is focus on the fact that action is key to both the manifestation of virtue that allows us to judge others and the fact that our assessment of moral matters is not consequentialist. This is because if it is activity and not securing our goals that generates true happiness, then what matters is not so much the outcome as the part we played in securing that outcome. As we will see this affects Ferguson's conception of what we should expect from moral philosophy. Ferguson's is a moral philosophy aimed at the practical. It is a philosophy for 'real life' rather than 'shadowy objects of fancy' (*Principles* 1: 296). Moral learning is not achieved from books or in the classroom, but rather is a form of exercise achieved from exertion.[10] Once we grasp this we also get a better sense of Ferguson's conception of happiness. We cannot be happy if we are not active.

Happiness

It is worth pausing here to consider Ferguson's view on the place of happiness in moral experience. We noted above that Ferguson was particularly preoccupied with the long-running philosophical debate on how to distinguish pleasure from happiness. For the most part he plays out the standard sorts of position he picks up from ancient philosophy, particularly Aristotle and the Stoic and Epicurean debates, but his various attempts to work through this thought are, as Eugene Heath (2006) has observed, interesting in themselves. One reason why they are so interesting is that in this discussion Ferguson reveals another feature of the linked empirical and normative project that he is developing. While he is unwilling to accept the identification of pleasure with happiness, he is certain that happiness is a central part of moral experience and must be reconciled, or at least in principle be reconcilable, with other elements of our moral life. The question for Ferguson is how to achieve this.

There is an additional reason to consider this point. In an extended discussion of the relationship between Ferguson's empirical and normative enterprises David Kettler (2005: 120) suggests that Ferguson, by virtue of his various commitments, was unable to develop a scientific and properly naturalistic account of morality. One of the key planks of Kettler's argument is that the refusal on Ferguson's part to make a direct association between pleasure and virtue cuts off the only substantive way to provide a convincingly naturalised account of morality. This is part of a wider problem that Kettler observes with the incompatibility of the various elements in Ferguson's argument: if pleasure is not the direct link between what is and what ought to be, then how does Ferguson hope to pull off the connection?[11] This is related to the question of how Ferguson can 'defend the possibility of a scientific moral theory unbounded by mere facts while insisting that all scientific knowledge rests on the perception and consciousness of facts' (Kettler 2005: 126). Kettler's answer is to suggest that there is no real solution to these problems and that Ferguson's system remains riven by such contradictions and tensions. Indeed, he develops the idea of 'complementarity' as a way of explaining Ferguson's argumentative strategy in the light of such apparently glaring contradictions. But everything we have noted in our study thus far suggests that Ferguson was well aware of the problem – in fact he appears to have designed the structure of the *Principles* around precisely this point – and it would be extremely strange if he did not at least think that he had avoided the issue that Kettler raises. As we will see below, it is not just that Ferguson thought he had avoided the issue, he thought he had a solution to it.

In each of the three versions of Ferguson's theory pleasure is assigned a distinct place in human life. From the *Analysis* onwards pleasure and pain are treated as physical manifestations of the 'salutary' and 'pernicious' (*Analysis*: 31; *Principles* 2: 7). These extend from the body to the emotions, with things that affect the emotions generating pleasure and pain. So pleasure and pain are among the chief incentives to action. We choose, not surprisingly, pleasure over pain and when we must the lesser pain and the greater pleasure. From here we see Ferguson's various distinctions between this fact of psychology and the moral 'fact' that happiness is not the same as pleasure. In terms of the discussion of the ancients Ferguson is clear that the Epicureans are wrong to identify happiness and pleasure and that this error led to the 'unnatural' outcome of preferring sensual enjoyment and sloth to activity.[12]

So happiness and pleasure are not synonymous but, in the tangled discussion in the late *Essays* we find them more intimately intertwined than the denunciations of Epicureanism might lead us to think. The conclusion that Ferguson hopes to reach is that virtue, goodness, perfection and happiness are not only compatible, but identical. So 'the perfection and happi[ness] of mankind [are the] same' (*Manuscripts* 5). They are 'one and the same point' (*Manuscripts* 162) or different divisions of the same thing talked about under different headings (*Manuscripts* 81). Ferguson is relatively consistent throughout his writing that happiness and virtue are identical. If these elements can be properly understood as different manifestations of the same phenomenon, then Ferguson must connect them to the identified fact of pleasure while maintaining the relationship but not identity between the two. Ferguson's way of doing this is to go back to the emotional experience of pleasure and pain. In the *Institutes* he discusses one aspect of this when he argues that good and evil 'imply' enjoyment and suffering (*Institutes* 141) or that: 'He is a voluntary agent, destined to act under the following wise restraint: That his hurtful dispositions are painful to himself, and his beneficial dispositions are pleasant' (*Institutes* 133).

Pleasure and happiness/virtue/perfection are not identical, they are implicated in each other, and here, as elsewhere, Ferguson assigns the origin of this order to providence. The means of this implication is actually found very early on in Ferguson's writing when he observes that: 'The sense of any perfection is pleasant; of any defect, is painful' (*Analysis* 31). All happiness is pleasant, but not all pleasure is happiness and the distinction is found through the notion of perfection and defect.

In Chapter 4 we'll discuss Ferguson's relationship to Stoicism in more detail, but for the moment let us observe that for all of the strong statements that human happiness does not depend on the attainment of perfection, nor is it entirely, as the strong Stoic position would have it, 'indifferent' (*Principles* 2: 82) to the external condition in preference to the contemplation of perfection, but it is related to the idea of perfection. Ferguson repeatedly attacks philosophers who promote resignation in the face of fortune and who advise against public life. Whether they be the more extreme adherents of the ancient sects or Christians who favour 'monastic retreat' (*Essays* 171), these thinkers are wrong in their conception of happiness, wrong in their understanding of human nature and, ultimately, 'may be suspected of encouraging a dangerous neglect of affairs' (*Principles* 2: 340).

It is in the more detailed fleshing out of Ferguson's conception of happiness that we see him depart most obviously from the Stoic inspiration for the happiness/pleasure distinction. Aurelius and Cicero's notion of duty and playing one's part within the city might seem obviously linked to Ferguson's more republican discussions, but the discussion of happiness is deeper than this. It is grounded in his observationally based moral science. Here, we find that happiness is necessarily related to that other key Fergusonian concept: action. For Ferguson genuine happiness is a product of action and exercise. This is a position held consistently throughout his writings. From the *Essay*, where pleasure and pain do not equal happiness and misery because only active exertion can make us happy, to the *Principles* where happiness is not the attainment of fortune but the exercise of the faculties, happiness is portrayed as active rather than restful – as striving and ambitious rather than retiring and relaxing. The central creed of Ferguson's moral thought is that 'to be happy, he must be employed, or have something to do' (*Principles* 2: 14).[13]

As we saw above, such activity can take many forms, but there is a qualitative preference for 'business' in Ferguson's analysis. We prefer serious engagement where our capacities are tested and exercised. For Ferguson this is both pleasurable and generative of happiness. When he writes that the 'the sole object of reason is happiness' (*Principles* 2: 64) he means that rational creatures seek happiness and that this is a principal object of their moral ambition.[14] Ferguson's next step is to seek an object for the ambitious action that will generate happiness, virtue and moral improvement. Again, that object must be something that fits with the nature of human beings. It must be something that can be identified by moral science as a universal aspect of human nature and which, however diversified in form, can be traced across human history. Ferguson moves immediately and consistently to the point which he holds as being uniquely, ubiquitously and ultimately the defining characteristic of the human: sociability. Humans are social and society is the stage upon which they act, so ambitious action is directed towards society because we are social.

Society

As we saw in Chapter 2, sociability is an established 'fact' (*Essay* 39) supported by 'irrefragable proofs' (*Principles* 1: 47). Humanity is, as he puts it in a particularly colourful phrase, 'doomed to society' (*Principles* 2: 17). A human being raised outside of society, or even a human being conceptualised apart from his fellows, is not a human being: 'the individual can no where shake himself loose of his species' (*Principles* 2: 329). Everything that makes us what we are as a species comes from our social nature. Man is 'indebted to society for every exercise of his faculties' (*Principles* 1: 269). A man in a wasteland who sees tracks is overjoyed, a meal taken alone is a necessity, but a meal enjoyed with others is a pleasure because 'the pleasures of society are the exercises of a social nature' (*Principles* 2: 15).

Moreover, as we saw in Chapter 2, the deeply social nature of human life means that sociability is intimately linked to the nature of morality. Man's opinions and habits result from 'the state of their society' (*Institutes* 263). Again, this is a position consistent across his writings from the *Analysis* where: 'Man is by nature the member of a community. His love of that community renders him a good member of it, and intitles him to praise' (*Analysis* 32), to the *Principles* where, as we have seen, society is necessary for pleasure, happiness and the human good (*Principles* 1: 20). It is in sociability, rather than pleasure, that Ferguson finds the link between the various elements of his thought. Humans are social. Humans are ambitious to pursue the moral good, they direct their actions to this and, because they live in society, they act morally in society. Ferguson's intimate linkage between the social and the moral is where he thinks he is able to connect the factual and the normative.

> Society, in which alone the distinction of right and wrong is exempli-
> fied, may be considered as the garden of God, in which the tree of
> knowledge of good and evil is planted; and in which men are destined
> to distinguish, and to chuse, among its fruits. (*Principles* 1: 268)

Or again:

> The great distinction of right and wrong, or virtue and vice, on which
> men experience such extremes of complacence or indignation, of
> esteem or contempt, is formed on the dictates of a social disposition,
> which receives, with favour and love, what constitutes the good of
> mankind, or rejects, with disapprobation and abhorrence, what is of a
> contrary nature. (*Principles* 1: 35)

Society is the 'atmosphere' or 'vital air' in which morality is 'kindled' (*Principles* 1: 268–9), it is the 'nursery' (*Principles* 2: 325) where we learn from our actions how we ought to conduct ourselves. If humans are naturally sociable then a human morality must be a social morality. We can say that they are social but Ferguson also believes that we require an additional argument about the choice of good or evil. This is simply because both good and evil exist in a social setting: 'To be in society is the physical state of the species, not the moral distinction of any particular man. It is the state of those who quarrel, as well as those who agree' (*Principles* 1: 24). Humans are destined to act in society and moral philosophy must identify which social actions tend to the good of society. It is not enough to say that evil is anti-social because even evil acts take place in a social setting.

Ferguson's argument runs from the observation that morality and basic moral distinctions are universal facts about human life; he combines this with the observation that human beings are active creatures who develop their capacities through activity, adds the observation that this activity is driven by ambition for better than we have at present, and that this ambition includes the ambition to be better people. He then attaches the fact that human beings are social, that their moral actions take place in society, and that the concerns of society are the main arena for the exercise of morally ambitious action – all of which leads him to the observation that the main characteristic of human morality is benevolence. He has arrived at the same conclusion as Hutcheson and Shaftesbury but by a slightly different path.

This is fortunate for Ferguson because it also provides him with the object of his systematic moral philosophy: that is to say, with a rule or criterion for the assessment of particular actions in their circumstances. This is a point that he makes consistently from the *Analysis* onwards.[15] The central task of moral philosophy is to identify the core elements of moral thought, to thus allow us clear conceptions of them and the relationship between them, and ultimately to allow us to order our moral thinking in the pursuit of the ambition for moral improvement in whatever circumstances we find ourselves. Before we look at some of the specific details of how Ferguson undertakes this project it is worth noting what impact the process has on individuals. As we noted above the exercise of moral judgement makes us morally 'fitter'. The more we live and act, the more opportunity we have to learn from our actions. So each human life is, in effect, a constant process of moral learning where we adjust and correct our conceptions of morality. As he puts it: 'It is the tendency of experience to exhaust the sum of possible errors, and to limit the choice at last to what is best' (*Principles* 1: 298). The choice of the chapter title 'the progress of moral approbation' (*Principles* 1: 300) is not accidental. Moral approbation is a process within the individual each time a judgement is undertaken, but it is also progressing in the sense of refining and improving in the lives of each individual and, crucially, in the lives of each nation and, ultimately, in the life of humanity itself.

Ferguson's moral philosophy seeks to identify the main elements of a successful process of moral judgement. There are two
sides to this: the abstract and the practical. The practical, which
we will explore below, is conducted in terms of a relatively com-
monplace account of the virtues. The abstract concerns the details
of a project for philosophers, detached from the advice given
for practical judgement. Ferguson's worry about modern moral
philosophy is that it has given up on one of the key elements of
ancient thinking, the idea of a single principle that lies at the heart
of moral philosophy. Modern thinkers find the idea of a single
greatest good implausible, or likely unknowable by anyone except
God. But Ferguson's hope is that by restoring the idea to a central
place in our philosophical thinking about morality we will succeed
in systematising our thought in such a way as to solve apparent
moral dilemmas.

Ferguson's project for moral philosophers is that laid down by
Epictetus as the discovery of a 'standard of judgement' (Epictetus
1925: 279). The criticism that Epictetus makes of the Epicureans
is precisely that they fail as philosophers because pleasure does not
provide a reliable and constant standard upon which to ground
philosophical argument (Epictetus 1925: 283). This, if we recall,
was precisely the charge that Ferguson levelled at Adam Smith.
Smith reduced moral judgement to conformity with the propriety
judgements of an imagined impartial spectator, and for Ferguson
this amounts to little more than a refusal to engage in actual moral
philosophy.

The worry, as he states it at the beginning of *Principles* 2 (5),
is that things we term good may be inconsistent with each other,
such that the choice of one may require the sacrifice of the other.
The principle which Ferguson's moral philosophy seeks is one
which will allow ultimate reconciliation of our choice between
goods, and to give this more substance than referring it to an
impartial spectator's opinion. Ferguson's project is an ambitious
one, it is nothing less than the creation of a consistent system of
moral thought which will establish 'a principle of estimation and
choice, upon which to determine every question of right or propriety relating to the affairs of men' (*Principles* 2: 6). When Ferguson
turns to explaining why he adopts this approach his most frequent
justification is that he is seeking a common denominator for the
structured understanding of moral experience. His belief is that
humans do in reality act as though they have such a principle in

mind. The philosopher should take this reality seriously and direct their enquiries to the identification of such principles.

Ferguson's three systematic books, the *Analysis*, the *Institutes* and the *Principles*, each contain a series of headings through which Ferguson examines the nature of good and evil, beauty and deformity, excellence and defect, vice and virtue, happiness and misery, to try to reach a conception of what is best for mankind that will allow us a sense of 'the Fundamental Law of Morality'. Crucially he adopts the view that many of the supposed clashes between elements of our moral thinking are not due to any fundamental contradiction but rather to the fact that we have developed different conceptual languages for different elements of moral experience. These different appellations refer to 'different aspects' of the same moral law and his aim is to find 'some one general principle the most likely to unite the whole' (*Principles* 2: 107). The terminology of the early versions from the *Analysis* and the *Institutes* refers to the attainment of this as 'probity'. A number of commentators have identified this as the point at which Ferguson brings together the normative and descriptive parts of his account.[16] While it is true that probity, or justice as it later becomes in the *Principles*, is a central bridging conception in Ferguson's thought, it is not the only bridge between moral science, moral philosophy and living a moral life. The two projects, as we noted at the start of the chapter, are more closely implicated than this.

So the task is clear enough: we need a 'standard measure' of wisdom and goodness just as we need one of length (*Principles* 2: 133). The identification of this allows us to adjudicate between competing elements of our moral judgement. Moral judgement itself is a fact and an underlying universal of human experience. And while our application of that judgement may be wrong or 'warped' (*Principles* 2: 134) in particular instances, the basic elements of morality are acknowledged by everyone. So: 'When the reality of any moral distinction is questioned, we naturally refer to the general sense of mankind on the subject' (*Principles* 2: 135). Individuals may disagree on the application of the moral categories in particular circumstances, but the universality of the acceptance of basic moral categories raises Ferguson's hope that we can systematise our thinking. This desire for moral knowledge on the part of the philosopher is both motivated by the desire to inform our practical moral judgement and constrained by the fact that we do not need this knowledge in order to function as moral beings.

Moral disagreement does not mean the disposition to morality is a question of information, in the *Essay* Ferguson goes so far as to state that even if the project of moral philosophy fails to identify the ultimate principle of morality, human beings will continue to live moral lives and act like such a thing exists.

> Can we explain the principles upon which mankind adjudge the pref-
> erence of characters, and upon which they indulge such vehement
> emotions of admiration or contempt? If it be admitted that we cannot,
> are the facts less true? Or must we suspend the movements of the
> heart which they who are employed in framing systems of science have
> discovered the principle from which those movements proceed? (*Essay*
> 37)

The argument here is a stock Common Sense position, like Reid's arguments for the reality of moral distinctions, and like his critique of Hume's aesthetics it is based on the notion that the inability of philosophy to account for something does not mean that the phenomenon itself is in any doubt, rather that philosophy itself is a limited exercise.[17] We should be absolutely clear that Ferguson is not saying that the truth about morality is to be found in common opinion. It is the fact of moral judgement and the reality of moral distinctions that are established from common life. The content of morality is something that is filled up by each individual as he grows and learns, and which is interrogated and systematised by the philosopher. As he puts it in the *Essay*:

> Man may mistake the objects of his pursuit; he may misapply his
> industry, and misplace his improvements. If under a sense of such
> possible errors, he would find a standard by which to judge of his own
> proceedings, and arrive at the best state of his nature, he cannot find
> it perhaps in the practice of any individual, or of any nation whatever;
> not even in the sense of the majority, or the prevailing opinion of his
> kind. (*Essay* 15)

At this point we should pause to clarify two related elements of Ferguson's account of the experience of moral judgement: reason and sentiment. Ferguson's criticism of Smith should lead us to expect him to reject moral sentimentalism, and indeed he does this, but he does not dismiss the reality of the moral sentiments. He attempts to categorise them as the pleasure we feel when we

perceive virtue or the good. While recognising that we are motivated by a diverse range of passions, which can be the subject of
'settled or habitual desire' (*Institutes* 77), and that these issue in
pleasure, we should not, as we saw above, mistake this pleasure
for happiness.

The point of all this is to show that, though sentiment is present
in our motivation and in our experience of moral judgement, it is
not the central or active element. This is because judgement is a
cognitive activity, it is discerning. It is reason or conscience that
guides our moral judgement. Each of us possesses an ambition to
do the right thing, and reason is what we use to identify the end
and the means to that end. Crucially for Ferguson this allows him
to preserve a central role for reason, and thus the possibility of
right and wrong in morality, while refusing to reduce morality to
reason alone. It is the job of moral philosophy to make this task
easier by clarifying the vocabulary of moral thought.

The Vocabulary of Moral Distinctions

Ferguson divides his discussion of the basic moral categories into
two conceptual languages: the language of moral laws and the
language of the virtues. It is this quite deliberate attempt to merge
ideas from the jurisprudential and humanist traditions that has led
to many of the accusations of inconsistency that have been levelled
at his overall system. But as we will see, Ferguson does not assume
a naive reconciliation; instead, he attempts to describe how these
two distinct elements in moral experience can be reconciled in
moral philosophy through the basic notion of benevolence that
arises from our natural sociability. Moral laws operate at the
'general' (*Analysis* 29) level while the virtues are the character
traits that facilitate moral action in practical circumstances.[18] The
clearest discussion of the moral laws appears in the *Institutes*.
Ferguson initially identifies two laws of nature: the first is the
'the law of self-preservation' (*Institutes* 91) and the second is the
'law of society' such that 'Men naturally desire the welfare of
their fellow-creatures' (*Institutes* 91).[19] Ferguson's discussion of
these two laws elsewhere in his work is partly a moral scientific
enquiry into the fact that they do in fact exist, and partly a moral
philosophical enquiry into how they relate to one another. They
are not, in his view, inconsistent: 'If the law of self-preservation,
for the most part, prevail, it does not follow, that the law of

society has no effect' (*Institutes* 92). There may be cases where we assert the right to self-preservation above the welfare of our fellow creatures, but there will also be situations, like the battlefield, where we prefer the good of society to our own self-preservation. In some cases the law of society will move us to beneficence, and in others it will merely restrain our self-regard and retard 'mischief'.

It is this, Ferguson believes, that is captured by the traditional distinction between justice and benevolence. As he puts it:

> Hence the rule by which men commonly judge of external actions, is taken from the supposed influence of such actions on the general good. To abstain from harm, is the great law of natural justice; to diffuse happiness is the law of morality; and when we censure the conferring a favour on one or a few at the expence of many, we refer to public utility, as the great object at which the actions of men should be aimed. (*Essay* 41)

As we noted above, Ferguson compares the laws of society and self-preservation as being akin to gravity (*Correspondence* 2: 482). Both operate through tendencies. The law of society draws us to actions that benefit the public good but this is balanced by the law of self-preservation and human beings are suspended between the two: the law of self-preservation is in some respects limited by the law of society. Bland statements such as we ought not wish 'what is wrong, or inconsistent with the safety of mankind' (*Principles* 2: 247) or that 'the virtuous have a common cause with mankind' (*Principles* 2: 169) need to be understood in the context of Ferguson's more complex account of the relationship between self-interest and benevolence.

Throughout his work Ferguson maintains the belief that humans have both 'selfish' and 'social' dispositions. Indeed the philosophical vice with which he charges Bernard Mandeville is precisely that he introduces a binary opposition between social and selfish which does not capture the reality of these dispositions or the nature of the relationship between them. Ferguson's argumentative strategy here is the same as that advanced by Francis Hutcheson in his discussion of malice. Following Hutcheson, Ferguson distinguishes between self-interest, selfishness and malice. Malice is 'the greatest bane of the human heart' (*Principles* 2: 398) and a defect or deformity of mind. To act maliciously towards another is morally wrong, but it is not the same thing as selfishness or self-interest.

For Ferguson self-interest arises from the first law of morality concerning self-preservation. This is perfectly natural and is in no way incompatible with the law of society. He cites Smith's *Theory of Moral Sentiments* in support of this, claiming that Smith has shown how self-interest and benevolence 'coincide' in moral philosophy (*Institutes* 115). The problem arises when this self-interest extends into selfishness, when it encompasses all of our attention and becomes 'the sole object of human care' (*Institutes* 99). Excessive focus on interest can distract us from society, but even then human nature is so deeply social that we are always associating with others and 'even while the head is occupied with projects of interest, the heart is often seduced into friendship' (*Essay* 40). So self-preservation can become selfishness through a 'mistake in the choice of our object' (*Essay* 54). There is nothing particularly novel or interesting about Ferguson's view on this. He is following Hutcheson's response to Mandeville and is treading the same turf as Hume and Smith's attempts to reconfigure the virtues to downplay the dangers of commercial activity. He is also following Hutcheson when he comes to discuss the nature of the law of society as manifested in the principle of benevolence.

As we have seen, Ferguson follows Hutcheson and Shaftesbury in identifying benevolence as the central principle of morality. Benevolence is an 'active principle' (*Principles* 2: 14), it is the 'specific excellence of man' (*Principles* 2: 34), his 'chief gratification' (*Principles* 2: 28–9), the 'greatest good to which human nature is competent' (*Principles* 2: 149). This 'principle of humanity' (*Essay* 40), or 'love of mankind' (*Institutes* 116) provides the content for morality. In the *Institutes* he develops a position that views morality as a combination of benevolence with censorial inspection. This combination is 'the principle of moral approbation' (*Institutes* 114–15). But just as censorial inspection requires intelligence, so moral approbation combined with benevolence must be directed by 'wisdom' (*Principles* 2: 28). This idea runs through the *Principles*. Benevolence is the basis of moral approbation but requires the support of the other virtues to realise itself.

Benevolence 'either inspires or requires for its support every other good quality of human nature' so he assumes that it is 'the fundamental or primary object of moral law' (*Principles* 2: 111) and that it underwrites the other virtues. This view is constant from the beginning of Ferguson's career and he seems aware that he may be coming close to the philosophical vice of simplification or over-abstraction in his treatment of benevolence. But his way around this is to stress the unity of the idea with other elements of moral experience such as the virtues. As he notes:

> We are thus disposed, for the most part, to simplify our conceptions, and to seek for some fundamental principle from which, if we secure it, every other requisite will follow; but the reality of any such principle, even in the government of human nature, may be doubted. The love of mankind, which we have assumed as the nearest approach to a general principle of virtue, requires the direction of wisdom and the support of courage. (*Principles* 2: 332–3)

One of Ferguson's main reasons for adopting benevolence as the principle of moral approbation was undoubtedly the fact of human sociability, but another feature is the fact that benevolence requires us to choose to act in the interest of others. Ferguson follows the traditional argument that beneficence cannot be extorted by force.[20] The point is that it is people who are judged morally, that is to say, when it comes to beneficence, it is character that matters regardless of the outcome. We can admire unsuccessful attempts to help others – which is the same as saying benevolence and not utility is the object of moral approbation. Later, in Chapter 5, we will focus on Ferguson's political thought, but here we should note that this conception of the nature of morality as both censorial and social explains why humans are political for Ferguson. If the 'greatest good competent to man's nature, is the love of mankind' then the 'consequences' of this are 'that the good of communities, is likewise that of the individual' and that the good of the whole is the good of the parts (*Institutes* 171). As we will see this links Ferguson's sociological considerations on socialisation to his normative philosophy.

Ferguson's moral philosophy, based on his response to the philosophical vices, includes a demand for clarity in moral thinking. But it is equally the case that this clarity must be of practical use for living a moral life. This leads Ferguson, in his lectures and the books based upon them, to engage in a modern version of casuistry or the identification and definition of good offices.[21] Censorial inspection involves us in judging a 'moral action' (*Principles* 2: 166) and the moral law – of benevolence – tells us what is good and therefore ought to be the object of choice, but it does so only in a general form. The virtues and reason are required to make proper censorial inspections and moral philosophy is required to 'guard the imagination against the admission of false apprehensions' (*Principles* 2: 173). Here again Ferguson draws on the established natural law vocabulary to distinguish the realms of jurisprudence and morality. The sanctions of morality are conscience, public repute, compulsory law and religion, while reason and virtue are required to make effective use of them in particular circumstances.

The law of nature informs us of what is the proper object of judicial punishment. Ferguson here provides us with a stock version of eighteenth-century natural jurisprudence, the details of which are of little interest. The law of nature provides for self-defence, limited to 'what is effectual and necessary' (*Principles* 2: 253), and a system of justice is central to human society. We will return to this, and politics, in Chapters 5 and 6. For the moment our interest is on the distinction between casuistry and the subject matter of compulsory law. If the 'necessity of keeping distinct the sanctions of morality from those of compulsory law is extremely evident' for duties such as gratitude (*Principles* 2: 368) because it is so important for the realisation that the duty is self-chosen, then it is equally so for the other duties. Ferguson's disavowal of the language of perfect and imperfect rights (*Correspondence* 1: 112) does not mean that he rejects the differential phenomenology of the negative demands of justice and the 'positive' duties of morality. Instead, his worry is that calling something imperfect suggests that it is less important or less of a binding duty.

Law and morality each have their province, but what really distinguishes them is the different sanctions: the sanction of duty, covered by casuistry, and that of compulsion, covered by jurisprudence. Now, as we have already seen, we cannot compel the fundamental moral law of benevolence, but a society without compulsory law cannot be moral in Ferguson's view. Jurisprudence is 'The first application of the fundamental law of morality to the actions of men, is prohibitory, and forbids the commission of wrongs' (*Institutes* 191). Ferguson then outlines the standard jurisprudential development of rights. This is a natural jurisprudence in the sense that Ferguson believes that it arises from the nature of things. Thus: 'Original rights are the universal appurtenances of man's nature, and coeval with his being' (*Institutes* 198). A natural jurisprudence is then set beside a newly realised account of casuistry.

If Ferguson is to create a modern casuistry then it must be one that avoids the errors, indeed the vices, of the ancients and the medieval. The schoolmen were just that, their knowledge had no use outside the schoolroom, their distinctions and quibbles were of little use to a man faced with actual moral actions and choices. To 'erect philosophy' into a system for sect votaries and not normal life 'is to mistake its nature' (*Principles* 2: 402).

Having set the methodology and the boundaries of moral philosophy, Ferguson proceeds in each of his books to fill in the content. In all three books, *Institutes*, *Analysis* and *Principles*, much of the content takes the form of a systematic statement and ordering of the virtues. The project looks very much like old-fashioned definitional argument. And it would be easy to assume that Ferguson is merely writing up his lecture headings in a desultory fashion. In one sense this is what he is doing, but in another he has a very clear reason why his philosophy takes this form. If we recall that he believes that he has a conception of philosophy that fosters clarity of thought for the self-fashioning of character, then we can begin to understand the intellectual basis of his moral pedagogy.

Ferguson is seeking to revivify and reconfigure moral vocabulary for the modern world. Both the *Analysis* and the *Institutes* contain a section on casuistry. In the *Analysis* the section 'Of Casuistry' defines the subject as 'casuistry treats of the stations, manners, and duties of men' (*Analysis* 38). But both here and in the *Institutes* Ferguson is quick to distinguish his notion of casuistry from the failed version of scholasticism. In the *Institutes* section 'Uses of Casuistry' he is clear that casuistry cannot replace a good disposition. The belief that rote learning of rules and disputes about the definition of terms are a productive mode of moral philosophy was the ruin of medieval Catholic thought. For Ferguson the end of casuistry is rather to define and identify general terms in order to facilitate clear argument and thought. And, not wishing to labour the point, the exercise must take place against the backdrop of moral science or it becomes sterile. This realistic philosophy needs a clear terminology. But the terminology must serve the analysis rather than become the subject of analysis.

The modern casuist aims for meaningful distinctions linked to actual moral experience rather than verbal hair-splitting. Only by linking this to moral science can we escape becoming the dupes of our own language. This approach will allow us to avoid 'Differences of Interpretation' (*Institutes* 183) by providing a clear set of underlying definitions. But there is a further feature of casuistry that Ferguson finds attractive. This is the idea that the definitions and generalisations are meant to inform moral choice rather than govern it. They are supposed to help us to find our duty in any set of circumstances. One key indication of this is the distinction between the subject of jurisprudence and casuistry.

Like Adam Smith, Ferguson makes it clear that part of the distinction between the province of law and the province of virtue lies in the amenability of the first to precise identification. Jurisprudence is more specific than virtue and can be traced like an axiom in mathematics.[22] It can thus be made the subject of compulsory law. The object of casuistry on the other hand is the identification of the elements necessary to determining our choice when it comes to pursuing our duty. The sanction here is not legal penalty, but the happiness or misery that arises from the knowledge that one is doing right or wrong.

As we saw above Ferguson believed that moral judgement was natural and that when allied to the notion of ambition prompts or motivates individuals to pursue what they regard as the good. Casuistry provides the conceptual language for the consideration of what this is. The two elements, the disposition to do good and the mental framework to understand what that is, must come together: 'The establishment of general rules relating to duties is a principal object of casuistry. But the best directory in human life is the disposition from which those duties proceed' (*Analysis* 41).

Ferguson's version of casuistry is intended to make the most of language while at the same time purging it of ambiguity. A modern casuistry must be a realistic and useful one. It should serve to clarify the terms of our moral thinking rather than obscure them in abstraction and verbal cleverness. 'Human nature no where exists in the abstract, and human virtue is attached, in every particular instance, to the use of particular materials or to the application of given materials to particular ends' (*Principles* 2: 419). Ferguson's development of a new form of casuistry is modest and realistic in its scope. The hope is not, as it appeared with some of the schoolmen, to encompass all of moral experience in a code of behaviour, but rather to clarify the terminology of morality and indicate its application in typical cases which arise in everyday life. Casuistry serves to point us away from the more egregious errors. It is basic schooling which makes us fit for the practice of moral judgement. 'It is the object of casuistry to prevent, or to correct, such errors, by pointing out the real tendencies of virtue and of vice in external actions' (*Institutes* 240–1). It serves as a useful guide but should not be mistaken as possessing the same authority as the laws of jurisprudence.[23] The rules identified by casuistry serve as a sort of intermediate between the attainment of a virtuous character and the sanction of the criminal law. Social pressure and not disposition or physical coercion have a role to play here. The result is an additional layer of social pressure which promotes adherence to the form of duty even if the character does not exemplify it. It is a necessary feature of a society of imperfect individuals.

This is yet another aspect of the central role that Ferguson attributes to sociability. Censorial inspection is, after all, inspection of others. Casuistry merely clarifies the informal rules of ordinary decent behaviour. We are influenced by socialisation and by the opinions of our fellows. As a result an accurate moral philosophy must take account of this and at the same time an effective moral pedagogy (as we will see in Chapter 4) must seek to put this feature of our social nature to good use. The sense of duty is not simply limited to the sanctions of religion and opinion, but it is also related to our loyalty to the magistrate as the 'principal object of that affection we bear to the society itself' (*Principles* 2: 379). 'Public spirit' understood as 'preference of public to partial consideration' (*Principles* 2: 381), is similarly enforced by informal social pressure as much as by character and virtue.

God

In Chapter 4 below we will discuss Ferguson's views on the place of religion in his scheme of moral philosophy in more detail. For the moment we can simply note that Ferguson is operating with a highly naturalised account of religion.[24] Ferguson's natural theology is attached to his moral philosophy, but it is almost always the case that God is in the background. He accepts that the Will of God must be the foundation of morals, but at the same time accepts that humanity cannot know this. In the *Principles* (1: 166–7) he argues that the actual experience of the identification of moral rules works the other way around: we decide what is right and then attribute it to the Will of God. The task of philosophy then is not a challenge to the established religion, but rather a support to its refinement. 'It is in search of a model, and of a patron of what is previously known to be right, that we arrive at our best and highest conceptions of the Supreme Being' (*Principles* 1: 167).

Medieval casuistry was over-prescriptive and excessively formal, it was too caught up in definitions and attempting to square its logic with scriptural support, but that does not mean that the practice of philosophy, properly reformed, cannot be compatible with a useful discipline of casuistry and with the teachings of revealed religion. In fact, it seems that for Ferguson the practice of philosophy brings us closer to God as it helps us see the order that he has created. As we will see below this leads Ferguson to his peculiar interest in the idea of providence. But the discussion of providence never becomes fatalistic in the Stoic mode. For Ferguson philosophy allows us to recognise God's will and to come closer to the truth in moral judgements. Even if we obey from fear of punishment, whether civil or religious, it nonetheless remains true that: 'Merely to obey, without a sense of goodness and rectitude in the command, would be greatly short of that duty which we owe to our beneficent Maker' (*Principles* 2: 171). God superintends the system and provides the sanction for the rules identified by moral science and moral philosophy, but these rules themselves are not derived from doctrine, rather they are the result of application to 'experience and observation' (*Principles* 2: 403).

Virtue

Before we embark on a brief examination of the content of Ferguson's discussion of virtue, we should pause to look at the mode by which virtue is experienced. Virtues are habits: they are socially acquired, unconsciously learned and may be inculcated through education. Habit arises from the 'concomitancy of things or circumstances' (*Principles* 1: 139). Humans are habitual creatures, they acquire habits, like skills, from practice and these habits become difficult to shift.[25] Our thoughts, and in particular our imagination, come to be 'confirmed' by habit to the extent that even when erroneous they 'are not corrected even by experience' (*Institutes* 62–3). But lest we form the mistaken impression that Ferguson is a hard determinist on habit we need to be clear that he sees a role for the correction of habits as well as their early inculcation through proper education. We can mend our habits and even make a choice of what habits we acquire. As Ferguson would have it: 'he may be formed by himself in the course of that life he adopts' (*Principles* 1: 225) and so 'in chusing what habits he shall acquire, he is in some measure the artificer of his own nature' (*Principles* 1: 227). Education can help us to acquire good habits, but it seems that Ferguson also believed that there was a role for philosophy in helping us mend our false conceptions and to choose clarity of thought guided by experience and observation.

As we have seen, Ferguson moves from the consideration of externally coerced duty in jurisprudence through social and religious duty sanctioned through opinion to individual character. Throughout, the core fact of human nature – that we are social – and the central principle of morality that flows from this – benevolence – have formed the spine of Ferguson's analysis. The discussion of virtue becomes central to this as the censorial inspection that characterises moral judgement is judgement of another's actions and intentions, of their character as manifested in their interaction with others. In the broadest terms Ferguson sets the scene by noting that virtues require both intellect and emotion. As he puts it: 'Capacity and parts refer to the Understanding; ardour and force to the Heart; both united constitute a natural superiority of character' (*Analysis* 23). The account here is straightforwardly Aristotelian.[26]

Virtue is the best state of an 'active intelligent being' (*Principles* 2: 45) and so we must direct ourselves to the elements of character rather than the external effects that follow from them. All of these demand action and the key to Ferguson's practical ethics is the identification of the virtuous character traits that allow us to play our part. This leads us to the cardinal virtues: Justice, Prudence, Temperance, Fortitude.[27]

Despite the shifts in terminology Ferguson's approach remains consistent. These are universal categories that apply to all humans and are not restricted to any one place or culture. Indeed, for Ferguson it is the universality of these characteristics and the universal admiration that they elicit that identifies them as virtues. As befitting their origin in his lectures, the *Analysis*, the *Institutes* and the *Principles* then continue on to anatomise the subsidiary virtues and duties which follow from the main distinctions. The analysis here shifts terminology and focus through the volumes, but the intention remains the same: to clarify the subsidiary features of each of the cardinal virtues and allow the audience to grasp them. The aim of these definitions might in one sense be taken to arise from the note-heading nature of the *Analysis* and *Institutes*. However, the approach remains the same in the *Principles*. We are given a little more detail to flesh out the headings, but they remain a skeletal framework. This, I want to argue, is quite intentional on Ferguson's part, because his aim is to provide a vocabulary in which his readers can think through their own thoughts on morality. It is part of his commitment to practical morality. His aim is not to paint a picture of perfect virtue, but to allow his reader to identify what the virtues are and then allow them to think clearly about them in their own censorial inspections.

Ferguson's account of virtue is, like his moral philosophy in general: intended to be both practical and realistic. As he stresses:

> It is of little moment to be told of a good, which we cannot command, or of an evil which we cannot avoid. Our object in every case, is to make such a choice of the things which are in our power, that is, of our own conduct and actions, as to do the best which the case can admit for ourselves or our fellow creatures. (*Principles* 2: 59)

Now while this partly reflects a Stoic-inspired injunction against the pursuit of things far beyond our control, it also connects to the idea that we are capable of improvement. This is not a counsel of despair that asks us to accept our fate. Instead, we are to act and in so doing realise the attainable aspects of virtue in whatever circumstances we find ourselves. We can approach virtue in any state of society or condition. What is important is that they are doing what they can in the sphere in which they are able to exercise influence. This is important for Ferguson because it underlines the fact that we should not mistake wealth for virtue. And he intends this to hold in both directions. The rich man may be more virtuous than the poor and vice versa depending on their behaviour. Nothing in the circumstances of either makes vice inevitable.

Even here Ferguson is stressing that his 'realistic' moral principles are also beyond most of us. One further indication of this is his acknowledgement of the partiality that we have for those close to us. We have particular duties to family and friends that, though they do not excuse us from our duties to strangers, carry special weight in moral considerations. Friendship and consanguinity are special moral relationships which Ferguson addresses in some detail.[28] Again, this discussion is underwritten by the stress on sociability that characterises all of Ferguson's moral thought. By identifying these distinct duties and their proper relationship to the other virtues Ferguson allows us to form a sense of moral perspective.

This reminds us that moral philosophy is a form of moral knowledge. It allows us to define virtue in general terms and to clarify our language concerning it. But if we are considering 'moral approbation' as the 'subject of theory' we need to place the virtues within a system of thinking about morality. For this, as we noted above, we need a 'canon' or 'rule' (*Principles* 2: 114–15) and we need to identify this before we talk about institutions such as jurisprudence or politics. We need to be able to place each element of moral experience in its correct place in order for us to see the relationships between them and to be able to come to a proper conception of the system as a whole.

The discussion is supported by an analysis of vice that stresses its opposition to benevolence. If we recall that, for Ferguson, emotion prompts human activity while extreme passions have the potential to misdirect our actions we can see why, while all excessive passions are to be 'reprobated' (*Principles* 1: 129), Ferguson is particularly concerned by the 'corruption' of self-preservation into self-love. This is precisely because the proper relationship between self-preservation, and indeed the special relationships of friendship and consanguinity, and benevolence are vital for a proper appreciation of how we should act. The point here is that vice, for Ferguson, is an error – the result of false notions that misguide or pervert moral behaviour.

To take an example, at several points in the *Principles* Ferguson points to the danger of mistaking celebrity for just moral approbation and entering into competition with others for fame rather than pursuing virtue. This can be corrected by 'the progress of information' (*Principles* 1: 182) and this in turn will allow us to 'Purify the mind of this taint, and most of the evils in human society are done away with' (*Principles* 2: 76). The problem here is one that can arise at any stage of social development. The problem is not so much wealth as the desire of fame for its own sake. We can then begin to see how the universal terminology of morality that Ferguson has developed can be put to use in a variety of different settings. If human nature is always open to 'the mixture of ill disposition, folly, or mistake' (*Principles* 2: 483) then the moral philosophy provided by Ferguson will always be relevant – so long, that is, as it remains 'user friendly'.

Conclusion

Ferguson's task has been to identify the proper role of moral philosophy and provide a practical system that can be of use in whatever circumstances we find ourselves. Humans are social and moral creatures and, despite the diversity of customs and beliefs, there is a set of universal moral concepts that lies behind all censorial inspection. Humans are 'deeply concerned' to find and apply the distinction of good and evil, and this is a form of knowledge 'no less than in the pursuits of physical knowledge, or the practice of arts' (*Principles* 1: 300).

But again, we need to be clear what type of knowledge we are referring to here. Moral philosophy is a task which can help to systematise and educate, but it cannot help to apply. Indeed the truth, for Ferguson, is that the moral, the good, the virtuous, the happy – all of these come from action and actions chosen by individuals without much philosophical reflection. The task of Ferguson's moral philosophy is not, in the end, to provide a prescriptive code of morality, but to make us all become the sort of people who are able to make the best of the situations in which we find ourselves. Ferguson is not saying that that such moral knowledge makes moral progress inevitable or moral corruption more likely to be avoided. The truth about morality exists for Ferguson, even if we cannot identify it or even approach it in our lives. Our moral knowledge is greater than that of the ancients but that does not make us individually or collectively better than them. What it does do is leave an accession of knowledge for those who come after us. So even though a society may fall into corruption or an individual sink into a life of vice, that continues to provide the empirical evidence upon which we can exercise our moral science in refinement of our moral philosophy.

Moral philosophy must be 'realistic' and it must have as its ultimate end the production of a useful guide for human moral judgement. The task is in part an academic enquiry, but more importantly it is knowledge of ourselves that will allow us each to make happy choices:

> Here. Also, we may presume that knowledge is power; and that, whoever is successful in the study of his own nature, as he may lay the foundation of a happy choice in the exercise of his will, so he may lay the foundations of power also, in applying the laws of his nature to the command of himself. (*Principles* 1: 3)

Now, as Ferguson has already told us that the distinguishing characteristic of humans is their moral faculty, we naturally find that the 'proper study of man' (*Principles* 1: 179) is not just man, but what men ought to do. Ferguson's demand that we have a solid basis for this in our understanding of human nature is coupled with a belief that history itself will act as a sort of school or evidence base for us to learn the nature of moral law. But as we will see in the next chapter the means by which we learn from history is not a crude moral message. Instead the description of people and events is another opportunity for us to exercise censorial inspection.[29]

If we want to promote the good we must get the factual study of human nature correct. This is true both if we want to identify what is good for human beings, but also if we want to discover the means best suited to promoting that good in particular circumstances. We need to reiterate the point that the study of existing behaviour does not place limits on what we conceive to be the normative laws that apply to humans. That we have not attained these laws does not diminish their strength.

The question to be explored in the normative project is the discovery of 'the excellence to which human nature is competent' (*Principles* 2: 44) which will allow the moral philosopher to determine the 'soil' in which he must 'sow' (*Principles* 2: 73). The aim of the moral philosopher is, at base, educational. It is to provide a clear set of principles which will clarify moral thought and banish self-deception and error: 'Moral science operates for our good, only by mending our conceptions of things, and correcting or preventing the errors from which moral depravity or misery proceeds' (*Principles* 2: 73).

Ferguson recognises that this educational project is the same as that of ancient philosophy. But the difference he adduces to his own system is that it actually undertakes what previous moralists only claimed to have done. Ferguson does not merely abstract and produce an ultimate moral principle from a priori argument – he believes that he has based it on observation. Thus, though his system will, as it turns out, provide an ultimate principle, that principle is grounded in observation of human nature. The project is not a guarantee of a complete moral system that will guide all action in all circumstances – nothing could achieve that – but the knowledge generated in trying to think about how best to live may act to move towards moral improvement. It might, then, create the sort of person who is more likely to be able to make the right decisions. The cultivation of a clearer way of thinking about the human condition, the exercise of self-control and the acquisition of good habits are the end of moral philosophy.

Notes

1. Significantly for those who would read Ferguson as a Stoic this passage is followed by a criticism of the ancient schools of philosophy which is predicated on their adherence to system rather than reliance on the evidence of the study of human nature (*Principles* 2: 401–2), a point which Ferguson returned to in the late *Manuscripts*: 'In Science we would Ascertain What is on the Whole most beneficial and safe or productive of most Enjoyment and least suffering' (*Manuscripts* 155).

2. Lisa Hill (2017: xix) claims that the Edinburgh lecture notes reveal that Ferguson was attempting to reinterpret classical moral terminology in 'ordinary discussion' with his students.

3. This is an image that Ferguson returns to in a letter to Sir John MacPherson where he likens self-interest and benevolence to gravitational forces in human nature (*Correspondence* 2: 370).

4. In the *Highland Walk* essay he suggests that the tendency to esteem the perfect and shun the defective in what relates to our own character: 'I would call it Ambition' (*Manuscripts* 52). This is interesting because it suggests that ambition has an object. Moral ambition is ambition to be better, and this must be directed at some conception of an end. But this is not an end that we need have a fully worked out sense of; indeed, in the *Principles*, when he distinguishes telos from instinct, he says that we have an 'instinctive intimation of an end' (*Principles* 1: 122). Animals have a propensity to pursue actions from instinct to use particular forms of behaviour without a sense of the end or purpose. Humans, on the other hand, while they may not conceive the detail of their object, are possessed of a sense that it exists.

5. We should also note that Ferguson also deploys the concept in his analysis of economics where activity is prompted by 'ambition

formed to that of necessity' (*Principles* 2: 423). Lisa Hill (2006: 97) points out that Ferguson uses this as a way to distinguish between ambition and interest: 'Interest is largely confined to the care of the body whereas ambition is generally directed towards progress, whether moral, intellectual or technical.' It is also worth observing that Ferguson's concept of ambition is his own. It is quite clearly not the same as that presented by Aristotle (1998: 88–9). Similarly, Ferguson's discussion of ambition is some distance from Cicero's generally negative view of ambition as a source of corruption (Cicero 1913: 67, 71). There are other places where the grand claims on behalf of ambition prompt Ferguson to roll back. In the *Essay* (244) he notes that ambition can lead us into crises, though he quickly follows this up with an argument that at least crises are active and prompt us to exercise and effort rather than retirement. This seems to suggest that ambition can be misplaced or misdirected, and indeed in the *Institutes* (176) he does use ambition in a pejorative sense.

6. For example, Lisa Hill (2006: 98) sees ambition as the key to Ferguson's perfectibilism.

7. See *Principles* (1: 315).

8. An argument made throughout Ferguson's career (*Institutes* 160; *Essay* 246; *Principles* 1: 186; *Principles* 2: 12, 88). See Smith (2008).

9. As he puts it in the *Essay*: 'The virtues of men have shone most during their struggles, not after the attainment of their ends' (*Essay* 196).

10. See Smith (2006).

11. Kettler's discussion of the tensions in Ferguson's system is partly marred by a contemporary assessment of the coherence of the arguments. For example, he thinks that Ferguson's account falls prey to a naturalistic fallacy, when it seems unlikely that any of the Scots, even Hume, had as clear a conception of the problem as post-Kantian analytic philosophy has developed. For a discussion of Ferguson on is/ought, see Jack Hill (2017: 106–7). For discussions on Ferguson's strict separation of is/ought, see Berry (2015: 294) and Garrett and Heydt (2015: 88).

12. Again a point that recurs throughout his *oeuvre*: *Analysis* (35); *Principles* (2: 21).

13. Fania Oz-Salzberger (2008: 149) makes the interesting point that this helps us to place the appropriate contrast in Ferguson's thought as between active and inactive rather than ancient and modern philosophies.

14. 'It appears, upon the whole, that just opinions, benevolent affections,

and serious engagements, are the preferable enjoyments of human nature' (*Institutes* 155).

15. 'A conduct tending to the good of mankind, is invariably right, independent of opinion or custom' (*Analysis* 40).

16. For example, Jack Hill (2017: 122) and David Allan (2006: 34).

17. 'It is fortunate in this, as in other articles to which speculation and theory are applied, that nature proceeds in her course, whilst the curious are busied in search of her principles' (*Essay* 37).

18. Eugene Heath (2009: 162) suggests that Ferguson actually has three laws of nature: self-preservation, society and progress, and that these are all laws of the will. He distinguishes these from what he calls the four 'law-like tendencies' (Heath 2009: 166): initiative (ambition), communicative (society), preservative (habit) and challenge (conflict). This is a slightly different terminology and ordering from that used by Ferguson himself and the following section presents an alternative scheduling of the same concepts outlined by Heath.

19. 'Systems have differed chiefly by deriving our choice of actions and characters, some from the law of self-preservation and others from the law of society: but the fact is, that the laws of self-preservation, and of society, when well understood, coincide in all their tendencies and applications' (*Institutes* 115).

20. See *Institutes* (235, 248) and *Principles* (2: 92, 287, 367).

21. Knud Haakonssen (1996: 159) refers to casuistry as a 'flimsy discipline' distinct from jurisprudence, and while this is certainly accurate, it is also the case that some flimsiness can sometimes be a virtue in allowing leeway to adapt to the situation at hand.

22. See *Principles* (2: 315). Talking of the law he states that it must be brought back to 'the use of a language which all men understand' (*Principles* 2: 481).

23. This, in Ferguson's view, was the error of the Catholics: 'The rule of casuistry cannot supersede the judgement and good disposition of a virtuous mind. Attempts to give casuistry this consequence, have proceeded from superstition, and tended to confirm the most slavish superstition, by multiplying external observances, that mislead the attention, from qualities of the heart, to matters of form' (*Institutes* 258).

24. Chen (2008: 171) points out that Ferguson's discussion of natural religion is not 'classically Christian', and that while much of his thought is underpinned by references to providence, this providence is itself highly naturalised. Kettler argues that this surface piety hides 'a deeply ingrained secularism' (Kettler 2005: 224). While, as Berry

(1997: 47) and Hill (2006: 43) acknowledge, Ferguson's construction of moral science means that the naturalistic explanations work as explanations without direct divine intervention, this view is questioned by David Allan (1993: 207–17, 228–9 n. 192) and Richard Sher (1985: 180, 403) who argue that the model for the idea of unintended consequences that dominates Ferguson's moral science is to be found in Calvinist notions of providence, a point that is also made by Chen (2008: 180) and Hill (1998: 43–4).

25. Silvia Sebastiani (2013: 30) notes the 'specifically Scottish' preoccupation with habit, once again placing Ferguson in the mainstream of the Scottish Enlightenment.

26. See Aristotle (1998: 142).

27. See *Analysis* (33), *Institutes* (242), *Principles* (2: 36–7). There is a final ordering of the virtues in the late essays: 'Industry, Frugality, Oeconomy, Temperance, Liberality, Charity, and Beneficence' (*Manuscripts* 269).

28. *Principles* (2: 361–4).

29. In a clear statement of his intent at the start of the *Roman History* he claims that he will provide the reader 'with models by which they may profit, and from which they may form sound principles of conduct, derived from experience, and confirmed by examples of the highest authority' (*Rome* 10).

4

Moral Education

Society itself is the school, and its lessons are delivered in the practice of real affairs. An author writes from observations he has made on his subject, not from the suggestion of books; and every production carries the mark of his character as a man, not of his mere proficiency as a student or scholar. (*Essay* 169)

In 1786 Ferguson's former student and frequent correspondent John MacPherson wrote to his old professor to offer his practical observations on the most significant moral lessons he had learned from his life. These lessons, he suggested, should confirm Ferguson even further in his system, and they provide us with a useful sense of what Ferguson's student thought were the main points in his pedagogy. MacPherson makes three points all of which will be familiar from the previous two chapters:

> 1st That the pursuits of an active mind are its greatest happiness, when they are directed to good objects, which unite our own happiness with that of our friends and the general advantages of society. 2d I have likewise experienced, that he who has not been in contact with his fellow creatures knows but half of the human heart. But such are the necessary taxes of occupation, of business, and perhaps of life. 3d That all that rests with us individually, is to act our own parts to the best of our ability, and to endeavour to do good for its own sake, independent of events, disappointments, or sufferings. (*Correspondence* 2: 224)

These were the chief lessons that MacPherson took with him from Edinburgh into his public career. Thus far we have focused on Ferguson's attempt to create a moral science upon which he would be able to construct a moral philosophy for a commercial civilisation. Along the way we have noted that Ferguson holds particularly strong views about the role and nature of philosophy. Moral philosophy, he declares in the *Institutes*, is the study of what ought to be, of the good or of virtue, but this study is not an abstract enterprise. The practice and content of moral philosophy are to be grounded in the real world. As we saw in Chapter 2, Ferguson divides the *Principles* into two volumes and the distinction between these is between the natural history of man and a moral philosophy for humanity. The two, in Ferguson's view, are linked. What is (facts) clearly informs what ought to be (values). Moral philosophy connects the study of human nature with social and physical circumstances such that the normative values that are its product are ultimately grounded in the science of man.

In this chapter we reach the third element of Ferguson's philosophy, the practical application of this system of thought in his role as a professor of moral philosophy. Ferguson was, by all accounts, a popular and well-regarded teacher.[1] Indeed, when his biographer Jane Fagg refers to him as 'a second-rate historian and moral philosopher' but a 'first-rate teacher' (Fagg 1968: 332; 1995: xxxvii) she is pointing to the central issue that we will explore in this chapter: to what extent was Ferguson's thought geared towards the classroom? The relationship between Ferguson's writings and his lectures provides us with an interesting insight into his view on the best form of education, as well as the limitations that constrain what we should expect from philosophy. Moreover, the conception of philosophy as an essentially educational exercise was, as Gordon Graham (2007) has pointed out, characteristic of the mainstream of the Scottish Enlightenment. Thomas Ahnert (2014) has highlighted the wider project of the acculturation or creation of a moral culture that lay behind the Moderate's conception of improvement and it makes sense to see Ferguson, from the Edinburgh moral philosophy chair, being central to that enterprise.[2]

Ferguson's interest in securing the foundations of moral philosophy in moral science is intended to generate a useful system of thought, useful, that is, for educational purposes. To this end he places at the heart of his understanding of human nature the idea that humans are moral creatures. This universally observed human character trait, the fact that we judge ourselves and others, becomes for Ferguson an indicator of the universality of morality. However, he admits that not all judgement takes the form of a principled moral assessment of others. Judgement may be mixed with other passions – he names envy as one possibility. It remains a fact that humans are 'censorial' by nature (*Principles* 2: 22) but these judgements may just as easily be subject to bias or error as they may be led by good principles. As a result, moral philosophy and moral science are an aid to accurate judgement and, more importantly, they come to form the basis for a form of character education intended to create the sort of gentleman who might, like MacPherson, make his way in the world and do the right thing.

If humans are naturally judgemental and this is an indicator of the universality of morality, then this will naturally affect the task of the moral philosopher. The task of the moral philosopher must be to identify the good and to clarify its nature from among the many actions and judgements of humanity and consequently to reduce the danger of error in the actual exercise of moral judgement.[3] The task of this form of philosophy is not to operate at the edges of human knowledge, rather it is to promote right thinking and the 'right' values among the community. The moral philosopher – if he is to fulfil his role in the community – must do more than identify principles to guide human judgement, he must ensure that the act of judgement itself is undertaken without any of the other principles (such as mentioned above, envy) that can be admixed with judgement.

This is closely related to another of Ferguson's repeated observations: that virtue, if it is to have any meaning, cannot be the product of compulsion. Virtue must be the result of choice, an expression of character. The task of moral philosophy thus extends beyond the identification of the 'good' and into the inculcation of a mental outlook or disposition to pursue the good and to make the 'correct' choices.[4]

Ferguson is wary of 'book learning' for a number of reasons which connect to his key concern with the notion of activity and his worries about the philosophical vices. The overarching concern is that we 'substitute the knowledge of books, instead of the inquisitive or animated spirit in which they were written' (*Essay* 205). There are dangerous practical consequences to this because it leads us to ignore the skills necessary for practical judgement, what Ferguson calls 'capacity' (*Essay* 32). It is here that we see Ferguson's moral science and concern for straightforward philosophical analysis come together. The point of the system that Ferguson has developed is that it can be taught in the classroom and then be taken from there and applied in the particular circumstances in which each student finds themselves. The provision of a clear conceptual vocabulary that can be understood by ordinary people gives them the means to think through the situations that they experience. In a sense Ferguson is not so much shaping the characters of his students from his lectures and books – he seems to accept that his students will shape their own characters as they go through life – instead he is providing them with the intellectual toolkit to do so.[5]

Ferguson's concern for the 'business' of everyday life leads him to focus on the old Stoic idea of the 'great school of nature' (*Manuscripts* 283). We are 'pupils in this school of human life' (*Manuscripts* 239) where we acquire the capacity to act effectively. What becomes important then is not so much that we possess a detailed moral code that applies in all circumstances, but rather that we possess the requisite character formed for engagement in the school of society.

This clearly relates to Ferguson's understanding of what it is to be human in just as intimate a way as his observation that we are naturally sociable or the idea that we are naturally judgemental. He observes that: 'The final cause appears to be, that the talent of man for invention should be employed' (*Institutes* 15). But this 'invention' must remain grounded in the practical if it is to be of use in the conduct of life. For moral philosophy to be a practical discipline it must be related to 'the business of real life' (*Principles* 1: 296) and consequently depends on 'capacity' rather than 'book learning'. Ferguson's interest lies in applied rather than theoretical philosophy precisely because 'Men are to be estimated, not for what they know, but from what they are able to perform' (*Essay* 33).

Ferguson's project begins to resemble that of Aristotle. Scientific observation allows for clarity about the various elements of moral experience, which in turn forms the basis for a more extensive character education. Much of Ferguson's work thus takes on the form of a moral anatomy. The identification and definition of aspects of human moral experience sits well with the textbook nature of the *Analysis*, *Institutes* and *Principles*. This anatomising is not conducted with a view to metaphysical hair-splitting, but rather with a view to providing a useful and clear guide to the human experience of moral judgement.[6] Ferguson's textbooks are intended to provide a rubric for moral judgement and decent behaviour. We might consider the definitional passages in the

Principles as an example of this. Ferguson takes great pains to trace out the practical forms of behaviour that are derived from particular 'virtues'.

This is the basis of the moral philosophy as pedagogy interpretation of Ferguson advanced by Richard Sher (1985: 166–8) which understands eighteenth-century Scottish moral philosophy as 'a far-reaching, didactic, character-building discipline' (Sher 1985: 168). David Allan (1993: 187, 201–2) stresses the humanist, and more particularly the Ciceronian, inspiration for this approach to moral philosophy, and traces its roots back into sixteenth- and seventeenth-century Scotland. It seems likely that Ferguson was conforming to the established practice set down by his predecessors, including Hutcheson at Glasgow, and his own teachers Archibald Campbell at St Andrews and William Cleghorn at Edinburgh, but also the teaching he would have experienced at the Perth Grammar School (and ultimately the educational musings that he would have come across in Cicero himself).[7] But in an important sense he is also tapping into a more widespread view on the nature and purpose of education that comes from Shaftesbury's desire to train an elite of gentlemen fit to lead the opinions of the rest of society and from Addison and Steele's project of polishing manners.[8]

Not only must the knowledge of what is good be identified and popularised, but the character of individuals must be shaped such that they will connect these standards with a mental outlook that will ensure their correct application. Sher's account of the 'training of virtuous Christian gentlemen and good British citizens' (Sher 1985: 314) reminds us that contemporary notions of moral philosophy are some distance from the normal view in enlightened Scotland. It is perhaps going too far to suggest, as Lisa Hill (2006: 12–13) following Nicholas Phillipson (1981) does, that Ferguson sought to reshape Scottish civic identity. The reality was somewhat more practical and at the same time more universal in its aspirations: it was to produce a cadre of well-educated and sensible gentlemen who could be trusted to run the institutions of Great Britain. The issue was not so much national identity as gentlemanlike behaviour.

Moral philosophy as a practical discipline requires the identification of sound principles and the dissemination of the mental outlook necessary to apply them consistently in the practice of human life. But more than this, the success of a nation depends on the possession of 'capacity' by its people. It is this possession of practical knowledge of the activity of social life that is vital to a healthy polity in Ferguson's view. Ferguson returns to the idea that those who would reform society based on speculation were both misguided and dangerous. He who 'has gone forth in search of speculative melioration, or improvement, not absolutely required to the safety of his country, is to be dreaded as a most danger-ous enemy to the peace of mankind' (*Principles* 2: 498–9). Far better, in Ferguson's view, to trust the judgement of well-educated practitioners.[9]

This Aristotelian focus on unarticulated 'skill' (*Principles* 1: 227) acquired from practice demonstrates that science is not the only, nor perhaps even the most, important source of knowledge for Ferguson. Our faculties are sharpened from 'use' (*Principles* 1: 20) and an active life provides the challenges which whet the blade of our 'capacity'. Situations which encourage repose invite intellectual decline and it is in the 'bustle' (*Essay* 33) of an active life that individuals acquire capacity, and for there to be 'bustle' there must be a degree of difficulty or potential conflict. The idea is, once again, that the development of skill requires us to face challenges or 'perplexity' (*Essay* 32): the best sailors are those who have experienced 'boisterous' seas (*Principles* 1: 177).[10] Lack of practice means lack of capacity, so the absence of opportunities, or the 'space' to engage in active participation, will reduce the possession of skills.

Teacher

For Ferguson, the primary role of the philosopher is as a teacher, and the task of the teacher is to shape character. Sher, referring to the final passages of the *Institutes*, has observed that: 'By "charac-ter" Ferguson means a people's degree of virtue or other guiding principle; by "condition" he means a nation's size and social struc-ture, which is closely bound up with its economic system' (Sher 1985: 193). Given what we have explored in the previous chap-ters, it seems that character actually refers to something broader than implied by Sher here. Character implies a mental outlook or set of psychological predispositions that direct the individual towards a certain set of values: it appears to involve the skills or 'capacity' involved in making the 'right' decision in a given set of circumstances as much as knowledge of the 'guiding principle'.

The virtues have an epistemic as well as a normative aspect, and Ferguson's Aristotelian notion of capacity allows him to explore this.

In the *Analysis* Ferguson argues that 'capacity and parts refer to the understanding; ardour and force to the Heart; both united constitute a natural superiority of character' (*Analysis* 23). Our conduct makes known our character and is the proper subject matter of the censorial inspection that is as natural to humans as social life. Thus 'character is the ground of estimation, and may raise or sink men to the Rank in which they are qualified to act' (*Analysis* 39).[11] Behaviour is the 'extended expression' (*Analysis* 39) of character where character is understood, not as the pursuit of some particular principle, but of the general mental outlook of a 'good' person.

The chief task of the practical moral philosophy that Ferguson favoured becomes the creation of the 'right' character which is predisposed to act well in the world. Lingering behind this, as we saw in the previous chapter, is the Stoic notion of self-command, or 'probity' as Ferguson refers to it in the *Analysis* and the *Institutes*. We are able to 'control' our own character and given the appropriate mental habits we will be able to make virtuous decisions in diverse circumstances. Indeed he goes further and argues that: 'The only direction on which men can rely in every particular case, is the discernment of a wise and benevolent mind' (*Institutes* 180–1). It is thus that we are able to judge how the same action has different moral implications in different cases (one example being the difference between self-defence and murder). Ferguson is clear that the findings of moral science are not as predictably general as those of natural science as circumstances intervene to alter the moral import of particular acts. This creates a problem for the moral philosopher as teacher in the sense that it becomes impossible to create a comprehensive moral code that answers all questions in all circumstances. As Ferguson puts it:

> Events, indeed, in the course of human affairs, are never determinable in the same manner with the events that regularly succeed one another in the mechanical system of nature. We know precisely at what hour the sun will rise tomorrow, but what action the caprice of thought and passion may lead a human creature to perform, at that or any other hour, is more than human foresight can reach, with any confidence above that of mere conjecture. (*Principles* 2: 346)

Human affairs are imperfect and, as a result, a degree of discretion is required when it comes to determining the morality of particular cases. Indeed this is perfectly in tune with the idea that we are naturally judgemental creatures. But what it quite clearly does not imply for Ferguson is any thoroughgoing subjectivism in moral judgement. Discretion in judgement need not prove an insurmountable problem to living a moral life in line with what Ferguson clearly believed were universal principles of morality. Given the right mental outlook or character, and an awareness of the nature of the world, we can expect that the complexity of human circumstances will not prove a barrier to making the 'right' choices or judgements. Given the right grounding we will learn not to confuse our 'interested' passions with the true bases of moral judgement.

Ferguson understands this relationship between knowledge and the exercise of the will as a form of power. The result is a situation where individuals can be trusted to 'do the right thing' when they have become men of character. This is coupled with the realisation that the ability to discern 'right' also requires strength of character or 'fortitude', understood as 'resolution' and 'force of mind' (*Institutes* 244). Furthermore, one must have the ability to discern what is right in a given set of circumstances and then to act in accordance with this. It is only in this way that the character is manifested and our fellows are able to pass judgement on our 'virtue' as individuals.

It is precisely this line of thinking that colours the eighteenth-century Scottish attitude to moral philosophy in education. The task of the university moral philosophy class is to shape the character of the students. But the stress that has been laid on the character-shaping side of this enterprise has obscured the fact that there was a structured set of ideas and arguments that Ferguson used to assist in this pedagogy. Ferguson's ambition was to provide a systematic vocabulary, a toolkit, which would allow his students to think about morality. This is significant for the purpose of our present discussion because the *Analysis* and the *Institutes* are effectively pedagogical textbooks while the *Principles* is similarly grounded in Ferguson's lecture series and has the clear air of didacticism about it. This has led some to interpret these books as less significant than the more 'philosophical' treatises of Hume, Smith and Reid. But in doing this we not only mistake the very point of Ferguson's conception of philosophy as practical, active and cleared of the dangers of the philosophical vices, but we also under-appreciate the role of the conceptual tools that he provides for clear thinking. There is more to Ferguson's moral philosophy than an attempt to inculcate good habits.[12]

Many of those who have judged Ferguson to be an ideologist and educator have perhaps mistaken a contemporary understanding of the task of moral philosophy for Ferguson's eighteenth-century Scottish view. The size of Ferguson's class was over a hundred students at its height (Sher 1985: 35), and as a result he was able to have a far greater influence on the public than many of his 'more gifted' contemporaries. By his own admission Ferguson put a great deal of work into his lectures and created a 'lively' (Sher 1985: 116) teaching style that was elaborated from a set of general headings that he continually revised throughout his career (*Principles* 1: v). Taken in terms of the prevailing purpose of Scottish moral philosophy Ferguson was clearly a highly successful figure.[13] He participated in shaping the character of generations of future gentlemen, but he also gave them the language through which they would think about morality.

The eighteenth-century Scottish fascination with the phenomenon of habit provided good moral scientific reasons for pursuing the conscious socialisation of children and Ferguson's interest in the role of habit in human life led him to recognise the unique value of shaping the habits of children to prepare them for successful engagement in the adult world.[14] As we saw in Chapter 2, Ferguson believed that humans were deeply influenced by habit and that, to a large degree, habit actually became a part of character. Habits are more readily acquired and retained at an early age, but they may also be changed gradually throughout life as different circumstances are experienced and adapted to through a 'change of disposition' (*Principles* 1: 224). Provided with the 'right' habits children would be able to adapt to the circumstances they experienced throughout their lives in the successful pursuit of their predisposition towards 'good' principles.

It becomes clear that the inculcation of good habits is best accomplished in a practical manner.[15] This, together with the preference for empirical approaches, explains why the subject of history lay at the heart of Ferguson's thinking. For Ferguson history is didactic in that it 'instrucks' on the 'Distinction of virtue and vice' and leads us by examples 'to Embrace the one and avoid the other' (*Manuscripts* 21). Ferguson admits that this is not the 'specific object' of those who write history, but in the hands of the pedagogue the lessons of the past are illustrative material. In the Roman history Ferguson clearly appreciates the didactic role of history. He uses history 'to furnish those who are engaged in transactions any way similar, with models by which they may profit, and from which they may form sound principles of conduct, derived from experience, confirmed by examples of the highest authority' (*Rome* 10).[16]

This attitude to the place of history in education is mirrored in Ferguson's general view of the past as 'an accession of knowledge' (*Essay* 33) to future generations. He is quick to note that this accession does not necessarily make us better people. But it does provide us with a greater body of evidence from which to draw moral lessons. When it comes time to exercise self-command and to shape our own habits we must be clear that the lessons of the past are drawn upon as a reliable guide in our reaction to the circumstances in which we find ourselves. In the lecture hall this meant combining moral anatomising with the lessons of history such that facts illustrate values. What we should also note here is that he does not view age itself as endowing institutions with any sort of mystical wisdom. The examples of history can be examined and utilised because they are factual descriptions of actual events. Ferguson's systematic account of morality provides his students with a consistent language through which to think about history and to consider the lessons that can be drawn from it.

We should be clear here that when Ferguson discusses shaping one's own character through self-command he is not contradicting his views on the influence of habit and custom on moral beliefs. We are largely socialised within the extant traditions of behaviour of the social group to which we belong. However, strength of character allows the gentleman to control his own behaviour in an appropriate manner and avoid the worst effects of the contagion of manners such as lead to mob behaviour. The influence of people like this, with the requisite character traits, thus leaves open the prospect of 'sensible' reform to existing behaviour.

It is precisely because humans naturally exist in social groupings that politics also becomes natural to them as a result of their experience of social life. The organisation of the *res publica* becomes a key focus of human activity and Ferguson asserts that: 'The reason and the heart of men are best cultivated in the exercise of social duties, and in the conduct of public affairs' (*Institutes* 291).

Politics becomes an important arena for the exercise of character because it involves activity that has as its specific goal the matters of common concern that are the most obviously 'social' concerns. It is precisely because politics involves explicit decisions about matters of common interest that it plays such a central role in Ferguson's consideration of the practical exercise of morality.

What this leads to is not a developed theory of the ethical value of group life like that seen later in Hegel and the German historicists.[17] In Ferguson's thought group life is a fact and we have social values because we are social creatures. He does not provide us with a prescriptive model of what an ideal society will look like any more than he provides a detailed metaphysics. It is not Ferguson's intention to provide a blueprint of the ideal political situation. Similarly he makes no attempt to mysticise the value of the group or its primordial ties of blood or heritage. The celebration of group life that we see in Ferguson's thought is a celebration of what he regards as a fact of human existence. Humans are social and the continued flourishing of human societies can be accounted for without recourse to mythical holistic devices such as *Geist*. When Ferguson refers to national spirit and the vigour and health of the nation there is nothing mystical implied: these are terms of generalisation, like Montesquieu's use of spirit, grounded in observations about the shared characteristics of a group.

Stoicism and Christianity

It is in the context of this didactic and practical dimension of Ferguson's thought that we find the best way to understand the role played by Stoicism and Christianity in Ferguson's system. The blend of Stoicism and Christianity that typifies the mainstream of the Scottish literati is adopted by them precisely because of its practical use in character education. The philosophers most often cited by Ferguson are Cicero, Marcus Aurelius and Epictetus, classic sources for Roman Stoicism, but the other feature that all three have in common is that their moral philosophy is conducted with a pedagogical intention. These are practical moralists with a message to convey.[18]

In the light of this the debates about the extent to which Ferguson's system of thought depends on the existence of a Stoicised notion of providence seem, in my view, to be misplaced.

Ferguson's references to providence, like his references to nature, point to a general deistic outlook, but they rarely, if ever, do any active work in explanation. Perhaps the clearest way of seeing this is to compare the language of the early *Sermon in the Ersh Language* with the later systematic student-focused books. The notion of providence there is well in line with the jeremiad sermon: as Richard Sher (1985: 40–3) has observed, the direct providential judgement of individuals and nations is invoked in explanation of geopolitical events. But later the term providence is stripped of this judgemental function and becomes an almost neutral term to explain the apparent existence of order and meaning in nature. More often than not it is a placeholder for the metaphysical indicating a point beyond which our science cannot see. 'The Author of Nature' and the argument from design are produced in Ferguson's work with little variation and the arguments for both the existence of God and his benevolence are covered in a perfunctory fashion. Studying order in nature, efficient rather than final causes, is his project.

The religious arguments would be expected in a series of moral philosophy lectures, but they play very little role in the workings of Ferguson's theory. The separate, but complementary, roles of professor and minister help to explain why Ferguson's books are relatively bare of Christianity. This feature of his thought is also tied to his comparative lack of interest in metaphysical arguments and his gestures towards arguments from the Common Sense school. There is a point beyond which observation cannot take us, and at that point the Deity might usefully be brought into the conversation.[19] Religious belief is treated in a naturalistic fashion as one of the universals of human experience, and while it may be going too far to say that Ferguson's references to providence are paying 'lip service' (Lehmann 1930: 86–7), it is fair to say that these arguments are given their due in the due place in the system, without any undue attention being paid to them or stress laid upon them.

Stoicism, or in reality the practical ethics of Cicero and Marcus Aurelius, also has a didactic function rather than a substantive function in Ferguson's thought. As Katherine Nicolai has pointed out, not only did he not 'warp the truth' (*Principles* 1: 7) to fit the Stoic system, he usually invokes it as an illustrative and educational tool.[20] Indeed Ferguson is quite upfront about this. He explains his attitude to Stoicism by citing Cicero's observation from *De Officiis* (1913: 7), that he uses it for pedagogical purposes in practical ethics (*Principles* 1: 8).

As befits a set of publications that had their origin in a lecture series, Ferguson uses the ancient schools to illustrate diverse opinions on the central elements of moral philosophy. The contrast between the Stoics and the Epicureans forms a useful tool to illustrate the issues at hand. Ferguson's reputation as a Stoic is based partly on his more hostile criticism of Epicureanism and fondness for quotation from Stoics, though even here we should qualify this by noting that the passages contrasting Stoicism and Epicureanism are often critical of both.[21]

The quotes from the work of Cicero and Marcus Aurelius are not intended to invoke the authority of these thinkers; instead, they are intended to illustrate a point that Ferguson has already arrived at in the light of his own system. Perhaps the most striking of these is the long extended quotation at the end of Volume 1 of the *Principles* where Ferguson effectively gives up talking in his own voice. Like Cicero, Ferguson sees the value of the practical ethics of Roman Stoicism, he doesn't sign up to any 'school' in the sense of committing himself to its principles in their entirety, nor does it make much sense to view him as engaged in a project which takes any other attitude towards Stoicism than it acting as a resource for his own pedagogy.

His education in a Scottish system which stressed Latin, humanist scholarship and, at university level, the natural law thinkers who were likewise steeped in Cicero in their attempt to produce a naturalised account of authority, would have made these ideas second nature to him.

Similarly, Ferguson's Christianity is an aid to character formation. The almost total absence of references to revealed religion in Ferguson's books and lectures places him firmly on the more secular end of a spectrum of religiosity that we see running across the main thinkers of the Moderate literati, but that said, there is nothing in the philosophical arguments in favour of religious belief that he does provide that would run counter to the mainstream of eighteenth-century Scotland. The natural religion arguments that Ferguson produced for the moral philosophy class would sit seamlessly next to the sermons of Moderate Kirk ministers inculcating revealed religion.[22]

Gentleman

Instead, Ferguson is calling for a certain sort of human character. He is interested in the development of the 'circumspect' gentleman (*Principles* 2: 464), the steady individual who engages in public affairs in a disinterested manner.[23] Our natural sociability leads us to restrain our 'selfish' or 'interested' tendencies (*Institutes* 91, 97) in favour of what we regard as the good of the community. This mental outlook or personality type, when writ large among the participating sections of a community, provides the 'public spirit' (*Institutes* 78).[24] This, of course, brings us to the language of citizenship that has so often led to Ferguson being considered as a member of the republican or civic humanist tradition. Ferguson's preoccupation with the militia issue has been well documented and it seems certain that he regarded the militia as an institutional means of diffusing and maintaining public spirit among the population at large. However, we should also understand that this most republican of policy instruments is advanced in such a manner that it falls well in line with Ferguson's wider philosophy. Indeed, Ferguson expends great energy in arguing that the militia is necessary for the military defence of the nation and the established government from the threat of France. But beyond the military arguments, Ferguson's political arguments are equally conservative. The first indication that all is not republican here is the absence of any real notion of citizen equality from Ferguson's discussion. In the *Essay*, despite his nostalgic rhetoric, Ferguson had already accepted Hume's argument that Classical Republicanism was made possible by slavery (*Essay* 152–5, 176; Hume 1985: 383). The equality of citizens was only possible because of the systemic inequality between citizens as a class and the rest of the population. Any modern attempt to actualise the republican ideals of old would be forced to support itself without the aid of an idea of natural rank or justified slavery.[25] Ferguson also reiterates the view that republics are appropriate for small states while at the same time acknowledging that such states are not appropriate in a modern context. The practicality of political participation in states of above moderate extent means that the act of political participation in a modern state cannot be like that of the citizen assemblies of the ancient world.

We then have the evidence of the very limited nature of the franchise in eighteenth-century Scotland and Ferguson's own failure to endorse the political movements that pressed for its extension. The militia was to be as much an exercise in rousing and reinforcing the existing order of society in the light of the challenges of the European war as it was a school for citizen virtue. The militia would provide an arena for public service that was missing for much of the population, but that was a distant second to the space being created for the extension of 'capacity' to defend the country. Ferguson is clear that there is to be an officer class to direct the masses, that this class will be drawn from the existing social hierarchy, and that the 'rabble' be excluded altogether (*Militia* 34). Like most of his fellow Enlightened Scots, Ferguson was convinced of the necessity of 'rank' in society and that, concomitantly, social stability meant stability in the system of rank.[26]

Class distinctions and conflicts within societies were inevitable in Ferguson's view and they form the basis of his rejection of democracy along good Aristotelian lines. However, the support for a stable class system is mitigated in Ferguson's case by the fact that the epithet gentleman refers more properly to character and education than wealth. While Ferguson fully admits that wealth-based class distinctions are an important factor in the social dynamic of every society, he is also clear that there are other forms of social hierarchy that do not necessarily depend on wealth. Ferguson argues that it is the vulgar who conflate merit with fame and wealth. The vulgar here are not simply the poor, but rather people of all levels of wealth who mistake the grounds upon which to judge their fellows. The correctly brought up gentleman does not fall prey to 'false notions of rank' (*Principles* 2: 100). As we saw above, character is the criterion for judgement of individuals and character is not obviously indicated in the displays of wealth that are taken by the vulgar as the markers of class.

In previous republican writing the idea of the gentleman was linked to the tradition of the independent landowning citizen. This citizen class, however divided by wealth distinctions, lived in a condition of formal legal equality. However, in Ferguson we have seen that the character of gentlemen is a product of the 'right' type of education and manners. It was eminently possible that many 'gentlemen' would not be entitled to vote by Scottish eighteenth-century franchise limits. Yet they would be able to conduct their part in public life as civil servants, teachers, soldiers, ministers and lawyers. Handled correctly their education would instil in them the strength of character that would allow them to act their part within the system as a whole. In a political system like Scotland with a severely restricted franchise and a deeply ingrained system of advancement through patronage, the opportunity for direct political participation was small indeed. Even more significant here is the fact that the scope of what was considered appropriate for government action was itself highly restricted. In the absence of widespread participation in the political process institutions such as the militia would play a key role in maintaining the group bonds and rank structures that were necessary for social stability. They would create the 'space' for virtuous behaviour.[27]

Institutions

Ferguson famously observed that most human institutions were the product of gradual evolutionary development rather than the result of deliberate rational design. In rejecting the contract model and the great legislator myth, he was not only rejecting the central planks of civic and natural law thought, but also making a case for a more accurate history of human institutions, one that he hoped would place the Whig settlement on a more secure footing than that provided by contract theory or the questionable claims of ancient constitutionalism.[28] In addition to this intellectual ground clearing, Ferguson, like Montesquieu before him, was faced with two alternative narratives of the best way to secure liberty: the ancient liberty of the active citizen and the new modern liberty of the rule of law. Readings of Ferguson that compare him to Hume and Smith tend to stress the view that Ferguson is more sympathetic to the ancients than the moderns, but the comparison is distorting. Ferguson is consistent in his view that both institutions and character are needed.

Ferguson is absolutely clear on the centrality of institutions. He states that 'political establishments are the most important articles in the external condition of men' (*Institutes* 284). Note, however, that the institutions are part of the external circumstances to which men must adapt themselves. Institutions do not reduce the need to ensure that men possess the correct character to be able to act 'correctly' in a given situation.[29] Even good institutions require the right sort of people to man them. In this sense Ferguson is setting himself up in opposition to Hume's more institutionally focused political theory. Hume's observation that men might be supposed knaves in order to develop knave-proof institutions (Hume 1985:

43) misses an important truth for Ferguson, that even with the best institutions and the clearest laws, the institutions must be manned and the laws must be applied. Circumstances require discretion.

This stress on the significance of individual character for the successful operation of institutions fits well with that reading of Ferguson that focuses on the republican exhortation to active citizenship. But it also seems to fit well with the interest in unintended consequences noted by the sociological readings of his work. It seems obvious that he rejects the idea of the deliberate reconstruction of society along 'rational' lines, and it seems equally obvious that he rejects a tradition bound model of political quietism. The stress, it seems, is on the gentleman as reactionary: reacting to circumstances in order to evolve the polity to deal with present conditions. A closer examination of the passages in Part Third Section 2 of the *Essay*, 'The History of Subordination', reveals that the view of evolution held by Ferguson is based on an understanding of social interaction that gives pre-eminence to individuals reacting to current exigencies rather than philosophers designing constitutional models. Here Ferguson underlines that even those politicians who believe that they are acting in the best interests of the nation 'do not always know whither they are leading the state by their projects' (*Essay* 119).[30] The possession of good Principles is for naught if it is not accompanied by the strength of character and capacity to act in the circumstances in which a people finds itself at a given time. The job of the philosopher is not to dictate the content of morality but to prepare the individual to make moral decisions. Human institutions are, in Hayek's (1967) paraphrase of Ferguson's phrase, 'the result of human action not human design' and acceptance of the factual reality of unintended consequences makes it even more important that those who are making decisions are armed with sound principles rather than detailed plans.

As we observed above, the limited nature of the franchise in the eighteenth century severely constrained the scope for participation in the political process. Added to this is the nature of Parliament in the eighteenth century. The function of Parliament at this time was largely to act as a check on the revenue-raising activities of the executive. The institution was not primarily seen as a body that passed legislation intended to shape or revolutionise society. As a result the participation in public life undertaken by most of the young gentlemen who passed through Ferguson's class would have little to do with the design of legislation or institutions.[31] Instead they would each assume their place in the system and be expected to act their part in the smooth running of society as a whole. Suitably trained, these gentlemen would be possessed of the character necessary to act well in whatever field they entered (a trope of thought that would later emerge in the idea of a generalist civil service). They would, as a result, be able to undertake the gradual and incremental reform of existing institutions in reaction to circumstances that could not be foreseen by their teachers.

Nicholas Phillipson (1981, 1983, 1987) has made the case that this aspect of the Scottish Enlightenment involved a systematic rethinking of the role of the citizen in post-union Scotland. With the parliament gone, active citizens moved their participation into other social arenas, and the flourishing clubs and improvement societies of Edinburgh and Glasgow provided a new outlet for social activity with Addisonian polite society replacing Ciceronian active politics. Christopher Berry (2003) sees this as part of a wider de-emphasising of politics in favour of the 'private' world of commerce, a point which encourages us to read thinkers such as Ferguson as advocating a 'space' that would become the modern notion of civil society (see below, Chapter 5). But we should also be aware that in Ferguson's case there is a political function to the rise of the non-political.

What we see here, at least in part, is the recognition that insti-tutionalised politics played a restricted role in the public life of eighteenth-century Britain. The tendency to identify the public with the political is a characteristic of the republican outlook. But if we view Ferguson as a teacher we can understand him as concerned with ensuring the existence of well-rounded individuals capable of successful and virtuous action in whatever field of life they find themselves. A gentleman possessed of the right char-acter will be able to make the correct judgement in a variety of circumstances. It is for this reason that Ferguson believes that true freedom cannot be defended by law alone, but must be supported by men of character willing to defend it. And it should by now be clear that this would not necessarily occur through formal politi-cal institutions. True freedom is enjoyed and sustained by men of character. In a stirring passage Ferguson argues:

> Liberty is a right which every individual must be ready to vindicate for himself, and which he who pretends to bestow as a favour, has by

that very act in reality denied. Even political establishments, though they appear to be independent of the will and arbitration of men, cannot be relied on for the preservation of freedom; they may nourish, but should not supersede that firm and resolute spirit, with which the liberal mind is always prepared to resist indignities, and to refer its safety to itself. (*Essay* 251)

Men of character acting in defence of their rights are the surest defenders of freedom. Institutional design is a secondary matter because, absent the 'right' type of individual, institutions cannot preserve freedom. When Ferguson notes 'The greatest and most extensive benefit which single men can bestow, is the establishment or preservation of wise institutions' (*Institutes* 318–19), he is not contradicting his rejection of institutional design. Instead, he is pointing out the limits of the scope of deliberate human activity and how such institutions emerge through gradual adjustments to present problems. Properly educated and habituated, the gentleman will be able to apply his knowledge of the laws of nature in whatever context he should find himself. Ferguson believed that this would lead to a rejection of political radicalism and hasty reform in favour of a gradual adaptation to the circumstances in which the nation finds itself through the reform of existing institutions. This is because the nature of a system of reactionary gentlemen that he has described leaves change up to the individuals best placed to make the 'right' decisions.[32]

Ferguson views the institutions of a free society as the best school for the individual. Given the right principles individuals would be free to shape their character as they acquired practical experience in the business of life. Institutions such as the militia provide the opportunity for 'schooling' the public spirit among those who are excluded from the formal political process. Politics is important and it does have its place at the heart of Ferguson's theory, but it is also important to note that the scope of the political is circumscribed far more tightly than the scope for public service. Ferguson thought that: 'Institutions that preserve equality, that engage the minds of citizens in public duties, that teach them to estimate rank by the measure of personal qualities, tend to preserve and to cultivate virtue' (*Institutes* 318), but the equality encouraged by these institutions bears little resemblance to the more radical democratic ideas that emerged from the English civil war or those which would gain currency during the French revolution.

What is interesting about this discussion of the respective roles of institutions and character is that it appears to acknowledge far greater scope for reform than we might suppose given Ferguson's conservative reputation. Ferguson puts his faith in correctly educated gentlemen to be able to make the correct decisions in whatever circumstances they may happen to find themselves. It is gradual adjustments made by these men in reaction to changed circumstances that characterises institutional evolution. This reactionary activism grounded in character takes the place of quietism and submission and the wisdom of the mystical old order at the heart of Ferguson's conservatism. Ferguson's Stoicism is, in truth, Ciceroneanism in that it depends on the reactionary gentlemen who man the institutions of society more than it depends on any notion of providence. He places the responsibility for the successful reform of society at the discretion of a class of activist gentlemen. Cicero and Marcus Aurelius are so prominent in Ferguson's works, not because they adopt Stoic positions, but rather because their projects of creating a practical ethics of active participation match Ferguson's own project.

In the *Institutes* Ferguson argues that: 'Those were the happiest republics, who educated virtuous citizens, to whom any power might be safely intrusted' (*Institutes* 315–16). It is the education of gentlemen of the right character that is held up as the true source of stable and free political systems. Those who would embark upon 'respectable public careers' (Kettler 2005: 7) after a suitable education would be the guarantors of the future stability and freedom of the state. The public-spirited gentleman is necessary for the success of institutions and it is for this reason that Ferguson's discussion of corruption is based around a fear of a 'fatal dissolution of manners' (*Essay* 238), caused by a lack of 'calls to attend' (*Essay* 237) to matters of public concern. The corruption of nations is a result of the corruption of the people and it is only by ensuring a steady stream of well brought up gentlemen that the system will be able to adapt to the challenges thrown up by changing circumstances.

What is interesting about this assertion is that Ferguson combines it with an argument that recognises the value of internal conflict in the political aspect of this process. As we will see in the next two chapters, conflict and struggle play a key part in Ferguson's thinking, but we must also remember when we explore this aspect of Ferguson's thinking that conflict is always undertaken under a system of rules. This is particularly true of his analysis of the internal politics of states where factional disputes cannot be allowed to threaten the constitution. For Ferguson, the rivalry and contention of public life is 'the school of men' (*Essay* 62–3) and as we learn best in an active life, so we learn most in contention with our fellows in pursuit of the public good.[33] In a classic description of Rome as an example of this Ferguson states that: 'Rome, which commenced on the general plan of every artless society, found lasting improvements in the pursuit of temporary expedients, and digested her political frame in adjusting the pretensions of parties which arose in the state' (*Essay* 121). It is these 'accidents' (*Essay* 123) that form the basis of political life.[34]

There is an obvious link here to Ferguson's theory of social evolution through unintended consequences. Political activity does not, and never in any meaningful sense did, involve everyone standing up in the assembly. This was always an idealised account of a lived reality where rank and precedence and other modes of power and exclusion were everywhere. Ferguson was perfectly aware of this and his educational vision was directed as much at the ministers, lawyers and officers as it was at the vanishingly small number of people who passed through his classroom on the way to Parliament.

The realisation of public participation, understood under the broader heading of doing one's bit in the place one finds oneself, is only possible if there are things to do – if there is a scene that demands activity – and it is this general distrust of peace and quiet that typifies Ferguson's active notion of public life. Freedom requires the interaction of men of character if it is to persist. As Ferguson puts it:

> The ultimate and essential security to liberty . . . is the character to be retained by those who have any considerable stake in the welfare of their country, a character by which they are qualified, in the last resort, to defend as well as to fulfil the ties of their station. (*Principles* 2: 493)

Ultimately it is these men of character, together with the institutions that they inhabit, that provide the true bulwark against both tyranny and revolutionary zeal.

Conclusion

We can see that the conceptual building blocks of Ferguson's approach to education place a great deal of weight on the pursuit of a practical moral philosophy that has, as its chief purpose, the production of guidelines for the everyday experience of moral judgement. These guidelines are not, on their own, sufficient to ensure the diffusion of good principles in society. They must be supported by the formation of a character that is equipped to apply principles in a variety of real-life circumstances. The ultimate end of this moral philosophy is the education of a class of generalist gentlemen imbued with the character to take their place in the public life of the nation. This public participation would, in most cases, not take the form of direct political participation. Hanoverian Britain was not an ancient, or even a Florentine, republic and the system hit upon in the aftermath of 1688 was one far more appropriate to a nation of Britain's extent than the republican tradition could provide. Ferguson updates the classical idea of the virtuous citizen and applies it to the correctly brought-up gentleman who acts his part in society, but whose part need not involve direct participation in political life. He is also aware that formal politics, though a key area of human activity, is not necessarily the sole proper arena for gentlemen that the Republican tradition can sometimes lead us to suppose.

Ferguson's politics were essentially those of a conservative Whig and the influence of Republicanism in his work needs to be understood as part of his commitment to the Hanoverian settlement. We can see him as adapting classical ideas in defence of the established system in eighteenth-century Britain. Ferguson's moral science and moral philosophy come together to support a system of moral education designed for the leaders of a civilised society. This view of civilisation is concerned with social stability, order, rank and continuity.[35] Properly educated gentlemen would act as the intelligent reactionaries driving social change.

In the end Ferguson provides us with the model not of a small republic, but with the means of stabilising and preserving an expanded commercial nation. His moral science is designed to produce a practical ethics which would train the new Hanoverian elite. It would not be an exaggeration to say that Ferguson's pedagogy is not so much a system for training good citizens as it is a system for training an officer class. It is tempting to wonder if the model for this sort of independent, virtuous, representative of the established order might not have been Ferguson's own father: a man in some respects a lone representative of order in a disorderly community. Such a man requires strength of character and confidence that he is capable of making the right decisions and it seems to be just such character traits that Ferguson was trying to foster in his students and readers.

Ferguson's combination of moral science and moral philosophy is designed to provide a solid basis for character education. His intention was to provide his students with the intellectual toolkit to solve the moral problems that they would face in the course of their lives. Ferguson's view of the scope of what we can hope to gain from moral philosophy is revealed in this: the lived reality of moral life involves a vast complexity of potential circumstances which render the minutiae of scholastic casuistry next to useless. Different elements of moral thinking – justice, benevolence, public utility, the virtues – need to be balanced in deciding a course of action in complex circumstances. Ferguson's system, with its last-stand common denominator of benevolence, is intended to help his students make the right sort of decisions in their practical lives.

Ferguson has been described as a Scottish Cato, a name indicating his perceived love of the Roman Republic, but his character judgement of Cato, like that of Cicero, recognised that both were committed to a doomed cause. Rome could no longer support a republican political system. The reality of Ferguson's own situation was that it was Cato's elitism and conservatism and Cicero's pragmatism and restless activity that provided the true lesson which could be applied in the setting of Hanoverian Britain. Ferguson's system of moral philosophy was intended to provide a basis for the development of the sort of character that Britain needed in its officer class: educated, self-aware, anxious to do their duty, and loyal to the existing system of politics and law. The notions of self-knowledge, capacity and self-command are so central to Ferguson's thinking precisely because they are the necessary conditions for adaptability. As he puts it: 'It is the merit of a School to prepare its Pupils for the Stations they are destined to fill' (*Manuscripts* 229).

Notes

1. David Allan (2006: 12) notes that during his tenure as Professor of Natural Philosophy the class grew from nine to eighty students, and

Richard Sher (1989: 249) points out that, when Professor of Moral Philosophy at Edinburgh, Ferguson's class was so large that he may have lectured on national defence to a larger audience than had read about it in the *Wealth of Nations*.

2. Ahnert and Manning (2011: 10) also point out that the idea of the cultivation of character was an activity distinct from that which went on in the university classroom or in the pages of a philosophical treatise. This fits neatly with the reading here that suggests that Ferguson saw his task as providing a conceptual toolkit to aid in such cultivation.

3. David Kettler has examined this aspect of Ferguson's thought as it relates to his practical bent. Ferguson can be viewed as an 'ideologist' (2005: 139) and as an 'intellectual' (2005: 170) as well as a moral teacher (2005: 99). He possesses the 'intellectual's concern for practice' (2005: 175) so that his moral philosophising is concerned with the identification of vice and virtue in everyday life. The only difficulty with this interpretation is that it imposes the vocabulary of post-eighteenth-century distinctions between philosophy and ideology onto Ferguson's thought in a manner that unhelpfully obscures the nature of his philosophical project.

4. Ferguson's philosophy rejects what I have called 'book learning' (Smith 2006).

5. Gordon Graham (2013: 519) has pointed out that for Ferguson moral education is necessarily 'self-education' as it involves thinking about how we think about morality. Katherine Nicolai (2011: 142) notes the same point in Ferguson's Edinburgh lectures where he argues: 'The facts must be verified by your own experience, the sentiments must correspond to the feelings of your minds ...'

6. Richard Sher (1985: 94) cites the letter from Bute to Home (7 August 1757) on employing Ferguson as a tutor to demonstrate how Ferguson's approach was the mainstream view of the role of education at the time. 'It is not Greek and Latin that I am most anxious about, 'tis the formation of the heart – the instilling into the tender ductile plant, noble, generous sentiments, real religion, moral virtue, enthusiasm for our country, its laws and liberties.'

7. Ferguson's contemporaries, including Fordyce, Kames, Gregory and Turnball, all adopt similar views in their writing on education.

8. Christopher Brooke (2012: 120) discusses the Stoic and Ciceronian origins of Shaftesbury's views on education.

9. See, for example, Ferguson's letter to McPherson on the philosophy of Sir J. Mackintosh: 'The specimen I have seen inclines me to think he

is one of the greatest moralists this island has produced and I consider the publick character as involved in his success' (*Correspondence* 2: 456). Richard Sher's description that Scottish moral philosophy 'was also a means of integrating piety, politeness, propriety, and knowledge, with a view to producing learned, genteel, virtuous young men whose religious, social, and political views would prepare them for happiness and success in post-Revolution, post-Union, Presbyterian Scotland' (Sher 1985: 91) is perhaps the best summary of the nature of Ferguson's teaching. But if we stress the pedagogical function we are in danger of missing the fact that for this to be successful, it needs to be built on a sound moral science and clearly argued moral philosophy. Sher's view is shared by Kettler (2008: 112–13), Allan (2006: 14) and Oz-Salzberger (2008: 147, 153).

10. This in part helps us to understand Ferguson's frequent approving comments on savages. His depiction of the atomised and mentally blunted ordinary worker in a commercial society is contrasted with the broader capacities of the 'savage' who not only possesses a wider range of capacities, but who faces perplexity on a more regular basis than his civilised counterpart. The problem is not so much the division of labour as the absence of difficulties to stretch the capacities of ordinary people.

11. And it is worth flagging up that Ferguson connects character with rank.

12. The heavily annotated lecture notes held in Edinburgh University Library show that Ferguson constantly refined the headings and definitions that he spoke from, apparently thinking through each topic anew with each delivery.

13. The object, as Eugene Heath has observed, 'is not novelty, but benefit to the student' (Heath 2006: xlviii).

14. Sher cites Ferguson as stating: 'Now is your time to begin Practices and lay the Foundation of habits that may be of use to you in every Condition and in every Profession' (Sher 1985: 117–18).

15. A similar view is expressed by Gilbert Elliot: 'It is full time to endeavour to bring education hence to the real business and purposes of life; and to teach our sons when boys, what we desire they may retain and profit by when they become men' (Sher 1985: 125).

16. Xandra Bello (2017: 15) has shown that Ferguson's own *Roman History* is a particularly sophisticated attempt to bring together causal explanation and accurate narrative to create the didactic 'space' to allow his readers to think through the general lessons of history.

17. For a discussion of Ferguson as an ethical thinker see Jack Hill (2017).

18. For explicit statements of this see Aurelius (1930: 53), Epictetus (1925: 163), Cicero (1913: 7).

19. Thomas Ahnert (2014: 5) has pointed out that the Scots are actually far less interested in arguments about natural religion than is often supposed.

20. The best and most detailed discussion of Ferguson's engagement with his classical sources is Katherine Nicolai's work and I follow her interpretation here. She stresses Ferguson's eclecticism and the fundamentally pedagogical nature of his interaction with ancient sources (Nicolai 2011: 90, 102). For Nicolai, Ferguson's aim was to create an easy to follow practical philosophy rather than a comprehensive system of philosophy. As a result, his discussions of the Schools are not appeals to authority but illustrations designed to allow his students to think through the issue at hand (Nicolai 2011: 147–8). This leads Nicolai to stress that Ferguson is not a Stoic, but rather someone who uses Stoic authors to illustrate positions he has already reached from his own observation (Nicolai 2011: 184), thus: 'Ferguson does not follow the philosophy of the Stoics, but uses them as a source when they agree with his views' (Nicolai 2011: 230).

21. See, for example, *Principles* (2: 4–5).

22. Even the arch satiriser of the Moderates, John Witherspoon, developed a similar curriculum at the College of New Jersey.

23. See also *Principles* (2: 404) for his definition of a gentleman. Again, the use of the masculine is quite deliberate.

24. In the *Institutes* Ferguson defines public spirit as: 'Public spirit is founded in benevolence: its object is indefinite, men, or intelligent natures, wherever they present themselves to our view or conception' (*Institutes* 78). Lisa Hill notes the connection between public spirit and 'participation in municipal affairs' (Hill: 166).

25. As highlighted by Fletcher of Saltoun's problem with the status of vagabonds in his attempt to provide a Republican solution to Scotland's economic ills. Robertson (1985) and Pocock (1983: 240) suggest that the militia issue held particular salience in Scottish thinking as a result of Fletcher's influence, but as we noted in Chapter 1, there is little evidence to support this and it is far more likely that it came directly from engagement with ancient sources and the standard pedagogy of Scottish schools.

26. Though we ought to be clear as well that this system of rank was

not, necessarily, so rigid as to prevent mobility between the ranks by gifted individuals, a point we shall return to in the next chapter.

27. Iain McDaniel (2013a: 11, 155–9) has suggested that Ferguson's interest in the militia was not the result of classical nostalgia, but rather part of an attempt to create a military aristocracy that would hold in check the imperialistic tendencies of the British state. McDaniel traces this idea to older German ideas of military chivalry. The true lesson of Rome then is the need for 'military-civil union and the forging of a public-service elite' (McDaniel 2013a: 176).

28. For Ferguson's rejection of the legislator myth see *Essay* (120–1), *Principles* (1: 264) and *Militia* (1).

29. Indeed, in the *Institutes* he notes that different political systems suit different national 'characters' in different 'circumstances' (*Institutes* 292).

30. This stress on reaction to circumstances clearly complements Burke's views on the nature of political life. For Burke circumstances 'are what render every civil and political scheme beneficial or noxious to mankind' (Burke 1987: 7). This leads him to favour circumspect men of practical experience. 'A disposition to preserve and an ability to improve, taken together, would be my standard of a statesman. Everything else is vulgar in the conception, perilous in the execution' (Burke 1987: 138).

31. Still less if we consider that Scotland had no Parliament of its own – a situation of which Ferguson heartily approved (Hill 2006: 217). We should also observe that Burke shared Ferguson's approval of elitist representation in Parliament (Sabine 1957: 513–14).

32. Sometimes one man can make a difference – as usual with Ferguson the example here is Cato. His individual action preserved the Republic longer than, in Ferguson's view, it ought to have been preserved on account of the changing character of the mass of the people of Rome. However, if the institutions of society are manned by correctly educated gentlemen, the need for heroic individuals will be reduced as the prevalence of manners will ensure the continued functioning of the system. Fagg and others have referred to Ferguson as a 'Scots Cato', and while the *Roman History* does show Cato in favourable colours, Ferguson's comments on him are not universally positive. Perhaps, given the project of moral philosophy which he set himself, especially with its pedagogical and practical focus, it would be better to see him as a Scots Cicero – a man determined to act practically and to preserve the existing order. A pragmatic politician

of conservative leanings who would be unwilling to give himself over to the defence of a doomed order like Cato (*Rome* 404).

33. As David Kettler (2005: 6) notes, conflict over the public good has a 'vital pedagogical function' to instil disinterested virtue. See also Lisa Hill (2006: 216) where she notes that civic and moral character are shaped in political disputes.

34. This leads Ferguson to conclude that free debate between good men is a secure basis for a political order. In a passage that interestingly foreshadows the younger Mill, Ferguson makes the case for the value of open public debate. 'The conversation of good men very often takes the form of debate or controversy; and it is indeed in this form they are most likely to receive from one another mutual instruction and improvement of thought. The freedom of conversation, therefore, whether relating to matters of public deliberation or private concern, is at once a symptom of just as well as of vigorous government' (*Principles* 2: 510). But again, such conversation does not need to take place in Parliament.

35. There may even be a case for seeing this as one of the first attempts to articulate the ethos that developed in the nineteenth-century British public service. It stands apart from the idea of a specialised bureaucracy based on the division of labour among experts. Ferguson repeatedly attacks the Chinese bureaucracy as a symptom of a weak, rather than a strong, state (*Essay* 214–15, 255). Roger Emerson (2015) provides an eloquent summary of this feature of Scottish Enlightenment pedagogy when he observes that it was intended to create men who would be successful in whatever walk of life they ended up.

5

Civil Society and Civilisation

The happy form of our Government; the sacred Authority with which our Laws execute themselves; the perfection to which Arts are arrived; the Extent of our Commerce, and Increase of our People; the Degrees of Taste and Literature which we possess; the probity and Humanity which prevail in our manners. (*Militia* 11)

Having outlined Ferguson's general system of thought we can now explore how he applies it to the ideas of civil society and civilisation. My aim in the following two chapters is to explore the idea that Ferguson's opposition to and doubts about commercial society have been unhelpfully exaggerated by the preoccupations of his interpreters. The tendency to read Ferguson as an enthusiast for ancient virtue has a long history, dating as far back as Lord Kames's comments on the *Essay* in a letter to Mrs Montague.[1] But if we expand our attention beyond the *Essay* and view his comments on commercial society in their own light rather than in comparison to those of Hume or Smith, as late expressions of the civic tradition or as anticipations of Marx, we see something rather different. As we proceed through the next two chapters I will offer the case for reading Ferguson as a partisan for civilisation, a proponent of commerce and a thinker whose orientation is not so much that of a critic, but rather that of someone aware of the fragility of the achievements of modern Britain and, as a result, someone intent on suggesting reforms that will preserve the system. The reforms proposed are directed at the gentlemen who would read his works and attend his lectures, they are grounded in empirically based moral science, and conducted in line with the goals of the activist moral philosophy based upon it. The project is the advancement of civilisation through 'the desire of establishments more complete, and more effectual for the peace and good order of society' (*Principles* 1: 207) and, as we shall see, such establishments can be assessed in line with a set of moral scientific measures of civilisation.

Perhaps the clearest way into our discussion is to note the two particular areas that Ferguson believes are characteristic of the success of contemporary civil society and civilisation. As he puts it: 'And if our rule in measuring degrees of politeness and civilisation is to be taken from hence [conduct in war], or from the advancement of commercial arts, we shall be found to have greatly excelled any of the celebrated nations of antiquity' (*Essay* 193). As Michael Kugler (1996) points out we should be aware of the 'if' in this statement which suggests that there are other relevant criteria of assessment, of which more below, but that said, Ferguson is offering us a clear rule for comparison in two areas and both of these share the same characteristic that places the moderns above the ancients: the rule of law. This chapter will cover Ferguson's idea of civil society and the following chapter will examine his account of civilised warfare.

Before beginning our discussion of Ferguson's views on civil society and civilisation we should conduct some conceptual ground clearing and note, as David Allen (2006: 143–4) has observed, that Ferguson, despite his widely acclaimed place in the history of the idea of civil society, does not share the modern understanding of the term, nor does he operate with a particularly detailed version of the concept.[2] Civil society became a matter of popular discussion as the Eastern European countries moved towards the end of communist rule. It was applied as a vague tag to all the various non-state social movements involved in pressing for political change. As the 1990s merged into the twenty-first century the concept broadened to apply to many non-violent political and social pressure groups. This understanding of civil society, as a category of association that stands against or separate from the political state, is a product of Hegel's attempt to systematise the modern state. Prior to Hegel the 'pre-history' of the terms equivalent to civil society tended to carry with them the implication of the totality of a political community. Thus we have Aristotle's *Koinōnia politikē*, Cicero's *Civitas*, *Res Publica* and *societas civilis*, Aquinas's *communitas civilis sive / politica* and Locke's civil or political society. In each case, no distinction was drawn between the civil society and the political society.

Hegel, who was deeply influenced by Ferguson's analysis of civil society, deployed the term in a specific technical sense in his own work.[3] *Bürgerliche Gesellschaft* was predominantly (but not exclusively) the realm of market interaction in Hegel's thought. Civil society comprises the economic interaction of the community and the institutional arrangements necessary for the pursuit of subsistence. In Hegel's terminology it deals with the system of needs through the concepts of abstract right and contract. It was the arena where individual particularity reached its peak as individuals interacted with each other and acquired the material goods that manifested their own personalities. As Hegel would have it: 'Civil Society is the [stage of] difference which intervenes between the family and the state', as such it is a creation of the 'modern world' (Hegel 1991: 220). It is true that the sphere was not one of total atomisation; business associations and Hegel's corporations and guilds provided the steps leading to the final dialectic realisation of human personality in the synthesis of spirit manifest in the state. In this sense civil society, though differentiated from the state in theory can only reach its full manifestation once the state has developed.

Marx took his understanding of civil society from Hegel, but he stripped it of the other features that Hegel had tentatively brought along with market exchange from Ferguson. Marx regarded civil society as the place of egoistic life that represented a schism between the private individual and the supposed unity of membership of a political community (Marx 1975: 220). The main thrust of Marx's concern with civil society lay in the contradiction between the egoistic activity of private individuals secure in their bourgeois rights and the sham of political equality promised by liberal constitutionalism. For Marx economic determinism in the base/superstructure model rendered civil society into an intellectual edifice deployed as a means of control by the bourgeoisie over the proletariat.

This sense of civil society was developed in the sociological tradition – particularly through Tönnies's distinction between the mechanical association of a civil or market society and an older form of organic community (*Gemeinschaft*). It led to the widely held view that civil society was a part of a modern state/nation/ society, but that it was also in some sense not the noblest aspect of human association. The sociologist Edward Shils (1997: 326) sought to account for the reversion to a discourse of civil society in the former communist nations as a product of a perverse form of cultural memory. The communist regimes, inspired by Lenin's take on Marx's hatred for civil society, sought utterly to suppress civil association (hence the title totalitarian). In doing so they unwittingly preserved the idea in two forms: first, in those associations that they continued to tolerate in the belief that they controlled them or in those that they drove underground and thus outside their control; second, in the official language of Marxism-Leninism civil society was demonised as the epitome of the self-delusion of the West and this very demonisation kept the concept alive (as Shils says, much in the same way Christianity keeps the idea of the Devil alive). Thus when the time arose where there was an opportunity to oppose and topple the totalitarian regimes of the Soviet Bloc the language of civil society was there for the taking as a manner in which to express grassroots, non-state action. More recent analyses of civil society, such as Robert Putnam's (2001) work on the decline of civil association, have continued this distinction between the civil and the political.

In what follows I want to stress the centrality of the idea of rule-governed behaviour to Ferguson's notion of the space that has become our civil society. In addition to political institutions and the law, politeness, manners and civility are key features of what Ferguson calls a civilised or polite or polished society. As Fania Oz-Salzberger (1994: xix) has noted, Ferguson's civil society is the polity itself, but not all societies are civilised. The analysis of civil society takes two forms in Ferguson's work: first, the 'natural history' or, more accurately, the stadial theory of development from savage through barbarous to civilised society; and second, the analysis of civilised society itself. This will form the structure of this chapter where we will move from a consideration of Ferguson's stadialism, through a discussion of the 'quarrel' between the ancients and the moderns, to the criteria of assessment that Ferguson uses to judge commercial society (population, manners, wealth, liberty) and his subsequent diagnosis of potential corruptions that could undermine the basis of a civil society. Throughout we will maintain the reading of Ferguson's project outlined in the previous chapters but applied to the subject matter of 'the manners of men, the practice of ordinary life, and the form of society' (*Essay* 168). Understood in this way, the civil is at the very heart of Ferguson's intellectual project. His natural history of man is an account of the progress of the species from 'rudeness to civilisation' (*Essay* 7). As Lisa Hill (2006: 69) has noted, Ferguson is among the first to make extensive use of the word civilisation in the English language. The idea, already in currency in the writings of thinkers such as Mirabeau, is particularly useful for Ferguson's purposes and his innovative use of it is as good a place as any to begin our discussion.

Civilisation

In considering what Ferguson regarded as the attributes of a civilised nation we must first strip away the inessential practices that may cloud our judgement and encourage bias. It is clear, as we will examine below, that Ferguson considered wealth, trade, increasing population, progress in the arts and sciences and improving manners as attributes of a flourishing civilisation. All of these, however, are perhaps best considered as effects of civilisation. Ferguson's attempt at moral science leads him to identify what he regards as the underlying universality that allows, or causes, these effects. The underlying cause for civilisation is law. As Ferguson would have it:

> The success of commercial arts, divided into parts, requires a certain order to be preserved by those who practice them, and implies a certain security of the person and property, to which we give the name of civilisation, although this distinction, both in the nature of the thing, and derivation of the word, belongs rather to the effects of law and political establishment, on the forms of society, than to any state merely of lucrative possession and wealth. (*Principles* 1: 252)

Throughout his career Ferguson is clear and unambiguous: the order and stability of expectations that are the product of a system of public law are the mark of civilisation.[4] The gradual development of generalised conventions of behaviour among a group is the start of a process of abstraction and institutionalisation that is the hallmark of any society that is to be regarded as civilised. Ferguson provides a theoretical explanation of the gradual evolution of law from primitive convention. The gradual process of the formalisation of law allows the development of social order and a sense of security that fosters the other improvements that Ferguson regards as effects of civilisation. Ferguson's analysis depends on the absolutely central role of the development of legal institutions to adjudicate in disputes. These, along with the development of a military chief to defend from external attack, are the origins of political institutions. As he puts it: 'The utility of some permanent recourse of this sort, would naturally lead to political institution … So that, while we suppose men to be associated from their birth, or otherwise cast into groups together, every difference or dispute would suggest the necessity or utility of political establishment' (*Principles* 2: 268).

Note here the reversal of Adam Smith's notion that commerce introduces good government (Smith 1976b: 412) and of the standard Marxian base/superstructure model from economic relations to legal superstructure.[5] It is important to note this at this stage as one of the most obvious characteristics of Ferguson's approach is his analysis of the dependence of the rule of law on the evolution of a very particular set of political institutions which are, in turn, necessary for economic development. It is this that leads Kettler (2005: 321) and McDaniel (2013: 97) to suggest that Ferguson's account of civilisation is inherently political. While this is undoubtedly true, it is not perhaps true in the way in which they intended. For example, when McDaniel suggests that Ferguson is redefining the term civilisation as part of a 'broader effort to maintain a clear distinction between economics and politics' (McDaniel 2013a: 97), he ignores the fact that Ferguson is making an explicit connection between politics as a cause and economics as an effect. It is true that his attention is focused on the underlying universalities of social life and how these necessarily lead to the functions of war leader and magistrate – shared recognition of these leads necessarily to the relation of co-nationality and the identification of interest with the group. But what different societies do with that is another matter. This stress on the political elements of civilisation cuts against the Marxist inspired reading of Ferguson as aligned with a supposed proto-materialist theory that emerges from stadialism, but it does not sever the economic from the political, as we will see. If there is a base/superstructure in Ferguson it is the political and legal that is base and the economic that is superstructural.

Civilised nations are those which have begun to produce a system of abstract law and an impartial judicial mechanism. The aim of this process of codification is the desire for security and order, the same desire that drives the human mind to seek classification of experience. This process, of political and legal refinement, is necessary to prevent the disorder and potential civil war caused by clan feuds and the natural human partiality to sub-national groupings. Crucially for Ferguson, we need to understand that the process is both informal, in the sense of habits and manners, and formal, in the sense of political and legal. Part of his analysis is a natural jurisprudence based on perennial social problems, and as we might expect of one whose moral science is so attuned to the diversity created by the different circumstances of different nations, he accepts that the law of nature will manifest itself in different ways in different societies. But in each case the characteristic is the rule-governed behaviour of individuals. In a civilised society 'every proceeding is conducted by some fixed and determinate rule' with 'the impartial administration of rules to particular cases' (*Essay* 159).[6]

Ferguson conducts the analysis of the evolution of modern civil society within a broadly stadial schema and against the backdrop of the 'quarrel' between the ancients and the moderns. In respect to the central role of the rule of law Ferguson is quite clear: the ancients did not develop the legal and political institutions to qualify them as civilised in the modern sense. He observes of the Greek *polis* that: 'It is indeed impossible, that they can be more civilised, till they have established some regular government, and have courts of justice to hear their complaints' (*Essay* 185). To the extent that they managed this they can be considered as civilised. The Romans, to the extent that they developed an operative legal system, can, likewise, be considered as civilised. The reason for this lies in his recognition that commerce and artistic achievement are the result of civilisation rather than constitutive of it. Civilisation is regular government and law – the Greeks and Romans began to develop this, but did not realise it to the level apparent in modern Europe. As we noted in Chapter 2, it is the literature and culture of Greece and Rome that lead us to view them as civilisations.

It appears to Ferguson that the gradual development of government is explained by the desire for social order. Those governments that have pursued this end have proved the most effectual in creating the conditions for human flourishing. Chief among the exceptions to this rule that Ferguson identifies is Sparta. Ferguson believes that the Spartans prevented crime by shaping the character of their citizens to such a degree that it virtually disappears from their range of acceptable actions. But the long discussion of the imagined visit to Sparta in the *Essay* does not conclude with the modern visitor choosing to stay. Instead, Ferguson's conclusion appears to be that, admirable as Sparta may be, it is not a relevant example for modern societies. Ferguson seems to be aware of his reputation as a partisan of the ancient world and as an enthusiast for barbarian virtue. But he takes some pains to distance himself from what he sees as a misapprehension. For example, in a letter to Henry Dundas he points out that:

> I am not partial to former times, or disposed to ascribe the virtues of men to Ignorance and Poverty: but rather believe that Ranks well employed are favourable to Virtue and Elevation of mind. No Nation surely ever exhibited a better Spirit than Britain has done in the height of its affluence: but there is no reason why that Spirit should be neglected or because they are a great Resource adopted as the only standard of Estimation and honour. (*Correspondence* 2: 481)

Civilisation is synonymous with the evolution of a codified legal system and a secure political order. The 'public offices of goodness' in such a 'civil and political society' provide clear guidelines regarding the acceptable relationship between magistrate and subject and subject and subject (*Principles* 2: 352–3). This form of social order provides the preconditions for the other attributes of a civilised nation and it is also responsible for shaping the manners of the inhabitants of such a nation. Civil behaviour can only develop in a civilising society. As Ferguson notes: 'The manners of a nation shift by degrees, and the state of civil policy and of commerce, at which we are arrived, have greatly affected our manners in this particular' (*Militia* 8).[7] What is interesting about this stress on law in Ferguson's understanding of society is that it provides him with a relatively neutral measure for cultural comparison. The greater the degree of civil order that is brought about by legal and political arrangements of a nation, the more civilised it may be considered.[8] It is clear that this objective criterion carries with it an underlying assumption about human psychology in civilised nations – it presupposes a degree of individual self-command among the group members. This submission to rule-governed behaviour and the institutions necessary for its enforcement on the recalcitrant are the badge of a civilised individual.

Ferguson's account is based on a gradual unintended consequences analysis. People acquired 'the habits of political life' (*Principles* 1: 201) before they 'had conceived any concerted design to establish a government' (*Principles* 1: 260). The original order of subordination and the political constitution are shared habits or conventions developed in response to the circumstances of each society. These 'received customs of their society' (*Institutes* 207) form the basis of political association with the two chief functions being protection from external threats and maintenance of internal order. Ferguson continues this theme of the restraint of violence and the submission to order in his attempt to provide a standard of behaviour that differentiates the civilised from the barbarous. In the case of his stadial analysis the central idea is that of property.

The Three Stages

As we noted in Chapter 2, Ferguson develops a moral science that seeks to account for the evolution of shared beliefs, customs and institutions from a universal human nature acting in the particular circumstances in which each society finds itself. Part of this account is a natural history of the evolution of human society. As he puts it: 'The inventions of one age prepare a new situation for the age that succeeds; and, as the scene is ever changing, the actors proceed to change their pursuits and their manners, and to adapt their inventions to the circumstances in which they are placed' (*Principles* 1: 58). But Ferguson's use of the terms 'ages' and 'stages' (*Principles* 1: 194) or 'state' (*Essay* 97) are rarer than his use of the term 'nations' (*Essay* 102). The reason for this is straightforward: Ferguson is not describing a species history where societies necessarily move through these ages. Instead he is describing a historical and contemporary world where different societies have acquired different degrees of civilisation. Lowland Scotland was civilised, the Highlands were not (yet), although they were not subject to the same conditions as the American Indians, and so might be counted as a separate type of society.

In the next chapter we will discuss in more detail the notion that different types of society have different ways of waging war, but for the moment let us confine our attention to the internal characteristics of each of his types of nation. For Ferguson we can identify three broad types of society: savage, barbarian and polished. The model is directly adopted from Montesquieu (1989: 290), but Ferguson makes some of his own refinements. Each society has its own characteristic beliefs and institutions, but the differences between them lie in the regulation of behaviour in line with law (particularly property law) and the regulation of the arbitrary use of violence. 'Improvement' in manners reduces violent expressions of self-preference and curbs acts of 'brutal appetite and ungovernable violence' (*Essay* 93). The management of violence is necessary for a society to cohere, and so how a society manages violence, how it does its politics, becomes vital to understanding its operation.[9]

Ferguson's inconsistent use of terminology does not present us with a serious issue in understanding his analysis of the types of society. We have 'rude' or 'savage', 'barbarian', and 'polished' or 'civilised'.[10] Ferguson, unlike Smith and Millar, does not defer to modes of subsistence to typify his distinction: the types are not determined by economics. Indeed, he does not appear to distinguish between hunting and shepherding societies, lumping both together in his analysis. Ferguson's interest in the legal and political structures and differences between them lead him to stress institutions at the expense of economics. In line with his views on avoiding ethnocentrism he does not dismiss savage and barbarian societies out of hand, noting that they have their own notions of virtue adapted to their condition and that some aspects of these are admirable. The types of society have their own notions of liberty, their own forms of government and religion, which can be identified from the records of history and the evidence of travellers. We noted above that Ferguson is careful about the development of 'conjecture': his moral science is intended to be based securely on generalisation from the evidence and so the depiction of the types of society and the movement from one type to another is undertaken with particular care. There is nothing inevitable, or indeed, despite appearances, anything deterministic or cyclical about Ferguson's account of the rise of civilisation. It is one thing to observe that nations have risen and fallen, but it would be quite another to believe that there was an inevitable force operating in this for Ferguson.[11] Stable legal and political orders are necessarily adaptations to the circumstances of each society, and Ferguson is clear that we cannot force a savage to become civilised because civilisation is a process of acculturation and socialisation into a society that has developed a rule-governed order.

Ferguson's earliest discussion of the schema appears in the *Analysis*. Here the criteria used to distinguish them are government and equality. In a savage society there is no government and no inequality; in a barbarian society there is both government and inequality and in a polished society there is both government and inequality, but these are regulated by 'Law and established forms' (*Analysis* 11). In the *Institutes* (28–30) the discussion shifts to one about the development of property in land. It is also here that we come up against another of Ferguson's confusing shifts in terminology. In the clearest statements of the three stages he states that there is no conception of property in a savage society. The immediacy that arises from that form of life precludes the abstract thought necessary for the idea of property to develop. In the *Essay* he discusses the situation of 'the savage, who is not yet acquainted with property; and that of the barbarian, to whom it is, although not yet ascertained by laws, a principal object of care and desire' (*Essay* 81), so the schema seems to be clear and similar to the *Analysis* view on government and inequality. But on the next page he appears to muddy the waters and suggest that some notions of property, and hence subordination, exist in savage societies. By the time we get to the *Principles* we see that the discussion of the origin of the idea of property leads him to admit that the idea of inheritance exists in rude ages where 'property is least established' (*Principles* 2: 239), but does he mean by this that some conception of property exists for the savage as well as for the barbarian?

Ferguson's apparent rowing back from a clear initial position is frustrating for the reader, but it is an inevitable feature of his more capacious categories of society and his movement between the distinctions of rude and polished, and savage, barbarian and civilised. There is a wide variety of examples of savage and barbarian society and without the focus on form of subsistence Ferguson's analysis is forced back onto the general notion of law. There is no government and no law in a savage society, there is some government and some law (but not stable property law) in a barbarian society and there is both government and law in a civilised society. But Ferguson has already indicated that society is not possible without the development of certain social features necessary for humans to live together in groups. What in reality he seems to mean is that there is no regular government and law in savage societies, and that there are the beginnings of regular government and law in barbarian societies, but only civilised societies have regular government and the law.

To be fair to Ferguson here, his account of property is not the only one that rows back from the claim that savages are so immediate as to have no conception of property. The same move is made by Kames in the *Historical Law Tracts* (1776: 88–156) and Smith in his *Lectures on Jurisprudence* (1978: 14–18) when they accept the existence of property in the immediate holding of a good in savage society but not in the sense of a formally recognised 'right'. For Kames and Smith there can be no concept of abstraction or futurity attached to this, so inheritance is unknown in savage societies. Distinction by birth can only occur where we have both government and a notion of inheritance. But for Ferguson the existence of property in 'moveable objects' exists in 'rude or savage nations' (*Principles* 2: 238). So the 'unrefining savage' (*Essay* 87) who goes in 'pursuit of no general principles' (*Essay* 88) has property conventions. The whole discussion is unsatisfactory, and is doubly so as it plays such a central role in Ferguson's analysis of what counts as civilisation. There is, however, one feature that might help explain what Ferguson has in mind. As we saw above Ferguson attributes a central place to custom and habit in his analysis. There is a case, albeit not one Ferguson himself makes, that the distinction that he is looking for is one of articulation – that the habit of property exists in savage societies without being formally articulated or understood in abstract terms. This would then allow Ferguson to see the barbarian and polished societies as refining existing habit and custom into formal law.

The movement from rude to polished societies also sees an increasing diversity in forms of human behaviour and the objects of their attention. In part this is an economic argument – savages and barbarians are more focused on subsistence than the polished but this argument is usually qualified by Ferguson.[12] Diversification is a result of the division of labour which is absent from savage and barbarian societies. As man becomes 'civilised' he loses the 'uniformity of manners' (*Essay* 179) we find among those in the rude state. In the *Essay* this takes a particularly strong form: 'Upon a slight observation of what passes in human life, we should be apt to conclude, that the care of subsistence is the principal spring of human actions' (*Essay* 35). The suggestion is that on a 'slight' or superficial observation our attention is drawn to subsistence as an explanatory feature, and while it is true that it preoccupies 'rude' nations, even here it is not the sole object of attention (as we will discuss further below in the section on commerce), and this is precisely because social life itself produces objects of concern beyond subsistence and chief among these is politics.

The Political and the Civil

Ferguson's understanding of politics sees it as a natural outgrowth of the sociable nature we examined in Chapters 2 and 3. We are naturally 'associating and political' (*Analysis* 9) creatures. Politics as a discipline applies to 'nations and collective bodies' (*Analysis* 45) and in particular to the analysis of the 'united force and direction of numbers' which Ferguson terms 'the state' (*Analysis* 45).

When he comes to analyse 'the offices of civil and political society' (*Principles* 2: 352) and 'civil and political institutions' (*Principles* 2: 263) it becomes clear that, though crucially related, the civil and the political have distinct meanings. Ferguson, again following Montesquieu (1989: 7–9), begins his abstract analysis of political societies by dividing them into two core relationships: that between 'magistrate and subject' and that between 'fellow citizens' (*Principles* 2: 271). Each relationship is then accompanied by its own form or mode of regulation. Thus 'political laws define the relative rights of magistrate and subject' while 'civil laws define the relative rights of private parties' and 'criminal laws direct the proceedings of the magistrate in supressing crimes' (*Analysis* 52). As a result, a civil society is also a political society in the sense that civilisation is impossible without the political order required for the rule of law. As he notes in the late *Manuscript* essays 'Civil liberty is the Security of all Civil Rights' while 'Political Liberty is the Form of Government proper to that security' (*Manuscripts* 217). Civil laws regulate the interaction of individual citizens, while political laws determine the scope of the government's power to enforce the terms of civil association. These developments are essential for the existence of a civil society. As Ferguson would have it: 'The establishment of a just and effectual government for the repression of crimes, is of all circumstances in civil society, the most essential to freedom' (*Principles* 2: 459).

The particular forms of the role of magistrate and citizen may be diversified but their abstract function is universally apparent: the key feature of political and civil association is the recognition and acceptance of the monopoly of force held by the magistrate. It is the nature of civil association that disputes between fellow citizens are referred to the magistrate. Citizens must 'refrain from any application of force on their own part' (*Principles* 2: 272).[13] Similarly the magistrate is obliged, under the terms of political association, to resolve disputes and apply the monopoly of force to defend the innocent. Such are the 'conditions implied in every political establishment, and without which society either cannot be preserved, or cannot be said to have received any political form' (*Principles* 2: 273).

These 'primary articles' or 'fundamental laws' (*Principles* 2: 286) are the underlying universalities of human social life: the conditions necessary for society itself to cohere. Ferguson believes that the obligations and rights that are produced by the recognition of political association are 'derived from convention alone' (*Principles* 2: 273). Thus, while the forms of political association may differ in different times and places, the form of the convention remains as an underlying universality of what it is to exist in a political and civil society. Moreover, behind this executive power ceded to the magistrate and the notion of rule-governed interaction lies the notion of a law of nature that, prior to political and civil association, indeed 'prior to convention' (*Principles* 2: 274), was the standard of proper behaviour and the origin of our perception of the rule of law. This is coupled with a keen awareness of the idea of law as a restriction of arbitrary behaviour. The magistrate in a civilised society does not have absolute discretion, he is limited by the law in both his judgements and his enforcement of them: 'Punishments applied according to some fixed rule of law, give stability to the principles of justice' (*Institutes* 228).

Although Ferguson has no developed notion of the modern sense of civil society, what he does have is an awareness of the functional difference of, and relationship between, the civil and the political. The language is taken from the jurisprudential tradition, but the recognition is there nonetheless. Each society develops its own reaction to these universal features of social life and as the society develops these practices and institutions become the shared inheritance of a people. Ferguson's notion of the nation and the development of national sentiment will be discussed in detail in the next chapter, but for the moment we should note that these shared customs and practices become part of our identity.

The study of politics becomes key to understanding what allows society to associate in a civil manner.[14] It becomes clear that only a particular form of political association is compatible with a truly civilised society – a despotic society can never be a truly civil society on account of the arbitrary mode of its politics. Mild despotism, or despotism 'in time of moderation or civility' (*Essay* 255), can continue without offending the people, but will collapse

into arbitrary government at the first sign of danger or controversy. Ferguson conducts a quite detailed consideration of the
relationship between political and legal authority and the use of
force as an essential feature of securing political order. The most
important condition is that the citizens must accept the authority
of the magistrate and believe him to be right in the exercise of
force. As he puts it: 'Violence is effectual to support the authority
of government, so long as the bulk of the people agree in opinion
with their rulers, and think the force of the state is properly
applied' (*Principles* 1: 215). Where the sovereign does not have
the support of the people, in cases like the Stuarts, or where it is
used in pursuit of ends where it is ineffectual, such as attempting
to 'dictate opinion' (*Principles* 1: 219), it threatens the stability of
society itself.[15]

The study of politics has another dimension for Ferguson. Citing
Cicero, he reduces political science to a single operative idea: 'Salus
populi, suprema lex esto, is the fundamental principle of political
science. If the people be happy, we have no title to enquire to
what purpose they serve, for this itself is the purpose of all human
establishments' (*Principles* 2: 411). To this end Ferguson proposes
an analysis of the politics of a civil society that applies four main
categories: manners, wealth, population and civil and political
liberty.[16] Each of these represents a potential indicator of the
level of advance attained by a nation. Underwriting the analysis
is the idea of universal principles of human behaviour that can be
identified as present in all human societies as laws of nature.

Manners

In what follows we will examine Ferguson's discussion of the
forms of behaviour proper to a civilised society, what he calls
'the relations and duties of men in civil life' (*Analysis* 29). To
understand the operation of a civilisation we must understand
'the manners, or political character of the people' (*Principles* 2:
414–15). We should be clear here that Ferguson is not privileging
the manners of one particular society in this discussion.[17] Instead
he believes that, underneath the diversity of external manners, we
can trace certain mental attitudes that are universal indications of
civilisation. The 'real standard of manners' (*Principles* 2: 376) is
to be found in the disposition to oblige. Lingering behind this is
the idea of a gentleman or of 'good breeding' (*Institutes* 250). This

is a term that 'implies a certain caution to avoid what is hurtful, or offensive to others, liberality, and humanity, or attention to oblige, and to anticipate the wishes of the modest and unassuming' (*Principles* 2: 404). Ordinary decent behaviour may differ across cultures, but the core motivations or dispositions of mind are the same.

As we saw in Chapter 3 Ferguson understands manners as habitual dispositions that are arranged under his discussion of the minor or derivative virtues. Such modes of thought are conditioned by the circumstances of the society and acquired by socialisation. The savage has manners as much as the civilised gentleman and a proper analysis must seek the underlying universal features of the 'manner' that exists behind the particular expression. The analysis is unremarkable and in line with traditional accounts ranging back to antiquity. He believes that these offices are manifestations of two aspects of goodness and provides the following division of offices: innocence has fidelity, veracity, candour and civility as its subsidiaries, while beneficence has piety, personal attachments, gratitude, liberality, charity and politeness.

These ordinary virtues are the expression of noble motivations. They derive from a 'principle of humanity' (*Essay* 40) that forms part of mankind's sociable nature. This is deeply significant for Ferguson's understanding of human moral behaviour. As we saw in Chapter 3, the sociological 'fact' of our social nature is what lies behind the development of a common moral code, but it also influences the content or tenor of that code. Good manners, whatever the form developed in different societies, are a manifestation of certain attitudes towards our fellow humans that emerge from the experience of group life and the natural attachment to the group that is characteristic of human existence. Put another way, ordinary moral behaviour contains an implicit recognition of value of other human beings and an exercise of self-command in support of rules of behaviour. For the purposes of our present discussion two of these are of particular interest.

'Civility is a guarded behaviour in the ordinary intercourse of society, to avoid giving offence' (*Institutes* 249). It applies to 'matters supposed to be comparatively of small moment' (*Principles* 2: 355). Civility descends from innocence and as a result takes what we might call a negative form compared to the positive form of politeness. Civil behaviour is manifested in the control of our actions and expression to avoid giving offence. It is not, according to Ferguson, the preserve of a particular class or rank, but is instead the sign of an individual who has experienced social life and developed a desire to avoid being rude. What makes civility interesting in this regard is that Ferguson is both expanding the ideal of the gentleman class and extending it to apply to all of the inhabitants of a civil society. As he puts it: 'Civility is a habit very generally acquired in the practice of society, where experience and knowledge of the world conspire to enforce the duties of good sense and innocence' (*Principles* 2: 357). Ferguson believes that those who sneer at the idea of civility as a form of hypocrisy miss the point. Civil behaviour is the product of human group life and represents a form of honesty in human interaction. Manners matter because they ease group life and the ordinary virtues of civil behaviour allow a stability of expectations in human interaction. The desire of avoiding offence allows interaction, and particularly 'conversation' (*Principles* 2: 358).

If Ferguson regards the practice of civility as the 'negative' desire to avoid offence, then its 'positive' counterpart is politeness, a 'disposition to oblige' (*Principles* 2: 374).[18] According to Ferguson: 'The polite is attentive to the habits, expectations, and feelings of those with whom he converses: He would prevent their requests, by anticipating the effects; and would conceal his own wants, where the knowledge of them might importune or distress those to whom he is unwilling to be troublesome' (*Principles* 2: 374). Ferguson believes that such modes of behaviour have come to be known as manners because they are concerned more with the way of acting than the end result. In this sense they may be considered as of a lesser importance than other virtues, but they remain indications of character, even if they represent the 'polish' rather than the 'essential constituent' of virtue (*Principles* 2: 378).

Ferguson constructs an interesting argument in favour of his position on this issue. He begins by admitting the vast diversity of manners even among polished nations. He continues to observe that:

> Like other external signs of disposition and meaning, manners have either an arbitrary or a natural connection with the disposition signified. Manners of the first kind depend merely on custom; and fluctuate, like language, or any other arbitrary institution. Manners of the second kind are such appearances and conduct as men of certain dispositions naturally assume. (*Analysis* 39)

Two points of interest are raised here. First, the analogy of manners as a language: this type of manners is specific to particular groups and once established as a rule within a group becomes the expected standard of acceptable behaviour. Second is the idea that there are certain universally discernible forms of well-meaning behaviour.

It is this latter form of manners that interests Ferguson. He advocates a 'when in Rome' attitude to local manners and denies that the form of any one culture's manners renders them superior to any other. What really interests him is the state of mind or motivation that is expressed in what he understands as 'good breeding'. It is the 'disposition or habit of doing that which is agreeable, or avoiding that which is offensive to others' (*Principles* 2: 162).[19]

This care for others allows us to pierce through the habitual conventions of specific cultures and to recognise that what is harmful to humanity cannot be considered as an expression of good manners. Manners themselves are an expression of concern for others; they may be warped by tradition or religion, but it can never be an expression of good manners to act in a pernicious manner. Ferguson argues precisely this point:

> Manners founded in nature are sometimes varied by custom, insomuch that different nations or ages require a different aspect, carriage, and conduct, in expression of the same disposition. A conduct tending to the good of mankind is invariably right, independent of opinion or custom. Even in case of arbitrary manners, we are bound, when the good of mankind will permit, to observe those of our country, as we speak its language, or wear its dress. (*Analysis* 40)

Again Ferguson advocates conformity in non-essential regularities of behaviour as facilitating the important value of group cohesion. This argument is coupled with his observation that manners arise and are perfected first where 'the intercourse of men is most close and frequent' (*Principles* 2: 375). Politeness is a product of town life. Manners are, by this reckoning, an expression of rule-governed behaviour and self-command: in other words they are a vital manifestation of civilisation or of a 'mind enlightened' (*Institutes* 154). But as we saw in Chapter 4, Ferguson believed that the best school of morality was participation in an active life. Thus the people 'receive instruction and habits of civilisation, in the midst of labours in procuring their subsistence, accommodation, and safety' (*Principles* 1: 241).

Wealth

As we noted in the introduction, discussions of Ferguson's views on commerce have suffered from an unfortunate tendency in the critical literature. This tendency is, quite naturally given some of the rhetoric in the *Essay*, to view Ferguson as having doubts about the social and moral impact of commerce and luxury. He is held up as more sceptical than his fellow Scots Adam Smith and David Hume and this view is often compounded by the Marx-inspired interpretation of Ferguson as the precursor of alienation theory. While necessary correctives to this view have been found in the more measured work of McDowell (1983) on Ferguson's attempt to develop a political system that would balance stability and commerce, and Berry (2009: 146–8) whose analysis of the coeval nature of political and economic activity in the *Essay* suggests that Ferguson saw them as inevitably linked, the temptation remains to approach Ferguson's views on the 'commercial republic' (*Essay* 154) focused on the critical aspects of his view.[20] In what follows I hope to avoid this by placing Ferguson's account within the wider context of the system of moral science outlined earlier in this book. The task here will be to examine the centrality of economic activity as it fits into the philosophical anthropology that Ferguson uses as the basis of his moral philosophy.

One important point to begin with is to note that the issue of economics is clearly one where Ferguson is more deeply indebted to the moderns than he is to the ancients. There is no trace in Ferguson's discussion of a view that holds commerce as disreputable – indeed, he is critical of Roman society for precisely this reason. The stress on the importance of political participation and military service that form the basis of the republican interpretation of Ferguson are not combined with a rejection of commercial life or an argument that it will inevitably lead to a loss of virtue. Economic activity is a core part of human experience and throughout his writing Ferguson adopts the same tripartite analysis of the objects of our material efforts. As he puts it: 'The external pursuits of men terminate in procuring the means of safety, or accommodation, or ornament' (*Institutes* 26).[21]

This analysis connects to another pervasive theme in Ferguson's writing. As Christopher Berry (2009: 146) has pointed out with reference to the *Essay*, Ferguson's conception of humans sees them as by nature artists destined to act on the world and, crucially, to improve it. This is connected to Ferguson's core observation that ambition is what drives human activity. Humans are ambitious to improve in a material as well as a moral sense. In terms of our material lives there is no order of priority for Ferguson. Humans always pursue the convenient and ornamental as well as the necessary. There is then nothing to be gained from saying that pursuit of subsistence is of an entirely different mode of activity from pursuit of comfort and beauty. Humans always will, and always do, pursue all three. As he puts it:

> The convenient and ornamental in their several forms, however rude, are studied in the same age with the necessary; and the same person, who subsists from meal to meal or the precarious returns of the chace, is, in the intervals of his necessity, no less studious of ornament in his person, his dress, and the fabric of his habitation, his weapons, or arms, than he is earnest in procuring his food. (*Principles* 1: 240)

The desire of ornament is an ever present aspect of what motivates human action and ambition creates 'a principle of progression' such that mankind's 'fancy' is 'rendered insatiable' (*Principles* 2: 39).

In the late unpublished *Essays* Ferguson takes this point even further, arguing of the growth of commerce that 'would have been impossible to forsee that it should Arise from the mere defect of Food Raiment and lodging under which Man compared to the other animals is made to labour' (*Manuscripts* 82). This view is consistent throughout his career, but where he goes next is particularly interesting. He observes that once subsistence is secure 'Contemplation and Science become Necessaries of Life to many And the first principle of Want which Caused the Germ of Intelligence to Spring is comparatively overlooked and forgotten' (*Manuscripts* 83). The link between the initial effort to secure subsistence and the development of the science is reminiscent of Smith's argument in the *History of Astronomy*, but it is worth noting here because we will return to it below. More interesting for the present discussion is that subsistence takes a back seat to leisure, convenience and ornament in Ferguson's account. This mode of analysing economic activity perhaps helps us to understand an additional reason for Ferguson not adopting the mode of subsistence-based stadial arguments of his peers.

Despite his reputation as a moralist, Ferguson does not appear to be interested in the sort of idle moralising that often coloured the luxury debate. This is partly because he has identified the urge to comfort and ornament as natural and universal. But it is also because he finds that 'it is difficult to draw the line of separation betwixt convenience and absolute necessity, or between articles of convenience and those of mere decoration and fancy' (*Principles* 2: 48). Indeed, the line seems to be different in different ages. As with his observation about caves and cottages (*Essay* 12), Ferguson operates with the idea that there is a universal human need for shelter, and an ambition to acquire it, but that very soon the rudest accommodation will be made more comfortable and ornamented. There seems, then, little sense in holding the accommodation of one age to be morally superior to any other. As he puts it: 'The *necessary of life* is a vague and a relative term: it is one thing in the opinion of the savage; another in that of the polished citizen: it has reference to the fancy, and to the habits of living' (*Essay* 137–8). This is an important point for Ferguson. Luxury is relative and if that is the case whatever corruption it may engender is not a product of the material good itself, but rather of the mental attitude towards it.[22]

As a result we see why Ferguson defines wealth in the way that he does. We are wealthy to the extent that we have secure subsistence and are free to pursue comfort and ornament in line with the conceptions of these held in our society. Following Smith's anti-mercantilism he argues that the wealth of a nation is not measured by the revenue of the state, but by the amount left to citizens to pursue subsistence, comfort and ornament, consistent with the provision of sufficient revenue to provide the services required of the state.[23]

If ambition is the motivation behind economic activity and subsistence, comfort and ornament are its objects, then we can apply what Ferguson has already told us about ambition (see above, Chapter 3) to economic ambition. First, ambition is insatiable. There is no stopping point or ideal level. Just as we will constantly attempt to become morally better, so too will we constantly attempt to improve our material situation. For Ferguson this links to the other great theme of his moral thought, the value of action. Action in pursuit of 'business' is just as healthy for the human character as action in other fields. Activity in the economic sphere is more important than the attainment of the goods sought: 'These labours and exertions are themselves of principal value' such that 'mere industry is a blessing apart from the wealth it procures' (*Principles* 1: 250). As we noted above, activity increases 'capacity' (*Principles* 1: 250) and 'skill' (*Institutes* 27), it provides us with a chance to exercise our talents.[24]

All of this leads Ferguson to a notion of improvement that sees it as an ever-moving and developing phenomenon. What matters if we are to recognise improvement is not the level of wealth acquired at any given point, as this will soon be surpassed by the drive of ambition, but when it comes to 'the real constituents of wealth' (*Essay* 221), provision of the necessaries of life and the scope for individuals to pursue ambition, it is possible to make comparisons. Ferguson's aim here is not so much idle moralising about the effects of wealth, as he accepts that innovation and industry are driven by ambition for wealth; instead, he is observing that the spirit of a people and their institutions can be compared on a basic benchmark of necessity, but that anything beyond that becomes misleading. This is because the comparison is about the character of the people rather than their material possessions.

Ferguson's observation that 'contentment is still of equal value in whatever condition it be attained' (*Principles* 1: 248) could be understood as a Stoic moralising injunction against confusing wealth with happiness. But if we read it in the light of our discussion here we might see it also as a criticism of the idea that contentment is in tension with wealth. Contentment is a value that can be obtained whatever level of wealth we acquire. We see another example of this when he discusses enjoyment: 'Habit reconciles mankind, or renders them indifferent nearly alike to their respective fortunes' (*Principles* 2: 51). Happiness and contentment have as much to do with character as with wealth. As a result corruption is not an inevitable consequence of either poverty or wealth. Rather it concerns the attitude that we have to each and to our place in society.

The point for Ferguson is not to prefer public service to wealth but rather to combine them. A society like Sparta where commerce is absent and dedication to duty total, however admirable in the abstract, is not what Ferguson is looking for. Such a society is unbalanced because it does not provide the opportunity for activity in a variety of arenas. For all of Ferguson's observation about the centrality of the political he is quite clear that the role of politics can complement economics. Politics does not need to concern itself with the incentives to economic activity. The natural

ambition of individuals will drive them to pursue their own interest in their own way. Ferguson conducts this discussion in two
directions: first, by linking it to the issue of population (as we will
see in the next section), and second by advising government to
avoid intervention in the economy.[25]

Industry is a vitally important arena for human activity and
so to dismiss it, and to dismiss the ends which act as incentives
to it, is a mistake for moralists.[26] The problem is not wealth nor
is it the pursuit of wealth. The problem is when this aspect of
human behaviour invades other aspects of our lives and takes over.
'Oeconomy', understood as 'the proper use of what fortune has
bestowed, whether the fruits of labour or inheritance' (*Principles*
2: 340), is a 'virtue' (*Principles* 2: 341). If increasing our fortune
alone were the virtuous thing to do then we would not despise
the miser. The role of the government is not to foster virtue in
commercial life. Instead, its role is to 'secure the property of its
subjects', to 'facilitate communications' (*Principles* 2: 426) and
to provide for national defence. Given security of possession each
individual will pursue their ambition in the best manner open to
him. It seems obvious to Ferguson that 'private interest is a better
patron of commerce and plenty, than the refinements of state'
(*Essay* 139). From what we have seen of Ferguson's comments on
commerce and wealth it looks extremely unlikely that he was concerned about any inevitable causal link between economic growth
and moral corruption. The problem is quite clearly not that commercial activity inevitably leads to a decline in virtue, nor is there
any demand in Ferguson that economic activity be regulated or
curtailed to prevent corruption.

Trade and commerce are linked to Ferguson's core explanatory concepts of ambition and activity, but they are also crucially
related to his third explanatory concept: sociability. Trade and
commerce are social activities and Ferguson's analysis of the division of labour, so often read as a paradigmatic account of the
sceptical view of trade as individualising and alienating, places
interdependence at the heart of his account of what he calls the
separation of arts and professions. The division of labour depends
on 'trust' that they can 'exchange' (*Institutes* 32) such that we rely
on others to help us provide for our needs.

Ferguson's explanation of trade and the division of labour remains
consistent from the *Analysis* to the *Principles*. Commerce is mutually beneficial exchange of surplus which allows specialisation and

this interaction creates interdependence. The result is a mutually beneficial exploitation of specialised knowledge. And, of course, here we see a link with yet another of Ferguson's favourite themes – that skill and capacity come from practice. Specialists focus their attention and cultivate their craft so that: 'They become skilled by continued application, and by subdividing arts and professions' (*Analysis* 47). This process is undirected and evolutionary. As Ferguson makes clear in the *Essay* (173), 'the progress of commerce is but a continued subdivision of the mechanical arts,' but the division itself is not rational, in the sense of foreseen and deliberately entered into, it is not 'natural' (*Essay* 174) in the sense of given by nature; instead, Ferguson refers to it as instinctual. But this is perhaps a misleading term. He is not here talking about instinct in the commonly accepted sense. That animals behave by instinct is closer to what Ferguson means by 'nature' in this passage. Instead he is pointing to something else. The idea that individuals specialise and trade without conscious thought on the interdependence that arises.

> Those establishments arose from successive improvements that were made, without any sense of their general effect; and they bring human affairs to a state of complication, which the greatest reach of capacity with which human nature was ever adorned, could not have projected; nor even when the whole is carried into execution, can it be comprehended in its full extent. (*Essay* 174)

Ferguson's account of the rise of commerce is of a gradual and piecemeal development of specialisation and the gradual extension of trade. As we will see below the basis of his analysis is again the core concepts of his moral philosophy: ambition, action, capacity and sociability. While Ferguson is keen to stress the material benefits of trade and how it links to his main concepts for social analysis, he is not blind to the problems that arise in a commercial and specialised economy. In a moment we will devote some time to examining the main thrust of his complaint about the impact of commerce. But let us pause here and look at one of his ancillary arguments as it allows us an interesting vantage point from which to view the main argument. One of the ways in which Ferguson expresses his worries about the division of labour is through the very feature of it that he believes explains the growth of production. Ferguson credits the development of capacity for a specialised task and the acquisition of specialist knowledge for the increase in production. But the result of this is that no one individual is in a position to possess access to the whole range of human knowledge. We become fitted to our professions and while 'a scholar or a merchant, may be each in his way a person of great sense and integrity . . . the one is not therefore qualified for a counting room, nor the other for a place at college' (*Principles* 2: 413). If, as Ferguson argues, 'thinking itself, in the age of separations, may become a peculiar craft' (*Essay* 175), then most of us will come to be reliant on the thinking of others.

Moreover, there is an inequality in the experience of specialisation. As he argues in the *Essay* (175), the genius of the master is bought at the expense of the workers. This passage has often been read as one of the parts of Ferguson that led Marx to cite him approvingly in *Capital*. And while it does seem that Ferguson is waxing lyrical on the move from a savage society where the individual possesses a wider range of skills and lives in equality with his peers, to a commercial society where individuals possess only partial knowledge limited to their profession and live in inequality, he is also observing something else: that commercial society is better than savage society. While we may not possess the range of skills of our predecessors we are able, through trade and sociability, to take advantage of far higher standards of the material provision of the necessities, conveniences and ornaments of life. This, according to Ferguson, is not a problem. That inequality exists in commercial society and that it is grounded in the acquisition of levels of 'capacity' is not, for Ferguson, much of a matter of concern – rank after all is natural. If the benefits of commerce depend on inequality, then Ferguson is perfectly happy to support that inequality. His concern is rather that the inequality and the specialisation might destabilise other institutional bases of the society. His concern then, as we will explore below, is that the legal and political order will become precarious unless two types of knowledge remain widespread in the middle and upper ranks of society: the knowledge of politics and the knowledge of war.[27]

The core preconditions of commerce are a stable government and an effective property law system. The 'protection of a common sovereign' (*Rome* 450) allows for the extension of the division of labour. Not only does the law protect property, but the prospect of commercial gain also makes individuals more law-abiding. This leads Ferguson to observe that merchants are 'inclined to peace' as it disrupts trade (*Principles* 1: 253). The link between commerce and peace in Ferguson's thought seems to be near wholly taken over from Montesquieu (1989: 378), but things are not as simple as they first appear.

Population

Ferguson's interest in population levels can be traced throughout his work. He is interested in comparisons of birth and death rates and in the level of infant mortality, and believes that population is one measure of the strength of a nation, pointing out that the Romans used the census as a measure of their national success.[28] He presents two reasons for this. First, want of numbers leaves a nation open to the threat of invasion; and second, a large population provides an indication of a wealthy society. To this extent the state may 'estimate its profits and its revenues by the number of its people' (*Essay* 173).

Ferguson regards increasing population as 'a great and important object' (*Essay* 60) of human activity, but he quite explicitly argues that it is not the proper subject of government policy. The main reason for this is that an increase in the population is an unintended result of the natural operation of human nature in a particular set of circumstances. As such it is an indicator of success and not a specific good to be sought by policy. Population levels grow where government is stable and order has been introduced by law. The only role for government as regards the level of population is to provide the stable conditions for the exercise of the natural drive to procreate. As we observed in the section on sociability in Chapter 2, the biogenic drive to procreate and the subsequent bonds developed during childcare that develop into families are a universal form of human behaviour. This drive to procreate is not a matter of choice but rather an instinctual drive that arises from biological functions. As Ferguson would have it: the 'increase of numbers is procured without consulting the mind, or the intention of the parties' (*Principles* 1: 28). Nature has not left the choice to reproduce as a matter of conscious choice for reproduction was necessary before the emergence of human rationality. The true significance of government for the growth of population is the provision of the security that allows people to raise families of their own. Population growth is made possible under the rule of law because the rule of law allows the development of wealth and increasing security of subsistence. Subsistence is secured with the generation of wealth, and wealth is generated in a stable political and legal context. Thus the security of the rule of law allows economic development which in turn allows 'mankind to subsist in growing numbers' (*Principles* 1: 253) and nations to defend themselves.[29]

This provides us with one clear criterion for the level of civilisation attained. Large populations are possible only with political and legal stability and the generation of wealth. Or, as Ferguson would have it: 'If population be connected with national wealth, liberty and personal security is the great foundation of both' (*Essay* 139). However, Ferguson cautions against placing too much weight on population as an indicator of national success. He points out that wealthy nations are few and that they become natural targets for the poor. If they are unable to defend themselves their wealth will not protect their offspring but rather attract danger.

Indeed, there is a sense in which the republican analysis of the movement from small to large, extended societies has obscured the real significance of the link between politics and population in Ferguson. In tribal societies, where the social bond is that of kinship, there is a clearer link between individual family numbers and the success of the nation. Modern commercial nations have lost the immediacy of this connection, but the loss is not one of the scope to participate in an assembly, it is the loss of emotional intensity in the experience of patriotism and community.

Moreover, Ferguson links the analysis of population to political stability in an indirect fashion through economic growth, but he also speculates that the link between secure subsistence generated by wealth and the level of population may, in certain circumstances, lead to a reduction in the rate of population growth. As Ferguson argues: 'Commercial nations have not any interest in the increase of population, except in so far the people are industrious or possessed of some profitable art. The idle, the profligate and the prodigal become, in proportion to their numbers, a source of public distress and calamity' (*Principles* 2: 418). To this extent a concern for the size of a population must be tempered by a concern for the form of their social union. Or, as Ferguson would put it: 'The value of numbers is proportioned to their union and character' (*Institutes* 265).

It is precisely here that we find Ferguson addressing one of the most consistent themes of his career. Ferguson's reputation as a republican, keen to promote participation, seems to sit very uneasily with his analysis of social rank. Ferguson was no democrat and it is this that has produced the supposed tension between his 'consistent anti-democratic stance' and his nostalgia for ancient politics (Plassart 2015: 125). But there really is not a paradox here. Ferguson's admiration for the Roman Republic and his analysis of its decline is based precisely on this issue. The fall of Rome in Ferguson's analysis is not primarily about faction or about empire, it is a class analysis of the corruption of politics. The problem, the central political problem, for Ferguson is keeping the mob under control. As he put it in a letter to William Pulteney, the crucial issue to the British system was to ensure that 'our Present Gamblers for Power are made to feel that they cannot rise upon the shoulders of the Mob.' Like Rome the solution 'is to try whether a Neutral Interest can be formed by men of Property and Family to Ward off the Evils with which the constitution is threatened in the Ishue of a Contest between Mobs and Military Power' (*Correspondence* 1: 88).[30]

It is here that Ferguson links his account of the populous society with his account of the development of subordination. Like his fellow Scots Ferguson regards rank and subordination as natural and inevitable features of all societies. A stable society is a society with a system of subordination. This in part reflects the acceptance of the role of magistrate, but more than this it reflects the reality of life in a social group. Ferguson's point is that if humans have always been social, then they have always had some sense of inequality and rank. In other words, there never really was a state of nature along Rousseauian egalitarian lines.

Ferguson's discussion of inequality is conducted within the three-stage schema of savage, barbarian and polished societies. In each case, however, he is careful to stress that the differences of rank do not introduce differences in kind between individuals. What I mean by this is that for Ferguson, rank is a social construct and, while it shapes the socialisation experienced by an individual, it does not impact on the fundamental aspects of character that form the basis of his criteria for moral judgement. Both the rich and the poor are 'haunted' by 'wishes for somewhat beyond his present condition' (*Principles* 2: 51). While birth and rank may be outside a person's control that does not mean that they are thereby incapable of displaying 'probity' and acting 'their part' (*Principles* 2: 48–9).

The different sorts of inequality that exist in each form of society are of interest to Ferguson primarily as features which impact on the stability of the wider social order. Rude nations are more egalitarian, but they are not completely egalitarian. Birth and rank exist there, but they buy little more than respect. Rank, then, is apparent in each of Ferguson's types of society. But it takes a different form and plays a different role in each. In an intriguing passage in the *Principles* Ferguson compares a huntsman to a beggar and makes an attempt to connect character judgement to his analysis of inequality. There are two interesting points about this. The first is an observation that he shares with Smith and which appears at a number of points in his work. This is the idea that the basics of subsistence are relatively easy to secure in most societies. Smith's beggar sunning himself by the side of the road has the kind of peace that kings fight for (Smith 1976a: 185), but his observation is premised on that beggar having access to the goods to supply his basic needs. We have already seen that Ferguson believes that the basics of subsistence are very quickly available in even a savage society and that our attention is drawn at the same time to convenience and ornament. In Ferguson's hands the beggar acquires our contempt precisely because his life seems easy. The huntsman who exercises effort and displays bravery in an activity which, in reality, he need not undertake to secure food is admired over the beggar because the beggar does not act.

This leads us to what Ferguson has to say about the poor. His attitude is perfectly conventional for his background. The poor are to be pitied and helped where appropriate. Deliberate action to help the poor must be moralised in form. For Ferguson 'gratuitous' support of the poor will remove the incentive to labour, and the incentive must be preserved or action will be discouraged. We do them no favours 'by enabling the poor to subsist in idleness' (*Principles* 2: 372). The distinction between the deserving and the undeserving poor is based on their capacity for action.

So there should be support for the sick and the old, and the duty to provide it falls on 'society' (*Principles* 2: 372). That observation having been made, Ferguson suggests that the only issues remaining are pragmatic questions of efficient provision. The absence of trade and the division of labour makes a society poor and more equal while the absence of conveniencies and ornamental goods is not entire – recall that Ferguson says we pursue them in every condition, but they are not present to an extent possible for them to act as an incentive for action. Competition and ambition provide the incentive to labour, and to the extent that equality reduces the grounds for both of these it also reduces the goods that this labour provides to the whole of society. Ferguson's account is based on the observation that inequality is both inevitable and desirable. The argument seems clear enough then. Inequality encourages activity and acts as the prompt to ambition and the desire to improve one's situation.

In the *Essay* Ferguson strikes a more cynical note. Here the observation is that unequal property needs to be combined with the dissemination of that wealth: 'We are therefore obliged to suffer the wealthy to squander, that the poor may subsist' (*Essay* 225). Ferguson's point is that both the rich and the poor have their role to play in this process. Again, this is an argument that is very close to Smith's arguments in *Wealth of Nations*. This argument has appeared before in Ferguson's work. In the *Pamphlet on Stage Plays* Ferguson discusses the differing offices of the rich and the poor and states that social order and the diffusion of wealth depends on us recognising and indulging both of these.

> Whilst from humanity we indulge the poor in their station, we ought from justice to indulge the wealthy in theirs, and to expect that they are to go on agreeable to the habits of living which belong to their station, and which in effect are necessary to the order and good of society, and to the maintenance of the poor.' (*Stage* 25)

But having said all this there is one argument in Ferguson which suggests that he did see commerce as a potentially levelling influence. In the *Principles* he observes that:

> The citizen of London or Paris is enabled, at a meal, to furnish his table with productions that have been supplied from climates and soils the most remote from each other. And we may fancy it to be the object of commerce, or the effect it might serve to produce, were its efforts completely successful, to level the conditions of men in all the variety of their situations; to compensate original defects by adventitious supplies; and to give every commodity a current, from the place at which it is superfluous or abounds, to any other at which it is wanted. (*Principles* 1: 247)

Commerce then plays a dual role. In one sense it exacerbates inequality of property holdings, but in another it promotes the circulation of goods in such a way that needs are matched as effectually as possible. The dearth of one place is met by the surplus of another, suggesting that, if commerce were given free reign, equality across nations would exist alongside inequality of fortune within nations. The broad outline of Ferguson's defence of commerce is essentially the same as Adam Smith's.

Civil and Political Liberty

The final comparator that Ferguson suggests is civil and political liberty. In a sense we can already anticipate that it will be implicated and co-mingled with the other criteria for comparison. And indeed we have already seen liberty anticipated in what Ferguson says about population and wealth. But Ferguson's discussion of, indeed his very conception of, liberty is conditioned by what we have already seen of his account of civilisation and the rise of law and manners. It is no exaggeration to say that Ferguson is a convinced and total advocate of a modern conception of liberty as a product of law: 'Liberty consists in the secure possession of what the law bestows' (*Institutes* 289) or in 'the security of rights' (*Institutes* 288).[31] He is consistent throughout his career that liberty is a social product and that the notion of natural liberty is meaningless. Liberty is a condition created by the security of social institutions and has, in Ferguson's view, no meaning outside this conception. Moreover, there is next to no trace in Ferguson of the republican notion of active participation or non-domination as characteristic of liberty. Instead, as we will see, participation is understood as a necessary means to defend the system of law.

Perhaps the clearest exposition of this view is found in his pamphlet on *Dr Price*. Ferguson criticises Price for abusing language in his attempt to support the American cause. Price's notion of liberty as 'the power of a civil society or state to govern itself by its own discretion' (*Price* 2) misses out on the crucial idea that the liberty of each individual to govern himself need not be realised in a system of majority rule. Price's notion of liberty as political self-determination leads him to a view that being free is doing whatever we collectively want. Political participation is, Ferguson admits, a good, but it is not liberty. Liberty should instead be considered as a condition created by the rule of law and the protection of rights:

it is not a power to act in whatever way we wish, but rather a set of defences and constraints that preserve my rights to what is mine. In this sense liberty is an artefact of civilisation, it is a product of politics, but it is not constituted by political participation.

In the background of Ferguson's argument here is a critique of democracy. A people have more liberty in a mixed system like that of Great Britain than they would in a direct democratic system. The idea is that as a people gain more political power their actions can undermine the rule of law that protects everyone in society. Indeed, this is the backbone of his analysis of the class conflict in the *Roman Republic*.[32] The problem is not so much that the army eventually came to threaten the Republic, but that the army and empire were adopted as ways of dealing with a growing population of poor citizens who became dependent and prey to demagogues and that this in turn destabilised the constitutional balance.

If liberty is a creation of law rather than an exercise of autonomy, then the institutions necessary to maintain the rule of law are necessary to the creation of liberty. It is here that we see Ferguson turn to defend the cause of the Crown. An effective executive that enforces the law and protects society from attack is a necessary condition of liberty. Liberty exists when security is provided without the exercise of authority tripping over into tyranny: it is a creature of the institutions that make that possible. As such it is a product of human action not human design, a fragile, accidental achievement of a particular institutional setting – and that setting is the post-1688 British mixed monarchy.[33] Ferguson's concern for the stability of the constitution, and his attempt to use history to account for its evolution, is absolutely within the mainstream of the views of the Scottish Enlightenment and much British political opinion of the day.[34]

There is also another persistent line of argument concerning liberty that runs through Ferguson's writings. He consistently argues against mistaking liberty and equality. Equality under the law does not mean equality of status or equality of fortune and the ideas should not be confused. This is important for understanding Ferguson's own account of how liberty works in the mixed system of British politics. That the system is unique and fragile is taken for granted and the problem that arises is how to stabilise the constitution. The answer arises from the creation of a stable system of rank where each order plays the role proper to it. Zeal for liberty, as he puts it, is not perpetual opposition to government, but realising that government has a role to play and needs to be strong enough to do it.

The ideal is the modern sense of liberty exemplified by Britain and here once again there are heavy shades of Montesquieu's (1989: 187) discussion of liberty as a sense of security. As Ferguson puts it, some European nations had gradually evolved a system that 'formed a new power to restrain the prerogative, to establish the government of law, and to exhibit a spectacle new in the history of mankind; monarchy mixed with republic, and extensive territory, governed, during some ages, without military force' (*Essay* 128). The successful defence of this system requires its citizens to understand, through moral science, its nature and the nature of the liberty that they enjoy. The agitation in America and of radicals like Price and Wilkes betrays a fundamental misunderstanding of the origin and nature of liberty. The defence of liberty requires that moral science demonstrate its origin and operation in the rule of law in a mixed constitution and that this be combined with a spirit of participation in the life of the country in a manner and a degree appropriate to one's station. Such participation secures liberty but does not define it.[35] The clearest statement of this comes in the *Stage Play* pamphlet: 'Every person does good, and promotes the happiness of society, by living agreeable to the rank in which Providence has placed him' (*Stage* 24). Ferguson's vision is not one of equal citizens meeting in the agora to direct the government of the city, it is the British mixed constitution. His understanding of liberty does not consist in an active citizen participating in political debate, rather his concept of liberty as the rule of law is partly secured by political activity. His concern, as Yasuo Amoh (2008: 83) observes, is to diffuse patriotism through all of the ranks of society without admitting every individual to an equal place in the decision-making process.

Having discussed the various suggestions that Ferguson makes for assessing the superiority of one type of political society over another we should return to our initial observation that there is no one set of institutions which will provide these goods in all circumstances. The institutions of a savage society will not work in a commercial setting, and vice versa. But the idea that wealth, population, manners and liberty are in general good things runs through Ferguson's work. With this in mind we can turn to the oft-stressed passages where Ferguson discusses the danger of corruption.

Corruption

The long-standing tendency to read Ferguson's view as that of the *Essay* has had a particular effect on the critical discussion of his views on the link between wealth and corruption. As we have noted above, taking into account the framing of the other three major works and especially the *Principles*, shifts the focus of Ferguson's analysis from the corruption of wealth to the corruption of character which can arise at any level of wealth.

In the *Essay* Ferguson admits to qualms about his ability to comment on commercial matters and admits that he is 'still less engaged by the views with which I write' (*Essay* 140). So while he does indeed worry that 'the desire of profit stifles the love of perfection' (*Essay* 206), that desire of profit can arise in any society at any level of economic development.

Ferguson's analysis of corruption relates to a very specific set of circumstances. The danger that interests him is that of a system of incentives where wealth is preferred to other goods such as friendship or patriotism. It is important to see exactly how Ferguson frames this in the *Principles*. The worry is that a situation arises where wealth comes to be the sole criterion of rank. He believes that a 'contagion of baseness' (*Principles* 1: 149) arises when the only ground of elevation is riches. Now, given what we have seen above about Ferguson's core concept of morality as censorial inspection, the problem is one of such censorial inspection being replaced by pecuniary inspection.[36]

Wealth has always been a means to compare ourselves to others – 'The value of riches is comparative; for it consists, not in any absolute measure of wealth, but in possessing more than other men' (*Institutes* 100) – but it has only been one among several possible comparators. The issue is precisely those aspects of Rousseau's critique of contemporary society that Smith highlighted when he discussed rank in *The Theory of Moral Sentiments*. The difference between Ferguson and Rousseau is that Ferguson believes that there are other genuine grounds for rank. In other words, society itself is not the basis for corruption, nor for that matter is commerce; instead, it is a particular form of commercial society that poses a danger.

The story as it has been told thus far is the story of the conceptual development of the 'sense of a public' (*Essay* 211) among a 'nation'. However, there are a number of potential threats to this development of public spirit. A number of social forces may contribute to 'weaken the bands of society' (*Essay* 182) and break the acquired sense of 'mutual dependence' (*Essay* 182) that binds nations together. It is usual at this point in a discussion of Ferguson to dwell on his Republican examination of how self-interested pursuit of riches can lead to alienation and a lack of public engagement. Civil disorder is more likely if individuals dedicate themselves to the pursuit of commerce to the exclusion of public matters. This self-regard leads us to 'break the bands of society' as we develop the division of labour and results in a situation where 'society is made to consist of parts, of which none is animated with the spirit of society itself' (*Essay* 207). This neglect of community leads to the possibility that the very society that has been the source of the development of human civilisation may be a casualty of its own success. But it is also worth noting that Ferguson believes that the 'bands' of society are weakened when savage societies become barbarian societies. This is in part a feature of the generation of larger social groups beyond the kin network, but it is also a feature of the increasing differentiation between individuals. In barbarian ages humans become more diversified, they are different from each other in terms of rank, and as a result the sense of unity begins to move from the tribe to the nation. Rank is necessary for stability in extended societies and the worry is that rank comes to rest solely on wealth.

Ferguson's moralising here is of a very specific type and has a very specific target. Political judgement is about more than the pursuit of wealth, it involves other aspects of character and capacity. This means that moralists should not waste time by seeking to reduce luxury or stifle economic development. He is quite clear about this even at his most sceptical in the *Essay*: 'The use of morality on this subject, is not to limit men to any particular species of lodging, diet, or cloaths; but to prevent them considering these conveniencies as the principal objects of human life' (*Essay* 234).[37]

The problem then is not wealth, but a society where wealth replaces honour and public duty as the central means of advancing ambition. Corruption and luxury occur at any level of wealth, the problem lies in the corruption of character where we come to ignore other important things. So 'we may find him become effeminate, mercenary, and sensual; not because pleasures and profits are becoming more alluring, but because he has fewer calls to attend to other objects ...' (*Essay* 237). And it is here that we see the return of Ferguson's central concept of action. Inaction arises from peace. It is political quietism that is the danger. The absence of 'public alarms' (*Essay* 244) creates the space for a corruption of the objects of ambition. A society where the people face no calls to act in the public interest is a society that will create the space for the corruption of the object of ambition. It is not the material goods, but the political situation that is the source of the danger.

Ferguson's worry is that this will eventually lead to a 'fatal dissolution of manners' (*Essay* 238) and that if we are to avoid it we must deploy moral science in the service of educating the upper and middle ranks in their proper duty. Moral science teaches us that we need to be aware that the growth of wealth has different effects on different political systems. Luxury, as he points out, affects republics and modern monarchies in different ways. This underlines his point about the link between ambition and rank – the different rank structures and dynamics in a republic and a monarchy will require different responses. The issue will become even more complex in a mixed system like Britain.

The balance that Ferguson is trying to outline is one between a moral science that accepts the reality of ambition for material comfort, but also the reality of other grounds of social distinction that arise from censorial inspection. The incentive to engage in politics is ambition, it is personal aggrandisement, but that aggrandisement arises from service to the public rather than the display of wealth. Ferguson's theory accepts the reality that we tend to associate wealth with personal excellence and poverty with meanness, and that wealth plays a role in the class structure of society. He also accepts that the urge to ornament is the root of the desire to display wealth that encourages ostentation. But the analysis of the effect of riches focuses not on the level of material wealth, but rather on the character of individuals. The vices of the rich are not the result of excess of riches but of having nothing to do – it is inactivity rather than wealth that is the issue for Ferguson. This is 'a defect of understanding, and a corruption of the heart' (*Principles* 2: 62).[38] The problem is a society where wealth has become the only basis of rank and honour, and where ambition is directed at wealth rather than public service as a means of acquiring distinction.

The subjects of property, considered with a view to subsistence or even to enjoyment, have little effect in corrupting mankind, or in awakening the spirit of competition and of jealousy; but considered with a view to distinction and honour, where fortune constitutes rank, they excite the most vehement passions, and absorb all the sentiments of the human soul: they reconcile avarice and meanness with ambition and vanity; and lead men through the practice of sordid and mercenary acts to the possession of a supposed elevation and dignity. (*Essay* 154)

Ferguson's concerns about civil society do not step much beyond the mainstream of the Scottish Enlightenment. Like Hume, he did not view all luxury as a problem, only luxury that became an overwhelming source of attention. He was not particularly worried by inequalities of wealth, only about such inequalities replacing other sources of rank such as honour and public service. Ambition drives forward the search for material improvement and the task for Ferguson is to understand how the dynamics of rank can be brought to bear in such a way as to preserve the order necessary for a free society.

Conclusion

Adam Ferguson does not possess an understanding of civil society that matches our own notion of the term. But what he does have is a sense that social activity and interaction, the 'civil', is just as significant as the political in the successful mixed constitution of Great Britain. Those who speculate that the notion of civil society, or at least the 'space' for such a concept, suggested itself to provincial intellectuals divested of a parliament seem to be on to something. The idea of an active citizen as a de-politicised clubbable gentleman pursuing projects of improvement is indeed something beyond that contemplated in the civic tradition. It would, however, be too quick to see this as a non-political or even anti-political move. There is a political purpose to Ferguson's argument here. For all of the focus on good laws and regulation as the basis of civilisation we should recall his account of moral education. Good institutions need to be manned, and their personnel need to be subject to the correct set of incentives. These incentives are the allures of public honour.

On Ferguson's account all societies are political, but not all societies are civil. Civilisation is an identifiable condition for Ferguson and it has its roots not in the level of wealth or in republican participation, but in the rule-governed nature of all social interaction. Politeness and civility are just as much features of a civil society as the rule of law. Ferguson's is a resolutely modern conception of liberty and citizen participation: republican liberty is of interest to him precisely to the extent that it might help secure the conditions of stability or balance in a society. For all of his talk of man's active political nature, the work being done in his political theory is being done by a system of laws supported by a population willing to defend them. While he may not provide us with a recognisably modern notion of civil society, he does have a clear vision of a civilised society, and it is one that depends on a modern conception of liberty under the rule of law. Despite his rhetorical flourishes in the *Essay*, Ferguson is consistent in his view that the problems of modern Britain are not to be faced by nostalgia for the virtuous republics of the past.

Notes

1. *Correspondence* (2: 546).
2. For discussions of Ferguson and the concept of civil society see: Keane (1988), Cohen and Arato (1992), Gellner (1994), Shils (1997), Varty (1997), Ehrenberg (1999), Boyd (2000), Oz-Salzberger (2001) and Berry (2003). Perhaps the clearest statement of the position of the concept of civil society in the Scottish Enlightenment is that of Christopher Berry (2003) who suggests that while Ferguson and his compatriots do not use the term civil society to apply to the precise modern phenomenon, they nonetheless do identify the 'space' that we have come to call civil society.
3. See Waszek (1988).
4. Leading Ted Benton (1990) to observe that Ferguson's understanding of civilisation focuses on the achievement of law and internal conflict resolution coupled with defence against external threats.
5. Several commentators have noted that Ferguson's stadial theory differs significantly from that of his peers, and that the difference goes beyond his apparent preference for three rather than four stages. David Allan (2006: 81) shares the view that Ferguson's stages are not based on economics like those of Smith, while Duncan Forbes (1967: xxv) points out that property has a less central role in Ferguson's account than Smith's, a point denied by Ronald Meek (1976: 150). Meek, rightly in my view, points out that, like Montesquieu and

Hutcheson, Ferguson does not 'privilege' property and subsistence (Meek 1976: 34–5). The result, according to Meek, is a 'highly idiosyncratic' version of stadialism (Meek 1976: 154).

6. It is also important to note that Ferguson's understanding of the social cohesion of groups is not based on some idealised sense of community that precludes internal conflict (a topic we will return to in the next chapter). Duncan Forbes (1967: 40–3) suggests that Ferguson is searching for a criterion of civilisation and that he finds it in the idea of community. But this seems more than a little idealistic. Ferguson is deeply interested in the bonds that people share as part of a community, but when it comes to civilisation it is rules and not sentiments that count. For example, he observes: 'We must admit, that the peace of society is, in many instances, evidently forced, and made to continue by a variety of artificial means' (*Principles* 1: 23). It is this fact that leads Ferguson to the analysis of the bonds of civil and political association that recognises the entirely unsatisfactory nature of social contract and great legislator accounts of the development of social institutions, but the use of force suggests that more is in play than a sense of community.

7. Among the key features that Ferguson identifies in the following passage are the fact that 'individuals are fully secured under the protection of the laws', 'wrongs are less frequent', 'private revenge is prohibited', family feuds are no longer settled by arms and self-defence using weapons is no longer necessary (*Militia* 8).

8. It is perhaps going a little far to suggest, as Jane Fagg (1968: 332) does, that Ferguson has a 'fully developed conservative definition of civil liberty', but it is certainly the case that the notion of liberty he advances highlights the stability-enhancing effects of the rule of law. See also Kettler (2005: 88).

9. Ferguson's debt to Montesquieu is particularly obvious in his stadial theory (Sher 1994: 391) and this does distance him from his fellow four-stage Scots. Christopher Berry (2013: 40) has pointed out that this is yet another example of Ferguson's shifting vocabulary, so much so that it almost seems that he has two distinct versions of the three stages. However, if we consider the general form of the theory, the desire for a heuristic to structure the analysis of the nature of society as such, rather than a deterministic theory of progress then the method is well within the mainstream. For a discussion of these general characteristics of Scottish stadialism see Berry (1997: 114), Chitnis (1976: 96) and Höpfl (1978: 37). Ferguson's, and others', use of the terminology of savagery and barbarism have been

implicitly criticised by Mary Poovey (1998: 24) who suggests it led them to be read as justifications for subordination.

10. On the etymology of civilisation see Bowden (2004).

11. I include providence in this as we saw in Chapter 3 that he abandoned the jeremiad after the *Ersh Sermon* (see the section below on corruption for a more extended discussion).

12. See *Principles* (1: 58–9).

13. Though Ferguson accepts that there will be difficult cases of self-defence that require discretion on the part of the actor and the judge (*Principles* 2: 249).

14. Explaining why Ferguson can comfortably agree with Hume that a civilised monarchy and a republic fit the bill. What makes a republic for Ferguson is the rule of law and not the status of citizens with regard to political participation. This is a point noted by Istvan Hont (2015: 77–8) who suggests that Ferguson's support for a modern monarchy as a republic fit for eighteenth-century conditions is aimed directly at those republican zealots who fail to see that they live in a republic. For a contrary view, that Ferguson did not understand new types of republicanism emanating from America, see Buchan (2003: 225).

15. See *Principles* (1: 216) for Ferguson's discussion of the Stuarts.

16. *Principles* (2: 408).

17. 'The naked inhabitant of the Pelew Islands accordingly appeared to possess all the attention to oblige, and all the reluctance to intrude or importune, which, in the polite circles of Europe, distinguish the accomplished gentleman' (*Principles* 2: 378).

18. Yet again the discussion bounces off of one in Montesquieu who expressed a preference for civility over politeness as: 'Politeness flatters the vices of others, and civility keeps us from displaying our own' (1989: 317).

19. 'Politeness is behaviour intended to please, or oblige' (*Institutes* 249) it is an expression of 'decency' and 'agreeableness' (*Analysis* 40) that says something important about our recognition of other people as worthy of attention and respect.

20. 'Where violence is restrained, he can apply his hand to lucrative arts . . . wait with patience for the distant returns of his labour' (*Essay* 95).

21. Or in slightly revised terms in the *Principles*, men act to secure 'necessity, convenience and ornament (*Principles* 1: 239). Wealth, or riches, are defined as the possession of goods that realise these pursuits. 'Riches consist in the abundance of things that conduce to safety, subsistence, accommodation, and ornament' (*Institutes* 31).

22. In a sense we might expect this from what he has to say about the link between comfort and ornament and vanity: 'In competitions of vanity, riches are more an object of *ostentation* than of *enjoyment* or *use*' (Principles 2: 51). The definition that he provides of luxury – 'that complicated apparatus which mankind devise for the ease and convenience of life' (*Essay* 231) – is similarly focused on this, while that in the *Institutes* is even more specific: luxury is 'consumption of mere ornaments' (*Institutes* 270).

23. Much of the discussion of economics in the *Principles* is straight-forwardly derivative of Smith's account in the *Wealth of Nations*. For example, Ferguson's discussion of tax (*Principles* 2: 435–7) is a near exact reproduction of Smith's argument from Book V of the *Wealth of Nations*. In the *Principles* Ferguson's discussion of wealth has shifted in the light of his reading of Smith. In the earlier *Analysis* the definition of wealth is given as 'by possessing in abundance the means of subsistence, or what may be exchanged for such means.' And while this is consistent with the measures of wealth which he applies – 'Riches depend on the possession of lands, materials, indus-try, skill, and numbers of people' (*Analysis* 460) or in the *Institutes*: 'That the state of a nation's wealth is not to be estimated from the state of its coffers, granaries, or warehouses, at any particular time; but from the fertility of its lands, from the numbers, frugality, indus-try, and skill of its people' (*Institutes* 276) – the shift to Smithian language in the *Principles* where he defines wealth as: 'The wealth of the citizen is measurable by the quantity of labour he can employ' (*Principles* 2: 421), is marked.

24. Ferguson observes that calls to strenuous activity prompt the great-est exercise of human capacity. In economic terms this means that: 'It is vain to expect, that the residence of arts and commerce should be determined by the possession of natural advantages. Men do more when they have certain difficulties to surmount' (*Essay* 116). This leads Duncan Forbes (1967: xxvi) to observe that: 'His whole philosophy was designed for an age whose danger, as he saw it, consisted in the absence of danger.'

25. 'The commercial arts, therefore, are properly the distinctive pursuit or concern of individuals, and are best conducted on motives of separate interest and private advancement' (*Principles* 1: 244).

26. As Ferguson argues: 'Moralists have talked so much of the variety of fortune, and of its inefficacy to happiness, that they may be suspected of encouraging a dangerous neglect of affairs' (*Principles* 2: 340).

27. Elazar (2014: 769–72) sees a tension between Ferguson's elitism and his more democratic impulses. This lends his consistent advocacy of the liberty of the moderns a conditional or hesitant air. Elazar (2014: 781) suggests that Ferguson's way out of this is to allow participation which is appropriate to the context of the society. While this is correct it obscures his commitment to virtual representation (Fagg 1968: 148). In contrast to this view the reading offered here suggests that there is no hesitancy, because Ferguson is a consistent elitist who was actively hostile to democracy.

28. For example, *Rome* (12).

29. The 'numbers of mankind in every situation do multiply up to the means of their subsistence' (*Principles* 2: 409). Three factors come together – 'the laws of propagation', 'security' and 'the means of subsistence' (*Institutes* 23) – to allow the development of population as an indicator of national success. Population increases 'in proportion' (*Analysis* 48) as a society secures subsistence.

30. Max Skjönsberg (2017: 18–20) cites this letter as evidence of Ferguson's distance from the republican tradition's idea of competing factions, of which more in the next chapter. Xandra Bello (2017: 60) makes an explicit link between this class and applying the lessons of moral science against demagoguery.

31. Max Skjönsberg (2017) and Yiftah Elazar (2014) have both made this observation, but in the case of the latter he sees it as a development of Ferguson's republicanism rather than a decisive move away from the civic tradition.

32. 'Their liberty sunk as their power increased, and perished at last by the very hands that were employed in support of the popular case' (*Price* 52).

33. The 'idle assumption of discretionary power' (*Principles* 2: 504) was what did for the Stuarts.

34. Though he is perhaps more open to the need for a degree of arbitrary power than Hume (McArthur 2005: 123–4). Even John Millar, supposedly the most radical of the Scots, was a convinced elitist who wanted to co-opt the middle classes to the defence of the constitution.

35. Lisa Hill (2009: 115–16) makes the excellent point that Ferguson constantly advocates participation, but never really explains what the appropriate forum for such participation will be. Whatever they were, Hill suggests, they would be absent from Scotland. Again, this raises the issue of the depoliticised participation advanced by Phillipson.

36. There are clearly classical precedents for Ferguson's analysis here,

but the qualifications on the way in which wealth and luxury prompt corruption suggest that he is not buying into the crude eastern luxury corrupted virtuous Rome story of the decline of the Republic. See, for example, *Essay* (235).

37. 'It appears, therefore, that although the mere use of materials which constitute luxury, may be distinguished from actual vice; yet nations under a high state of commercial arts, are exposed to corruption, by their admitting wealth, unsupported by personal elevation and virtue, as the great foundation of distinction, and by having their attention turned on the side of interest, as the road to consideration and honour' (*Essay* 241). Ferguson's point is exactly the same as that made by Hume in his attack on vicious luxury (Hume 1985: 279).

38. 'The wants of nature are easily supplied, and the gratification of uncorrupted appetite is fully consistent with the higher and better pursuits of human life: But the voluptuary in acquiring habits inconsistent with these pursuits, is debauched by his imagination rather than by the force of his appetite, or by the solicitations of Sense' (*Principles* 2: 342).

6

Civilised Warfare

We have improved on the laws of war, and on the lenitives which have been devised to soften its rigours; we have mingled politeness with the use of the sword; we have learned to make war under the stipulations of treaties and cartels, and trust to the faith of an enemy whose ruin we mediate. (*Essay* 190)

In this chapter we will examine the second of the modern world's claims to have 'greatly excelled' (*Essay* 193) the ancient world: the conduct of warfare. Ferguson's deep interest in war, conflict and military matters has long been noted as a peculiarity of his writings, but discussions of this aspect of his thinking have rarely attempted to place this concern within his system as a whole. The most obvious way to do this, given what we have discussed in the previous chapters, is to see war as one of the underlying universals of human experience. And this, indeed, is what Ferguson thought it was. A science of society needs to have an account of war at its heart if for no other reason than that it has been a perennial feature of human social life. Mankind is 'disposed to opposition' and 'doomed' to conflict (*Essay* 28), war becomes 'a principal occupation' (*Essay* 197) because the 'possibility of discord and war is entailed upon human nature' (*Principles* 2: 410). Individuals experience an 'urge to subjugate' (*Principles* 1: 238) that can be traced through human history, as demonstrated by the fact that the earliest records of history are the records of wars.

Ferguson's analysis of war also includes a series of observations of its potential usefulness to humanity. So while the 'will of providence' (*Principles* 2: 502) seems to dictate that nations will go to war, it is also true that people will 'happily' do so. There are two sides to Ferguson's account of the benefits of war. The first refers to the strengthening of internal bonds in the face of external threat, and the second refers to the balance of power between different nations. We will return to the second of these below. The first is central to Ferguson's whole analysis. His oft-claimed influence on the idea of conflict sociology emerges in his development of a theory of group cohesion from external threat: 'Without the rivalship of nations, and the practice of war, civil society itself could scarcely have found an object, or a form' (*Essay* 28). While Ferguson is not unique in this observation he is more extensive and sophisticated in his development of the idea than any thinker since Machiavelli. Animosity between groups is a key force that creates internal cohesion to the extent that nations deliberately make war to maintain national unity. The Romans and, Ferguson believes, the post-Revolutionary French are able to maintain unity and avoid civil war only because they have united against a common external threat.[1] What is interesting about Ferguson's approach is that he dwells on the constitutive function of the bonds that exist among members of a group. Ferguson's account stresses the role of this sort of emotional bond in a fashion that is designed to stress not only its ubiquity but the centrality of it to human character. The failure of social contract theory and other explanations of the origin of political society is brought home to us by the fact that they cannot account for the emotional bond of belonging in a language of rational choice. As Ferguson puts it: 'Men are so far from valuing society on account of its mere external conveniencies, that they are commonly most attached where those conveniencies are least frequent; and are there most faithful where the tribute of their allegiance is paid in blood' (*Essay* 23). Ferguson's theory is an account of the operation of national sentiment, or to use the terminology we have developed here, it is a moral scientific account of the development of patriotism. Patriotism is an other-regarding virtue in Ferguson's account, it is an expression of sociability and benevolence, and so he is able to claim that 'War itself, which in one view appears so fatal, in another is the exercise of a liberal spirit' (*Essay* 29). As we saw in Chapter 5, action in the service of our country is an indication of individual and national health; and the same is true of war, it provides us with an arena for virtue.[2]

National Origins

One of the most marked features of Ferguson's thought, and one of the reasons he has been interpreted as both a founding father of sociology and a precursor of Romanticism, is his focus on the idea of the nation and his attempt to account for the forces that produce national sentiment. Once again the concern runs throughout his works, but in the *Principles* he devotes a dedicated chapter to nations. The account dwells on the 'naturalness' of nations. As he puts it: 'The human species, though disposed to associate, is disposed to separation also' (*Principles* 2: 293). This leads him to identify the nation as 'any separate company or society of men acting under a common direction' (*Principles* 2: 294).[3] Such formations arise gradually as people 'reluctantly' (*Principles* 2: 294) associate for safety over a long period. Ferguson is willing to recognise that the initial motivation to associate in larger groupings arises from 'expediency' (*Principles* 1: 34) and a desire to secure order and security. But his account goes on to stress how the long-term evolution of group customs leads to a process of habituation and identity formation that becomes vital to understanding human beings.

One of the ways that Ferguson seeks to reinforce this is by developing an argument that nations are, by their very nature, a bond between people. This idea is apparent as early as his first publication, the *Sermon preached in the Ersh Language*, where he argues:

> By a Man's Country is meant that Society or united Body of Men, of which he is a Member, sharing all the Advantages that arise from such a Union. Not merely the Soil or Spot in which he was born, as it is too often understood by many. On this supposition, the Love of one's country, which has always been esteem'd the most manly Virtue, might be rejected as a mere Whim or Prejudice. No: The Name of Country has a Meaning more sacred and interesting. It was not for the Place of their Nativity that *Jacob* exhorts the *Israelites* to play the man: It was for their People and for the Cities of their God. (*Sermon* 6)

Being a part of a nation is by its very nature a sense of belonging and kinship. The relationship between co-nationals is not to be understood on pragmatic or utilitarian terms because that is not the essence of the relationship nor is it how it is experienced.

Nations have their origin in conflict and, as they separate, they develop distinct customs and habits. These distinctions reinforce the sense of difference that is vital to Ferguson's account of the origin of national sentiment and, so Ferguson stresses, the idea that sociability and socialisation in one group is premised on opposition and conflict with other groups. This is as true for primitive societies as it is for developed societies, by which we can understand that the dynamics of group conflict are part of the constitutive structure of political communities. If the nation is 'an object of the most ardent affection' (*Principles* 2: 18), then we come to understand the vivid example that Ferguson uses in the *Essay* to illustrate the depth of national animosity. When he describes the dead father of a Spanish peasant who wishes to rise from the grave to fight his country's enemies (*Essay* 27–8) he is indicating not just the depth of national feeling, but also its connection to the past. National identity is a connection between current co-nationals, but it also represents a link to the shared past and achievements of a people. These sentiments, while forming the basis of the social bond, are also volatile and difficult to manage.

In the *Essay* Ferguson outlines the implications of this for politics. First, he observes that national sentiment is not the creation of politicians, but the natural result of group life. As he notes: 'Prejudices and national passions; it is among them that we find the materials of war and dissension laid without the direction of government, and sparks ready to kindle into a flame, which the statesman is frequently disposed to extinguish' (*Essay* 27). Politics has as part of its task the management of the expression of national sentiment. But this management cannot be blindly cosmopolitan, for the very thing that makes humans social is the division into different groups and the potential for conflict between those groups. It is here that we see the basic contradiction between Ferguson's account and that of the Stoics. Ferguson's agents are deeply embedded in communities and not the 'citizens of the universe' (Epictetus 1925: 65) of Stoic ethics.

Politicians must learn the basic lesson that: 'It is in vain to expect that we can give to the multitude of a people a sense of union among themselves, without admitting hostility to those who oppose them' (*Essay* 29). Love of country is so much a part of human psychology that the cosmopolitan ideal is, for Ferguson, far-fetched: 'And it would seem, that till we have reduced mankind to the state of a family, or formed some external consideration to maintain their connection in greater numbers, they will be for ever separated into bands, and form a plurality of nations' (*Essay* 25–6). An end to international competition or the rivalry of nations would 'break or weaken the bands of society' (*Essay*

29) at home. But this feature of political cohesion also involves the danger that unscrupulous populists will exploit national sentiment for their own gain.

To understand the dynamic of national identity we need to understand how it is driven by what Ferguson, following Montesquieu, calls 'national spirit' (*Essay* 200).[4] As we saw in Chapter 2, the internal bonds of national identity are the product of a process of habituation and socialisation which create 'prevailing opinions' (*Principles* 1: 218). These prevailing opinions are embedded in the sentiments of the people to an extent that they shape the character of each nation. Lest we think for a minute that Ferguson finds this observation regrettable, we should note that he also regards it as necessary for the development of individual intelligence and character. A man who does not feel himself to be part of a nation is not, in Ferguson's view, a rounded human being, nor is he in possession of the cultural resources that can be derived from 'the peculiar genius of nations' (*Essay* 30). This leads Ferguson to his interest in national character and national spirit. A healthy national spirit has 'vigour' (*Essay* 201) and it may 'sicken from want of exercise' or from 'langour' or 'listlessness' (*Essay* 204). The moral scientist is able to observe that: 'National spirit is frequently transient' because of 'voluntary neglects and corruptions' (*Essay* 212).

The vigour of a nation's spirit may be a collective phenomenon, but it also manifests itself in the spirit and character of individuals. It is here that we begin to see Ferguson linking his moral science to his normative moral philosophy. Human beings are by their nature social. The 'good' for human beings is a social good and so the 'health' of a society not only reflects the health of individual character, but to a great extent shapes the character of individuals. For an individual to experience a corruption of his character may both contribute to the corruption of the national character and be a consequence of the corruption of national character. If human beings are social, and if their morality is likewise social, then to act in public 'seems to be the principal calling and occupation of his nature' (*Essay* 33).

Ferguson's interest in national spirit and corruption certainly derives a great deal from the republican tradition of thinking about the experience of politics. But what is not perhaps so apparent is what Ferguson does with the themes that he draws from that tradition. Unless we appreciate a number of significant modifications and additions that Ferguson makes to the civic humanist and republican traditions we will fail to appreciate the extent to which they cohere with the rest of his thinking. Lisa Hill (2006: 27) has suggested that Ferguson's engagement with republican ideas is 'highly qualified'. This seems right and part of the aim in the rest of this chapter is to interrogate the extent to which republican and the 'civic' interpretations are helpful in understanding Ferguson's thought more generally.

Civilised War

Ferguson was, by his own declaration, a 'Warlike Philosopher' (*Correspondence* 2: 433). This preoccupation with warfare is often considered through the lens of Ferguson's supposed republicanism and his ardent support for a citizen militia. However, Ferguson's interest in war runs far deeper than the militia question. From the records of history Ferguson concludes that war is a universal aspect of human group life. Our natural sociability leads us to divide into 'troops and companies' (*Essay* 21) and these groups become the object of mutual suspicion and contention. Group rivalry renders war a perennial aspect of human experience but the mode of warfare changes as the form of social life develops. Warfare, like other aspects of human behaviour, becomes subject to regularisation through convention. As a result, the modern pursuit of war is regulated by conventions such as the declaration of war and the development of notions such as a 'just' war and the 'right' and 'wrong' conduct of war. These 'laws of war' (*Institutes* 230) represent one of the achievements of civilisation. Even in the conduct of violence a civilised nation constrains its behaviour by rules of correct behaviour.[5]

Ferguson's analysis takes place within his three-stage schema of types of society.[6] War is endemic to savage society and takes the form of a life or death struggle between tribes. The cause of such war is not gain, as evidenced by the North American Indians among whom warfare is constant yet property undeveloped; rather wars are fought from a desire for conflict and glory, such that savages appear 'addicted to war' (*Essay* 96). In rude societies 'the great business is war' (*Essay* 142) and social rank is determined by military success. Among barbarian societies the mode of war is different. The development of a notion of property and the increased sophistication of social organisation provides greater scope for organised force. Barbarian wars are fought for gain and lead to a gradual agglomeration of social groups into larger and larger associations. War is a tool of national enrichment and the extension of national control over larger and larger geographic areas. Barbarians are better organised and by dint of superior arms and technology they are able to overwhelm savage nations. Ferguson recognises that the way in which we wage war changes through time and however hardened by battle a savage society may be they will eventually be overcome by the greater organisation and use of technology of a barbarian army. In turn barbarians will themselves be overcome by the superior drilling and firepower of a civilised army. As was so amply demonstrated on the field at Culloden, an army trained in barbarian warfare suffered from serious disadvantages.[7]

> Rude nations in general, though they are patient of hardship and fatigue, though they are addicted to war, and are qualified by their stratagem and valour to throw terror into the armies of a more regular enemy; yet, in the course of a continued struggle, always yield to the superior arts, and discipline of more civilised nations. (*Essay* 93–4)

When Ferguson argues that war has been 'brought to perfection' (*Essay* 149) in civil society he means not only that the technology of war has improved, but also that the regulation of warfare has improved. If we are to look for the most obvious indication of civilisation we are to find it in the decline in arbitrary violence. Ferguson's point is not so much that wars are less likely to occur, rather it is that when they do occur they will be of a categorically different type: modern war is rule governed violence.

It is Ferguson's contention that civilisation has led to our manners becoming 'mild' (*Militia* 8). With particular regard to warfare this has led to an advance, 'by degrees', of the principles of war, from 'Ferocity' and 'Desire of Rapine' in barbarous ages to 'milder principles' in modern Europe (*Militia* 7). To illustrate this 'progress' Ferguson undertakes a comparison between the modern and classical conduct of warfare. The notion of glory in war no longer includes the absolute destruction of one's enemies as depicted in the Homeric epics. It is this regulation of the pursuit of warfare that Ferguson holds up as a prime symbol of modern Europe's claim to civilisation. Ferguson believed that this applied both *in bello* and *ad bellum*, with rules covering the conduct of

war and with the notion of the only legitimate war being to correct
a matter of right rather than conquest.

In the *Analysis*, the *Institutes* and the *Principles* Ferguson includes
a chapter on the modern system of warfare. Much of the detail of
the discussion follows directly from that of Grotius, Pufendorf and
Hutcheson, but Ferguson's particular interest leads him to focus
on the rules that govern the conduct of war rather than those that
govern the recourse to war. He begins by noting that though the
outbreak of war generally renders agreements between nations
void, their interaction continues to be regulated by conventions
surrounding the use of force. A state of war does not prevent the
conclusion of treaties regarding the conduct of hostilities, nor does
it excuse the hostile parties from the conventions of acceptable
battlefield behaviour.[8] These principles are agreed by 'all civilised
nations' (*Principles* 2: 305), but they are also complemented by a
less formal code of behaviour that regulates what may be expected
during a war: what we might call battlefield manners. The chief
article here is that a surrender be accepted (and meant) in good
faith, for without this act of mutual honesty there would be an
insufficient degree of trust to end any conflict and all wars would
end only with the 'extermination of an enemy' (*Principles* 2: 305).

The absence of an enforcement agent in a time of war does not
lessen the strength of these conventions: Ferguson believes that
they exist as a law of nature and, further, that the law of nature
limits the conduct of warfare in line with the principles of natural
justice. As he puts it, the law of nature 'directs a choice to be
made of such means, as being effectual, are least hurtful to the
parties against whom they are employed' (*Principles* 2: 305). It
follows that certain practices can never be considered as legitimate
means of warfare: 'use of poisoned weapons', 'infecting springs or
supply provisions' and 'breach of faith'. These particular prohibi-
tions arise from the failure to provide the 'option of submission'
(*Principles* 2: 307). The offer of the option of submission acts as an
indication that war is conducted to correct a specific violation of
principle and is not, like savage or barbarian warfare, a struggle to
the death or a conquest for profit. The object of modern, civilised
warfare is victory not destruction. The idea of 'quarter' is central
to Ferguson's thinking about the superiority of modern warfare.
To refuse quarter in such circumstances is regarded 'amongst civilised nations as an object of detestation and horror' (*Principles* 2:
308). Respect for surrender is supported by an obligation towards

those held as prisoners who should be provided with accommodation and subsistence, though they may be detained to prevent escape, and the expense of holding them may be considered as part of reparations.

Modern soldiers respect one another: they are no longer involved in tribal blood feuds driven by the dictates of personal honour or moved by a desire of rapine. Modern warfare is conducted without 'unnecessary severities' or 'any personal exasperation of those involved' (*Principles* 2: 295). This is possible because wars are no longer understood as matters of survival. Modern nations are assured that they will not be put to the sword or, as in antiquity, enslaved. The treaties of surrender necessary to end a modern war, the mutual good faith that allows them to take place and the notion of war for victory and not destruction have altered the nature of war. It has become regular and civilised. Conquest does not bestow a right to anything beyond proportionate reparation for the original wrong and the expense of conducting the war. There is no mass slaughter, no enslavement of whole populations and no wanton destruction. The most open expression of violence between groups of humans has been made subject to law.[9]

Ancients and Moderns

Ferguson's comparison of the modern way of doing war with the ancient is the basis of his strongest claim about the superiority of modern civilisation. Civilised warfare is 'the principal characteristic, on which, among modern nations, we bestow the epithets of civilised or of polished' (*Essay* 190) while the ancient nations have 'but a sorry plea for esteem' (*Essay* 189) in that regard. Leniency in war was absent from the Greek practice despite their attainments in other areas related to civilisation. The Spartan social model with its training for war is similarly rejected as inappropriate for modern conditions; however admirable the vigour and spirit of the individuals produced by the Spartan system, the form of warfare that they engaged in remained lawless in Ferguson's view.

Ferguson's admiration for Rome is also tested in respect to war. Rome was clearly not civilised or lenient by the modern understanding of the conduct of war. For all the admiration of Roman citizen soldiers, the destruction of Carthage was a 'horrid' example of Roman warfare (*Rome* 83). Even laying aside his moralised account of the decline of the Republic into civil war and military despotism indicating the political dangers of empire (*Rome* 135, 144, 150), Ferguson is straightforward in his evaluation that the laws of war in the ancient world are 'defective' (*Rome* 88).[10] In the *Militia Question* pamphlet (5–6) Ferguson is even clearer. He argues that the example of Rome is not comparable to the modern situation as modern war and modern politics have a more highly developed rule of law.

Moreover, Ferguson makes the case that its present appearance in Europe is not an accompaniment to the return of learning and economic advance. Instead, the regulation of warfare by rules is a product of earlier stages of Christian society and, more specifically, by the development of chivalric codes of correct behaviour for soldiers.[11] Ferguson goes on to conduct a comparison between the depictions of glory in classical literature with those in medieval romances. He is well aware that these examples are drawn from fiction, but he believes that the imagery that they embody permeates ancient and modern societies, acting as a medium for the transfer of differing attitudes to the conduct of war. Victory in the myths of the ancient world led, more often than not, to death or enslavement; in the European Romance it led to generosity, gentleness and forgiveness. The development of chivalry and the phenomenon of the gallant veneration of the female in the growth of Christian Europe fundamentally altered the practice of warfare inherited by the modern world.

Ferguson admires the ancient republics, but his admiration is conditional. He is aware that they have been idealised, and that modern conditions are quite different. For all of his praise of Athens, Sparta and Rome, Ferguson was perfectly willing to admit that they were marred by the 'cruel distinction' (*Essay* 177) of master and slave which impacted on both their political systems and their way of conducting warfare. The leisure that allowed the citizen to devote himself to politics and war was dependent on the exclusion of the vast majority of those who lived in the state. It is important to note exactly what Ferguson is arguing for here. He is objecting to slavery and suggesting that modern nations not only have a superior and more inclusive political order, but they also have a superior way of conducting wars.

He is not saying that the limited franchise of eighteenth-century Britain is ideal, nor is he saying that a universal franchise is desirable or that the British military is flawless. But he is acknowledging the British Constitution and attitude to war is an advance on the ancient world. We'll return to this below, but before that an examination of Ferguson's preoccupation with Rome gives us an interesting insight into how his thinking develops on this matter. One of the key observations is that he dwells on the implications of rank distinctions within the citizen class: 'The distinctions of poor and rich are as necessary in states of considerable extent, as labour and good government. The poor are destined to labour, and the rich, by the advantages of education, independence, and leisure, are qualified for superior states' (*Rome* 93). But what Ferguson goes on to do with this is to develop a 'class' analysis of the forces that drove the fall of the Roman Republic. The gradual squeezing of the middle class between the interests of the rich and the poor created a dynamic that drove the Gracchi and the eventual rise of Marius, Sylla and Caesar. In the case of Marius, Ferguson's analysis focuses on his admission of the poor into the legions. Later this becomes the more widespread practice of bribing the poor in order to secure political power.[12] This awareness of the class dynamic orientates Ferguson's discussion of republics. Rome's success in the early republican period lay in its ability to maintain the belief that it decided rank by public service not wealth. As this belief retreated with the process of colonial expansion and militarisation the reality of class power differences exerted itself.

The 'ruinous progress of empire' (*Essay* 62) gradually arose from a desire for security, but in time it became a source of corruption among the people and an imbalance in the Roman constitution leading inevitably to civil war. Ferguson frequently holds this up as an example in his more general opposition to empire. Ferguson suggests that empires are the result of a 'ruinous maxim' (*Essay* 148) by which a nation is tempted into imperial expansion in pursuit of security, wealth and prestige. In the case of Rome imperial expansion gradually brought about a change in the political order. But even here we see Ferguson thinking beyond the republican tradition in innovative ways, because he begins to consider the internally destabilising effects of a system of manners that privileges military glory.

Ferguson's interest in Rome points him to one significant exception in his story of civilised warfare: the possibility of civil war. Such wars are often conducted in what may otherwise be considered as a civilised nation and produce more violence and bloodshed than external wars because they involve the breakdown of, or conflict over, the legal conventions of a nation. As Ferguson notes on the end of the Roman Republic: 'More blood has been shed in an age of boasted learning and politeness, than perhaps has been known to flow in any equal period of the most barbarity' (*Rome* 404). The events of the seventeenth century and the Jacobite risings of the eighteenth century were very recent history for Ferguson and the Scottish Enlightenment more generally, so it is unsurprising that he takes a particularly dim view of civil wars.[13] Ferguson regards civil war as a disaster where factional interest overwhelms patriotism and strikes at the very source of virtuous character. His strong views on the American crisis and his advice for total war against the colonists in the case of their not backing down (*Correspondence* 2: Appendix H) suggest that Ferguson's obsession with stability and the rule of law lies behind his enthusiasm for things martial. Iain McDaniel has shown how Ferguson was deeply concerned by the danger of Caesarism in Europe in the 1790s, but the horror at the breakdown of order and civil war is there from the *Ersh Sermon* onwards. When military service becomes the only route to status and wealth, the danger of military despotism looms large. This is one lesson from Rome, but the breakdown of law inherent in a civil war was another.

Ferguson shares a common eighteenth-century view that the model of the Republic with direct citizen participation is inappropriate to the size of modern nations, but in addition he observes that there is probably an optimum size for national sentiment and that this is not necessarily the small size of the ancient republics. He pays some attention to the effects of living in larger-scale states on the nature of the national bond and individual character, and while he admits that it may be stronger in smaller states, he is willing to grant that it has prospered in 'states of a moderate extent' (*Institutes* 266).[14] His problem, as drawn from the example of Rome, is when this becomes over-extended. When Ferguson tackles this issue in his pamphlet in reply to Richard Price (23) he does indeed argue that smaller-scale political societies are better, but this is combined with an argument that Great Britain has yet to reach an extent that is problematic.

Ferguson links his discussion of political participation to another element of his normative schema – action. The danger for Ferguson is that citizens become inactive and this failure to play one's public role will 'weaken the bands of society, and, upon maxims of independence, separate and enlarge the different ranks it was meant to reconcile' (*Essay* 182). This feeds into his point about faction, dispute and debate. It is through being roused in internal contests that the vigour of the political system and the national spirit is maintained. We should, he observes, 'dread the political refinements of ordinary men' (*Essay* 209) when their end is repose or peace. The stability of the political system can be maintained through the internal debates – conflict is natural and healthy if maintained in the correct institutional bounds. Once again we have a fine balancing act – we need to preserve the health of the national spirit through active exercise, but we must do so without descending into civil war or apathetic quietude.

Machiavelli and Montesquieu

Much of the modern history of political thought has been concerned with tracing Machiavelli's influence on later political thinkers and part of the larger argument of this book has been that this move in the history of political thought has led to an overemphasis of certain aspects of Ferguson's thought, so it is worth reiterating the grounds for this argument. Laying aside the possibility that Ferguson's analysis is derived directly from the common shared source of Livy, and the particular genealogy that Pocock and others detect in early modern political thinking via the political thought of the civil war period, we find that Ferguson's analysis of Roman history is not, perhaps, as republican as it might first appear. We can see this if, instead of dwelling on the well-trodden path of Machiavelli's republican views on militias or on political corruption, we focus on his view on the centrality of war, violence and conflict in human history. Machiavelli treats war as natural and seeks lessons from the Roman experience of war. He is interested in martial virtue and yet is dubious about empire. But throughout his writing the significance of war and conflict remains a paramount concern for a successful polity. As he puts it: 'I have said elsewhere that the security of all states is based on good military discipline, and that where it does not exist, there can neither be good laws nor anything else that is good' (Machiavelli 1987: 491). Machiavelli starts his *Discourses* with an account of the early formation of Rome, arguing that the city owed its origin to a defensive union. And this is precisely the point that is central to Ferguson's later analysis.

Several Machiavellian themes can be found in Ferguson's *Roman History*, which is notable for its focus on military matters and in particular the care with which battles are described.[15] Two of Machiavelli's themes form the spine of Ferguson's analysis of the fall of the Republic. The first of these is that the vigour of the Roman political system was a result of competing factions, particularly the plebs and the senate. J. G. A. Pocock (1975: 194) has referred to this as the 'daring and arresting' hypothesis that 'the disunion and strife among nobles and people was the cause of Rome's attaining liberty, stability, and power – a statement shocking and incredible to minds which identified union with stability and virtue, conflict with innovation and decay ...' Pocock traces the influence of this argument on a central plank of republican thought where it provides a counter to those who were wont to argue that a kingdom divided in itself cannot stand. Machiavelli had suggested this in a short chapter in the *Discourses* (Book I, Ch. 4 'That Discord between the plebs and the Senate of Rome made this Republic both free and Powerful') but the analysis pervades Ferguson's *History*.

On one level Ferguson's *History* can be read as a stock morality tale about the corruption of a republic by the luxury wrought in imperial expansion. But it is also a careful analysis of the intersection between domestic politics and the practice of war through the medium of unintended consequences. For example, he argues: 'The Senate frequently involved the state in war, in order to suspend its intestine divisions, and the people as often took occasion, from the difficulties in which the community was involved by its enemies, to extort a compliance with their own demands' (*Rome* 17). The process of external conflict helped to mould Rome's internal politics, but it also provided a means for national unity and the health of the nation as a whole. 'Resentment to a common enemy', Ferguson argues, produced 'transient unanimity' (*Rome* 22); external threats 'calmed for a little time the animosity of domestic faction' (*Rome* 111); and the absence of external threat led to 'public tumults' (*Rome* 122). Ferguson also draws on Machiavelli's extension of this argument into an observation that 'discord in a republic is usually due to idleness and peace, and unity to fear and war' (Machavelli 1987: 360) to develop his line of argument against inaction.

What Ferguson brings to both of these Machiavellian observations is a more sophisticated moral scientific analysis on the important role of conflict in political cohesion and its relationship to the generation of national sentiment. But what is particularly noteworthy here is that he combines the specific lesson of the narrative history of Rome with the generalisation of the Scottish Enlightenment method of conjectural history. And he does this in a way that reveals his, admitted, debt to Montesquieu.[16] *The Roman Republic*, like much of the rest of Ferguson's work, is studded with references to 'national spirit'. The term is employed in line with the classic sense of Montesquieu's: 'Many things govern men: climate, religion, laws, the maxims of the government, examples of past things, mores, and manners; a general spirit is found as a result' (Montesquieu 1989: 310).[17] Montesquieu is himself developing an aside from Machiavelli when he considers the influence of the 'customs' (Machiavelli 1987: 517) of a nation on the character of its people and his analysis of the spirit of the laws becomes, in Ferguson's hands, an analysis of national spirit and is used to trace the 'vigour' of a particular national spirit in the *Roman Republic*. Ferguson is then able to look at the evidence of history and trace examples of the impact of war on the health of a nation's spirit.

Montesquieu's *Considerations on the Causes of the Greatness of the Romans and their Decline* (1734/1748) is an attempt to make sense of the history of Rome that is deeply influenced by Machiavelli. The usual themes of republicanism, the danger of corruption from Empire and the superiority of militias are present. Montesquieu even alludes to the conceptual framework of *virtú*, *fortuna* and *necessità* and often takes points over near verbatim from Machiavelli. However, his analysis does begin to go beyond the Florentine's and it does so by refining the 'scientific' nature of the enquiry. This more sociological enquiry is not concerned so much with the interaction of individual *virtú* with socially determined *fortuna*; instead, it is an attempt at institutional, cultural or social explanation that seeks the 'general causes' (Montesquieu 1965: 169) behind the experience of nations. Montesquieu adopts the notion of national spirit to provide the explanatory framework of his account. The fortune of Rome is to be understood as a necessary result of the expression of the spirit of that people. As Montesquieu would have it: 'Many precedents established in a nation form its general Spirit, and create its manners, which rule as imperiously as its laws' (Montesquieu 1965: 198).

In the case of Rome we are examining a 'nation forever at war' (Montesquieu 1965: 27) and again our two themes of unity as a result of opposition and the danger of peace are prominent in the analysis. As Montesquieu observes, 'When Rome conquered the

world, a secret war was going on within its walls' (Montesquieu
1965: 83). These 'agitations' (Montesquieu 1965: 88) among the
people are taken as evidence of the vigour or health of the polity.
Montesquieu is under no illusions that the actual causes of many of
the particular conflicts were a combination of the personal ambition of specific leaders or the attempts of the Senate to 'distract'
the masses with war abroad. Here the account is straightforward.
When faced with an external threat, real or created, the people
came together to defend the common good: war 'at once united
all the interests in Rome' (Montesquieu 1965: 45). The greatest
evidence of this is that 'during the civil wars, which lasted so
long, Rome's external power kept growing steadily' (Montesquieu
1965: 107). The view is that the Roman political turmoil over the
republican period fed expansion; indeed, Montesquieu cites the
evidence of how Roman expansion slowed and its spirit weakened
during the decemvirate.

> No state threatens others with conquest like one in the throes of
> civil war. Everyone – noble, burgher, artisan, farmer – becomes a
> soldier, and when peace unites the opposing forces, this state has
> great advantages over those with nothing but citizens. (Montesquieu
> 1965: 107)

Notice that the argument here is that a people used to conflict
are likely to be successful in war. But this is not quite the same
point as that the civil dissension in politics is the source of military
success. Indeed, it is actually closer to the other, more general,
argument that we are tracing: that war has beneficial unintended
consequences and that peace is potentially dangerous. This is a
point that Montesquieu picks up from Machiavelli and makes an
explicit lesson from Rome. Prolonged peace is bad for the martial
skills of soldiers and citizens, but, more importantly, Rome was
'less burdened by civil wars than by peace, which united the views
and interests of the leading men and brought nothing but tyranny'
(Montesquieu 1965: 104). External conflict, it would seem, was
also necessary to preserve the liberty and unity of the people.
This is demonstrated by the different attitudes towards war in the
republic and the empire:

> In the days of the republic, the principle was to make war continually;
> under emperors, the maxim was to maintain peace. Victories were

regarded as occasions for worry, involving armies that could set too high a price on their services. (Montesquieu 1965: 123)

The result of the success of Rome's spirit and institutions was that it became a powerful empire but this eventually led to a situation where the institutions that promoted growth were unable to manage the empire once it had been secured. For this reason Montesquieu, like Livy, Juvenal and Horace before him, traces the start of Rome's corruption to its first permanent campaigns outside Italy (more precisely the war with Antiochus). When imperial rule was in place the great period of expansive war was over and the experience of luxury, but more importantly the experience of peace, hastened Rome's corruption and eventual fall.

Empire

As we noted above Ferguson was concerned that imperial expansion unleashed forces that created real dangers for political societies. If 'the tendency of enlargement to loosen the bands of political union' (*Essay* 208), then we should be sceptical about empire.[18] As Iain McDaniel (2013a) has discussed at some length, Ferguson does take the lesson of Caesarism from his study of the fall of the republic and worry that it may indeed be Europe's future. But as we saw in the previous chapter the account that he gives of the impact of luxury does not straightforwardly fit into the traditional moralised account of the fall of Rome, nor, as we will see, does his defence of the militia fit straightforwardly into the narrative about the danger of standing armies.

There are plenty of examples of Ferguson making use of the language of corruption and luxury to account for a lack of civic engagement, but the temptation of luxury is something that is always present. No one society is more likely to be prey to the potential corruption and selfishness inspired by the pursuit of luxury: the 'epidemical weakness of the head, or corruption of heart' (*Essay* 226) can occur in any society. In the *History* he does indeed dwell on the widespread corruption of both rich and poor: the rich were 'nursed in luxury, and averse to business, petulant in safety, useless in danger, impatient to be at their villas in the country, and their amusements in town' (*Rome* 287), while the poor were also carried along by 'the torrent of servility by which all orders of men were carried' (*Rome* 316). Corruption is 'weakness of spirit' (*Essay* 231), and so the moral scientist is interested in identifying the springs of national vigour to avoid a decline from corruption into despotism.

Ferguson's problem, as we explored in the previous chapter, is not wealth per se, nor is it the pursuit of material ambition. The problem is when these become the sole basis for distinction in society. This can only occur in a situation of extended peace. Peace allows the decline of martial 'vigour' (*Essay* 202) such that 'these calm and halcyon Days . . . lull us so entirely asleep' (*Militia* 11). Ferguson's concerns show us another form of corruption that arises in situations of nascent empire. The danger of wealth becoming the only measure of social distinction is paralleled by the danger of military glory becoming the only measure of social distinction. In a militarised society the route to wealth and acclaim is conquest and a society where military rank is melded to civil rank, like Bonaparte's France, is just as corrupted as a society where wealth is the only path to distinction.

In an interesting and revealing discussion in the *Essay* (244–5) Ferguson notes that we need to be careful in our discussion of public spirited action. The temptation is to contrast it with self-interest or with factional interest. But, knowing what we do about human behaviour we should accept that many people enter public life because they are ambitious or because they desire fame. Ferguson's central political observation is that a successful political system must be set up in such a way as to ensure that the way in which such people get what they want is by acting in the public interest. But his prescription is not a return to small-scale republics. For a variety of historical reasons that path is closed. We are where we are and nations and national sentiment exist. They must be worked with in an appropriate institutional setting to ensure a stable form of government able to respond to the challenges of a shifting political situation.

It is here that Ferguson brings together the knowledge acquired from moral science, together with the capacity acquired by political practitioners, to invoke the possibility of passing censorial inspection on nations. The manners, understood as the general character, of a nation can be subject to moral assessment just as an individual can be assessed on his character. This task allows us to reflect not just on other cultures, but crucially, on our own:

... that wherever the manners of our country are dangerous to its safety or have a tendency to enfeeble or to corrupt the minds of men; to deprive the citizen of his rights; or the innocent of his security; it is our duty to do what is for the good of our fellow creatures, even in opposition to the fashion and custom of the times in which we live. (*Principles* 2: 154)

Ferguson was convinced that the 'salutary' (*Principles* 2: 154) would be sufficient to provide us with a 'scale of *merit*' (*Principles* 2: 162). Some things, for example human sacrifice (*Principles* 2: 154), are beyond the pale for Ferguson. We must assume that those who engage in such practices are capable of knowledge of the law of nature, but their ignorance of the law does not protect them from censure. The point of censorial inspection, after all, is to judge. Morality is judgemental, and some things are so evidently contrary to the happiness, health and security of humans that we can exclude them and refuse to excuse those who engage in them. As we saw above, Ferguson was fond of the naturalistic language of vigour and spirit to describe the relative success or health of nations and ages. But he was also aware that 'national spirit' or the 'national virtues' (*Essay* 146) were generalisations. When he talks of the 'spirit of the times' (*Rome* 16) he is aware that this spirit is embodied in particular individuals who share a social space at a given time. The task of the moral philosopher is not so much to condemn individuals or nations as it is to learn from them and use them to illustrate the findings of moral science. Censorial inspection is a judgement, but it is a judgement that adds to our own stock of moral knowledge.

Corruption: Faction

The republican interpretation of Ferguson, along with the proto-sociologist interpretation, both stress the significance of his interest in political faction and conflict. Perhaps the first thing to underline in discussing Ferguson's account of politics as an activity is the awareness that the institutions and practices of political societies evolve slowly over time through the unintended consequences of social interaction. Political change occurs 'with perfect blindness to the future, or ignorance of the consequences which are likely to follow' (*Principles* 1: 314). Nations which have become civilised owe the origins of their civilisation to earlier ages of 'paroxysms of lawless disorder' (*Essay* 230). Ferguson does not just pay lip service to the idea of a balance between factions existing in a mixed constitution, he actively connects it to his unintended consequences analysis to argue that 'the claims of party' 'may be considered as the great legislator of nations' (*Essay* 131).

This is a common theme in Ferguson's work. In the *Principles* he suggests that 'legislature in this form is a continued negotiation' (*Principles* 1: 304), while in the *Essay* he argues that 'law is literally a treaty' (*Essay* 159) between the various parts of the nation. Similarly the public interest is often best secured by individuals defending their own interest in the political disputes of the day. The 'agitations of a free people' (*Essay* 62), within the proper bounds, is the sign of a healthy political society, and 'balance' (*Essay* 125) is all. Law and political institutions, like national spirit, are the product of the interaction of individuals and communities reacting to their circumstances. But all of this needs to be balanced against other pressing arguments in his work. In a letter to Sir John MacPherson, Ferguson bemoans the fact that the British system works through party conflict rather than the cooperation of disinterested citizens.[19] But he accepts that this is the reality. Moral science tells us that this is a fact and that the idealised account of citizen participation disinterestedly debating the public good is inaccurate and to continue our analysis as though it were the case is a dangerous mistake.

As we have seen Ferguson's analysis of the development of the Roman constitution is basically a class analysis of the growing influence of the people and its impact on Rome's mixed constitution. Ferguson's frequent references to this fact of moral science together with his support for active political life and interest in conflict have led many to interpret him as an early advocate of the healthy nature of faction and party conflict. But as Max Skjönsberg (2017: 14) has recently argued, this is an exaggeration of Ferguson's interest in factions. It is true that Ferguson worried about passivity in the population, and those devices designed to maintain social order might suppress healthy political action. But the political action that Ferguson envisages is action within the constitution. His analysis of the development of civilised society is as deeply influenced by Montesquieu's analysis of the British constitution as it is by his analysis of the fall of the Roman Republic. The separation of the powers and functions of government and their balancing is vital to the constitution and the movement of any faction to favour one part of the population or one branch of the government has a destabilising effect.

The *Roman History* gives us clear examples of what Ferguson has in mind. His account of the changes that the Roman political order experienced is constantly directed against the 'vindictive spirit of party' (*Rome* 327) and 'the progress of ruinous faction affecting popular measures' (*Rome* 196). The argument becomes even more pronounced in the *Principles* where the concern is the danger of the 'mob' (*Principles* 2: 292, 478). In his discussion of a right to rebel against tyranny Ferguson brings himself to the interesting position that the risk of granting such a principle is that it opens the door to constant instability. Formalising such a right is dangerous precisely because 'so far are we from being able to state any speculative or abstract position that may not be abused' (*Principles* 2: 291).

Revolutionary circumstances may very well arise, but philosophy and even law cannot control them or direct them. In a revolution the mob will have its day and the elite pick up the pieces after the ensuing civil war.[20] Ferguson's view seems to be that the danger of codifying a right to rebel is too great as it will lead to demagogues constantly invoking it. Instead the reality of such circumstances is acknowledged, but the detail left helpfully vague. It has been suggested that Ferguson's political thought became more conservative in response to events in France (Kugler 2017) but, as we have seen, this reading sits uncomfortably against his equally strong views on the American Revolution and Jacobitism. The truth is that Ferguson was always an advocate of gradual and careful political reform and an opponent of revolutionary change. His preference is to work with the material that we have and adapt it in response to problems as they arise – to repair the building we have rather than start afresh, to borrow an image he uses from the *Analysis* to the *Principles* – and this indicates a very different attitude to politics than that of the more radical thinkers like Richard Price.

What then does Ferguson have in mind? It is clear that he accepts the historical reality of the role of factional conflict in the development of political institutions. It is also clear that he wants to argue against passivity on the part of the population, but it is just as clear that he is concerned about political factionalism and is an advocate of the centrality of law and political stability. We may find a clue to resolving this puzzle in the discussion in the *Essay* when he dwells on the elements of the British system that preserve liberty. The stress is on the diffusion of power through institutions such as juries and habeas corpus. These institutions check the abuse of power and depend, for their realisation, on the active participation of the people. The 'vigour and jealousy of a free people' (*Institutes* 297) expresses itself through a range of political and social participation beyond the classical model of the citizen in the assembly. If government itself is the gradual result of an evolution that responds to the circumstances of each nation, then the media of that evolution are the lives of ordinary citizens acquiring the 'the habits of political life' (*Principles* 1: 201). The actual constitution is the product of political action, while talk of the spirit or design of the constitution is 'mere constructions of speculative men' (*Price* 13). Politics is a practical activity, and it is also a reactionary activity for Ferguson. It is the collective response to problems experienced by the group and these problems are best solved by those who are actively engaged.

As we saw in Chapter 4, Ferguson's educational philosophy was focused on the creation of an educated and independent officer class. Merchants are not the most important component of the middling ranks for Ferguson: professional men like him were more significant. He is seeking the creation of a society with a clear order of rank and where political influence is limited to the middle and upper classes. The middle classes are to be educated to be virtuous generalists who will manage the public order in pursuit of honour and advancement.[21] The talents that he speaks of are the talents to act in the interest of the state and the same thought lies behind his suggestions for a system of public honours. This motivates the various classes to play their proper role. But the class system must be sufficiently flexible as to admit those skilled in public service to rise. The danger is not wealth per se, but when money acts as a proxy for ability at anything other than making money.

Statesmen and Warriors

Ferguson's commitment to the campaign for a Scottish militia has been well documented and explored in relation to the themes of republican political thought. However, the precise nature of his militia proposals is, in significant respects, at odds with some of the main themes of republican political thinking. For a start Ferguson's consistent argument throughout his career is for an armed population. His aim is to 'revive and defuse the Love of

Arms among our People' (*Militia* 19), with a view to 'every Sober Landholder and householder to have a stand of Arms in his House' (*Correspondence* 1: 224). The militia is to be drawn from this, but the central point is that all are armed and all know how to shoot. The promotion of sport and target practice will develop the capacity of each individual, and governments should not be afraid of the wide ownership of arms among their population (*Essay* 256; *Militia* 21–3).[22]

Secondly, the long-standing political argument against standing armies as a route to military rule is also severely modified in Ferguson's analysis. Ferguson, as befits a professional soldier of a decade's service, did not argue for the removal of the standing army. Instead he saw the proposed militia as an accompaniment to it. The key, as he argues, is that we manage an armed population, a selective militia and a civilised army.[23] The population will only acquire capacity in arms if they actively use them and this is the basis of Ferguson's detailed militia plans. Ferguson is very clear that the militia must itself be civilised and wedded to the existing social hierarchy. The system of rank in society must be replicated in the militia – as he puts it: 'We are very happy in the Degrees of Subordination already established in Britain ...' (*Militia* 37) – and an orderly militia will replicate that order.[24] Moreover, it will be limited in size and scale, essentially covering the propertied classes and respectable working classes. The 'most deserving of our People' (*Militia* 53) can be trusted to form the militia without suspicion that it will turn against the public. Ferguson also provides detailed accounts of the provision of a system of honours and recognition which both incentivises service and provides a basis for rank and honour through public service.[25] But Ferguson's argument rarely strays into the mode of citizen virtue. For the most part his argument is about marrying military preparedness with internal political stability – the mob were to be excluded from the militia which was there to be wielded against them if necessary.[26] The worry that a Scottish militia might have raised in the English after the events of 1745 is an abiding concern of Ferguson's, not least because he believed that such a militia could have prevented the rebellion. The argument is also directed towards the fear of invasion by the French, and Ferguson's main argument is that an armed population will be a secure defence against invasion.

As Ian McDaniel (2008) has noted, Ferguson's reaction to the French Revolution and the subsequent 'Paradoxical War'

(*Correspondence* 2: 321) was bound up more with his concerns about the reformed nature of the French army as an external threat to Britain than it was with the prospect of revolution at home. Indeed, as Anna Plassart has noted (2015: 140), it does raise an interesting puzzle: why would a thinker apparently so keen on republican spirit and martial virtue distrust a system that bound the state and the army so closely together? As both McDaniel and Plassart argue, the answer to this lies in the danger of empire that Ferguson saw as the inevitable outcome of the French system. A system of promotion within the ranks and the merging of the state with the army have militarised the state and rendered it a permanent threat to Britain precisely because the only way to pursue ambition in Napoleonic France is through military service in war, recreating the pressures of economic conflict that led to Rome's expansion.[27] Ferguson's ideal military model for Britain involved both a standing army and an armed middle class, whose independence secured them from careerism; combining these two models would allow for a diffusion of military skills designed to discourage invasion. Ferguson's aim was to create a balance that preserved wealth, public service and military skill in Britain.

The most commonly invoked republican theme in Ferguson's thought is the concern with the separation of the roles of statesmen and warriors. Again, this locution can be found across Ferguson's works (*Essay* 84, 180, 217; *Manuscripts* 40; *Rome* 127, 450; *Principles* 2: 334). The abiding concern, often read in conjunction with Ferguson's views on the dangers of the division of labour in commercial society, is that a society that separates the roles of warrior and statesman is inhabited by those who are in some sense 'mutilated' (*Manuscripts* 40) or 'feeble' (*Rome* 450). One way of reading Ferguson's concern here is to stress the passages where he dwells on the loss of martial virtue: where the skills of the statesman and warrior are contrasted to those of the 'clerk and accountant' (*Essay*: 214), or where 'citizens and soldiers might come to be distinguished as much as women and men' (*Essay*: 219), leaving the 'polished' prey to the 'rude' (*Essay*: 215).

When civilisation reduces military spirit it prepares mankind for 'the government of force' (*Essay* 219). This is the traditional lesson of the Carthaginian reliance on mercenaries and the corruption of the Roman Republic in the face of military rule.

But even this passage in the *Essay* is not, perhaps, quite what it seems. Take, for example, another rhetorical flourish where

Ferguson argues that: 'But to separate the arts which form the citizen and the statesman, the arts of policy and war, is an attempt to dismember the human character' (*Essay* 218). What are being separated here are the arts of the statesman and the arts of the warrior, and again the source is Cicero (1913: 77): 'For arms are of little value in the field unless there is wise counsel at home.' This is not a general concern about alienation as the proto-Marxist reading might suggest, nor is the point one about effeminacy in the republican fashion. It is about the capacity to be a successful political actor.[28] If war is inevitable and endemic then those who rule must have knowledge of the sword. The characters of statesmen and warriors are distinct, but the characteristics of each are required to fulfil the role demanded of political actors. As we noted in Chapter 4, Ferguson's conception of capacity from active engagement suggests that the requisite skills are acquired in practice. Moreover, both of these arenas are perfectly conditioned for the vigorous exercise of capacity. War and politics are, in this sense, good for us. The 'heart beats high' (*Essay* 107) in war and politics and this is a healthy thing in Ferguson's view.

Ferguson returns to the theme in the late *Manuscripts* when he observes that politicians must fight and soldiers must take part in government: 'Short of this he is no more than a Clerk in office and a Buble in Council. The Warriour as at Rome may occasionally only change his Gown for the Sajum but without knowing how to graft his services on those of the State is a mere prize fighter and Bully, whose only form of proceeding is mere Violence or Force' (*Manuscripts* 39).[29] And this is interesting because it returns us to the theme of civilisation. When he discusses the nature of life as a citizen and as a solider in the *Essay*, he notes at the same time the desire to separate civil and military authority as being against the 'most important lesson of civil society' (*Essay* 143). But this lesson goes in both directions, as military rule is impossible without a political structure. As he remarks in the *Roman History*, 'the considerations of civil justice, and the respect which is paid to some form of political subordination, are necessary even to the discipline and order of a military establishment' (*Rome* 410).

The rounded character must have experience and knowledge of both functions, or as he puts it in the *Militia Question* pamphlet, the aim must be 'to mix the military Spirit with our civil and commercial Policy' (*Militia* 3). The bulk of the argument in the *Militia Question* pamphlet is based on military necessity rather than citizen virtue. The argument running through the rest of Ferguson's work about the value of acquiring the habits of a statesman and warrior is also a pragmatic one: the defence of the nation depends on the skill sets held by statesmen and warriors. These should be 'required as ordinary accomplishments of the citizen' (*Principles* 2: 414), even if we are for the most part dependent on a standing army. And it is worth re-stressing here that Ferguson, as befits his own decade of service as a professional soldier, is not opposed to standing armies. He is not, then, drawing on the republican concerns of the civil war period. For the most part his argument is simply that no professional army could maintain an occupation if attacked by a well-armed and drilled militia. The ambivalence of Ferguson's comments about the superiority of the British professionals fighting the American militias deepens as the conflict proceeds. But the overall line of his argument is about the lack of leadership by the government.

The division of labour can enhance the particular skill sets of a professional soldier and a professional politician, but what it cannot do is keep together two functions and skill sets vital to sound government. In the *Manuscripts* he observes that it was the Ancient's superior knowledge of human nature that led them to keep the two roles together (*Manuscripts* 33, 148). If we examine the details of Ferguson's plan for the militia we find that it is structured around the existing power and class relations of society. One aim of this is clearly to ensure that the militia remains loyal to the state and preserves the status quo, but the other is to ensure that those who will be likely to have greater decision-making influence in the state will have experience of higher command functions. Ferguson's repeated concern for the roles of statesman and warrior to remain united reflect his belief that a politician who is ignorant of war would be unable to successfully direct the nation in one of his core activities. Similarly, a warrior who is not connected to the political system becomes little more than a mercenary and, as a result, less effective as a soldier. Ferguson addresses the point directly in the *Roman History*: 'Although the functions of state and war were entrusted to the same persons, yet the civil and military characters, except in the case of a dictator, were never united in the same person. The officer of state resigned his civil power before he became a soldier, and the soldier was obliged to lay aside his military ensigns and character before he could enter the city' (*Rome* 192). The same individual acts in both roles and has experience of both activities, but recognises the distinct, yet complementary, nature of the statesman and the warrior.

Reading Ferguson as an opponent of standing armies is a mistake, although he did worry about a standing army falling into the wrong hands; his response to this was not that of the English Commonwealthmen or even of Machiavelli himself. Ferguson believed that both a militia and a standing army were necessary for the defence of Britain and that such a combination should be led by a trained officer class who might move between careers in the military and the civilian world. Ferguson's own military service and the military careers that he advanced for all of his sons was not militia service. Indeed, in 1799 Ferguson was actively involved in planning for his son James to avoid undertaking militia service by hiring a substitute so that James could pursue his studies with a view to an eventual professional commission (Fagg 1995: xi).

Rank and the Idea of a Gentleman

One way we can begin to think about this is through Ferguson's attitudes towards the idea of citizen equality. Ferguson's moral science had convinced him of the universal reality of inequality and rank in society. The idea of a society of political equals does not match the reality of social life: 'The idea of men in any society, great or small, having ever assembled upon a foot of absolute equality, and without exclusion of any individual, to dispose of their government is altogether visionary and unknown in nature' (*Principles* 1: 262). Some groups, whether women, children, slaves, the poor, are always excluded. Even where the franchise is more extensive, decisions are made by a majority not unanimity. Ferguson's point is that these restrictions do not come from the consent of those to whom they apply, but from the exercise of power upon them. Ferguson accepts that the exercise of power, the fact that two may 'over-rule one by the superiority of force' (*Principles* 1: 263), does not provide a normative argument that such an exercise of power is 'right'. But it is a fact of any type of society that such power relationships exist. What this means is that a politics that seeks to abolish or ignore the reality of rank and power differences is unrealistic – it is not paying attention to what the evidence of moral science tells us about the reality of social life. This has important lessons for how we conduct politics and what we should expect from it:

> But the object of reason never can be to abolish the relation of power
> and dependence; for this nature has rendered impossible; but, to guard
> against the abuses of power, and procure to individuals equal security
> in their respective states, however differing in point of acquired or
> original advantages. (*Principles* 1: 263)

The distinction of ranks is natural, unavoidable and permanent.[30]
The question then is how the reality of ranks is combined with
the shared sense of national belonging and the answer is clear
for Ferguson – that all are co-nationals, but that each has his
own place and role to play in the life of the nation. The 'stability'
(*Principles* 1: 303) of the political society depends on the higher
ranks being admitted to the government of the whole but, crucially, Ferguson possesses a fluid account of the ranks. People can
rise through service to the public – much, one imagines, as he saw
himself, his fellow Moderate literati, and his hero Cicero as doing.

> Distinctions of rank, for the most part, are taken from birth or prop-
> erty; and we may censure the rule, but cannot reverse it. It is even
> fortunate for mankind that a foundation of subordination is laid,
> too obvious to be overlooked by the dullest of men, or by those who
> stand most in need of being governed. But, though property sometimes
> overpower both ability and every other merit, yet there are occasions
> in which it must give way to either. At elections and county meetings,
> men of fortune predominate; but armies are commanded, and states
> are governed by men of ability. (*Principles* 2: 473)

The way that Ferguson advances this argument is to stress that the
protection of the rights of co-nationals is the protection of unequal
holdings and statuses, but he does so while pointing out the need
for a route to influence by men of capacity. If we are to respect
the rights of all, and those rights are different, then any attempt
to 'level' would be 'repugnant' (*Principles* 2: 463–4), but we must
also keep an eye on the pathways that allow men of capacity to
rise when they are needed.[31] Ultimately Ferguson reaches the same
conclusion as Aristotle: that those who have a stake in the country
are most likely to be relied upon to act to preserve the country.

> But the ultimate and essential security to liberty, or guard against the
> disorders which are equally fatal to the state of the magistrate as to
> those of the privilege of the people, is the character to be retained by

> those who have any considerable stake in the welfare of his country, a character by which they are qualified, in the last resort, to defend as well as to fulfil the ties of their station. (*Principles* 2: 493)[32]

As each society has its own unique set of circumstances and dynamics, its own culture and institutions, its own 'character' (*Institutes* 292), then the form of government must be adapted to the condition of the people. These adaptations are always imperfect because 'no human institution is perfect' (*Essay* 176).

The great question of political science for Ferguson is how the political system is adapted to the circumstances of the people. If benevolence is the *summum bonum* and if it is such because of our social nature, then this leads to a political principle which supports the greatest participation by the greatest number consonant with the circumstances of the society and dependent on the continued attainment of political stability. If the poor are a rabble, as they may become in a corrupted nation, then admitting them to political influence would be a disaster. This is not to say that all citizens cannot engage in some form of public service, for example by serving in Ferguson's militia or by participating in political discussions if not holding political office. It is simply to say that there are limits to this and those limits are set by the desire to ensure the stability of the political system.

> And we may now also assume that forms of government may be estimated, not only by the actual wisdom or goodness of their administration, but likewise by the numbers who are made to participate in the service or government of their country, and by the diffusion of political deliberation and function to the greatest extent that is consistent with the wisdom of its administration. (*Principles* 2: 509)

This, then, is Ferguson's view. That what counts as participation can be 'service' rather than direct political participation. Engagement in political deliberation might take a variety of forms, and the extent of those admitted to participation is limited by the desire to maintain stability and the rule of law in the society. Faction and division in political assemblies is what drives the national spirit, but it is competition within the rules. Political liberty in a modern nation like Britain is secured by 'representation' and 'deputation' (*Principles* 2: 468); it proceeds by debate and is settled by majority vote. The people's 'share' can be through representation, through public debate and through service, but not through direct participation.

It might be thought that by the time Ferguson set down this argument in the *Principles* the events of the years immediately prior to 1792 produced this strong conservative position. But as we have seen already, Ferguson possessed this view in his response to the Jacobites in the 1740s and events in America in the 1760s and 1770s. Similarly, the claim that Ferguson moves from an early enthusiasm for democracy in the *Essay* to a later support for rank (Kalyvas and Katznelson 1998: 180; McDaniel 2013: 568) seems to be mistaken – the same attitudes appear consistently across his work from the *Sermon* to the late *Manuscripts*. Ferguson is interested in what can be learned from the Republican tradition, and from Rome in particular, but at the end of the day he is a pragmatic Whig defending the constitution and its mixed nature, keenly aware that it exists in a delicate balance. The overwhelming preoccupation with stability and the insistence that political form must be adjusted to circumstance places critical distance between Ferguson and the more idealistic of the Radicals like Richard Price.

We've spent some time looking at Ferguson's link between the exercise of individual virtue and public spirit. What we have seen is a wedding of Ciceronian civic moralism with a highly developed sociological account of the generation of the nation and national sentiment. We might then suppose that Ferguson viewed political life in instrumental terms – for what it could add to the potential for moral virtue. But this is not the case. Ferguson views humans as socially constituted and so inevitably faced with conflict between and within social groups. What drives us in our political action is public spirit, but the way that we secure the good of society is by preserving and reforming the inheritance of our nation. The key political virtue for Ferguson is not liberty, nor is it citizen virtue: it is stability.

As he puts it in the *Principles* (2: 474–5) 'Stability is of more consequence than any advantage to be gained by change . . . Too much fluctuation, or frequent transition from one set of rules to another, is, of all circumstances, the least consistent with that sense of security in which the possession and engagement of liberty consists.' Ferguson is at his most Machiavellian, not when talking about citizen virtue, but when recognising that the good of stability must be secured in different ways in different contexts. The British system of mixed government under the rule of law provides liberty but it also, if kept in balance, provides stability. Stable government and the defence of the existing institutions are also the backbone of his defence of a militia. It isn't really the effect that participation has on the individuals, it is the way in which the institutions breed responsible and rounded political participants and at the same time secure the nation against invasion. Ferguson does not regard the British system as perfect or without its dangers, but he recognises that perfection is not something that is ever realised in human affairs.

Patriotic Liberty

Patriotism, public spirit and action come together to make politics a realm for the realisation of the best features of human character. Hardship, trial and effort are just as vital to the exercise of public spirit as they are to our other character traits. Like war they provide us with an opportunity to display ambition in the service of the community such that 'the most happy men, whose hearts are engaged to a community' (*Essay* 59) are able to realise this aspect of their nature in political service.

In the *Institutes* he offers the following definition of public spirit: '1. A faithful discharge of any office intrusted for the public good', '2. A continual preference of public safety, and public good, to separate interests, or partial considerations' (*Institutes* 251). While this appears suitably bland it is worth noting that the definitions are wedded in the discharge of existing roles and stations in society. Ferguson was particularly worried by the idea that someone who committed themselves to a political ideal that they saw as in the public interest would develop revolutionary fervour. 'The Zealot for liberty has run into the wildest disorders, and adventures, under pretence of promoting it, have found their way to the most violent and pernicious usurpations' (*Principles* 2: 457). As we saw in the discussion of Richard Price as an exemplar of a philosophical vice, this is a mistaken sense of liberty. Ferguson's sense of liberty as security of rights under the rule of law is civil liberty and the issue of political liberty is to be answered by considering which political order is best fitted to the circumstances of the people in question. In the case of Britain, Ferguson clearly thought, that system was the mixed constitution arrived at following the civil wars. Liberty is not equality, it is not direct participation in an assembly and it most certainly is not democracy. The lesson of Rome was that liberty is threatened by 'the prevalence of democratic power' (*Principles* 2: 464) and the danger to liberty is 'arbitrary power' (*Principles* 2: 464) wielded by whatever part of the community. The opposite of arbitrary power is civilised power.

Ferguson's notion of a mixed form of participation and wide public debate leads him to view political freedom as essential to encouraging political 'conversation' which is a sign of a 'just' and 'vigorous' society (*Principles* 2: 511). His ideal is a society of 'vigorous, public-spirited, and resolute men', one where 'virtue is a necessary constituent of national strength' and one which allows us to 'sustain in the same person, the character of the senator, the statesman, and the soldier' (*Essay* 213). The character of the people is a 'national resource' (*Institutes* 267) which allow them to react to the circumstances of the nation. Healthy nations need good institutions, good laws and above all good people.

Ferguson's role in all of this was as a moral educator, the trainer of the next generation of men who would continue the stability of the British system. As he wrote to Henry Dundas, arguing that election to Parliament should be contingent on militia service:

> Or in other words the sword tho powerful should be directed by Justice. For this I know not any security so effectual as that of placing the sword, When Education, the sense of high Rank, And a mighty Station in the preservation or order, have already placed the virtues of Candour, magnanimity and Justice. (*Correspondence* 2: 473)

We are now in a position to get a better sense of what Fania Oz-Salzberger (1994: xxiv) has called 'Ferguson's cautious restatement of classical republicanism'. What we find is that Ferguson was indeed an admirer of the ancient notion of a republic where the citizens were sovereign and where these citizens devoted themselves to the public. But he was also aware that modern nations were not ancient republics. Indeed a significant danger might arise if modern societies tried to organise themselves along the same lines as the small, ancient republics. In the *Essay* Ferguson cautions against 'the misplaced ardours of a republican spirit' (*Essay* 71) and he was clearly preoccupied by the destabilising impact the revolutionary and democratic movements had the potential to pose. This was in 1767. His commitment was indeed to a publicly engaged population, but that engagement was counterweighted by the mixed constitution, the rule of law and a set of institutions designed to protect the existing system of rank. Reward for public service should be the true measure of the citizen, but the type of service which was appropriate varied depending on the individual and his station.

Conclusion

These final two chapters have sought to interrogate the assumptions frequently made about Adam Ferguson's attitude towards commercial society and the influence of republicanism on his thinking. My aim has not been to deny that Ferguson raises issues about commercial society or that he deploys arguments from the civic tradition. The question has, instead, been whether these are the most accurate or dominant set of concerns in his writing. The focus on the rule of law and regulation as the central aspects of civil society and the necessary conditions for the appearance of commerce suggest that a civilised society is one where 'every proceeding is conducted by some fixed and determinate rule' (*Essay* 159). Law and security go together and so political establishments are necessary to create liberty. Viewing Ferguson as a late entry in the civic tradition or as an early figure in the sociological tradition obscures his genuinely novel contribution: an attempt to understand something universal about human experience and to do so within his wider system of moral science.

This book began with a suggestion that if we dethrone the *Essay* we are left with a somewhat different impression of Ferguson's overall thinking. But even in the *Essay* we find that his discussion of the division of society into classes and how they become 'mutual checks' (*Essay* 154) occurs within the system of law. When Ferguson argues that 'the boasted improvements of civil society, will be mere devices to lay the political spirit at rest, and will chain up the active virtues more than the restless disorders of men' (*Essay* 210) he sounds like a classical republican thinker. But when he expands on his understanding of politics we find the account of rank and the centrality of law and stability to civilisation to be so pervasive that he sounds more like a mainstream figure of the Scottish Enlightenment. His account of the evolution of political systems expands the range of social factors involved beyond the mere 'political'. By stressing the importance of habit, custom and manners he underlines the fact that rule-governed behaviour, civilisation, is more than formal political participation.[33]

The trends in the history of political thought over the last fifty years coincided with a revival in Ferguson's reputation and an increasing interest in the Scottish Enlightenment. While this has had many positive effects on Ferguson scholarship, it has also tended to lead to Ferguson being read through certain lenses. While Ferguson is clearly drawing on the example of Rome and the republican tradition that has developed from it, he is doing so within a peculiarly Scottish and British context. His republicanism, if we can call it that, is the republicanism of someone who has the hindsight of the civil war and the commonwealth, of the covenanters and the Jacobites, of the New Model Army and military dictatorship. It is also the republicanism of a man who served ten years in one of the regiments of the new professional British Army. Ferguson's republicanism then is not the republicanism of someone who opposed a standing army, it is the republicanism of someone who sees the need for both a standing army and a militia. His republicanism is not that of a Rousseauian dreamer looking for a return to small republics where all can take part or discover the freedom as non-domination that contemporary historians and philosophers regard as characteristic of the republican tradition. For Ferguson freedom was freedom under the rule of law in a nation of moderate extent, and politics was civilised to the extent that it took place in a rule-governed manner. The idea that Ferguson was in anyway sympathetic to the idea of a self-governing direct democracy of equals being appropriate for Hanoverian Britain is an almost entirely misplaced sense of the main thrust of his politics. Reading Ferguson as a backward-looking, nostalgic, thinker is just as much of a mistake as reading him through later intellectual developments like alienation. The problems he faces are those of eighteenth-century Britain and the need to preserve the fragile constitutional balance that secured civilisation. He sought to do that by creating an educational system that provided a scientific and philosophical toolkit for those who would take leading roles in society. Ultimately the positions that he adopted were much the same as those of his fellow Scots who were thinking through the same problems.

There is a danger in trying to impose order on Ferguson's thought: a danger that one systematises the system at the expense of recognising the tensions in his thought. My aim has been to see beyond the difficulties that emerge from Ferguson's own presentation of his ideas, but in doing so to avoid reading too much consistency into his thought. Throughout the preceding chapters there has been an attempt to read Ferguson as more centrally located in the Scottish Enlightenment than has been the tendency in recent years. The imperfectly expressed project of science, philosophy and education revealed here remains constant throughout his career and places him firmly in the mainstream of the literati. Far from being an outlier, Ferguson might actually be understood as the archetypal enlightened Scot.

Ferguson believed in the value of civilisation, and in particular of the historically evolved settlement of Britain, and he wanted to be certain that its achievements were secured by identifying the dangers that it faced. He believed that we needed both good laws and good men able to react to the unpredictable unintended consequences that characterise human social life. He was clear eyed about the destabilising forces at work around him, from the danger of demagogues and the mob to the perpetual threat from abroad, and believed that the securest defence against them was the creation of an educated elite who would recognise the need to blend law and order, increasing wealth and military security.

David Kettler (2005: 348) suggested that perhaps the best way to understand Ferguson's thought was through the developing idea of civility. This, it seems to me, is correct. Ferguson understood what he thought was the basis of the desirable features of modern society and that these are the blessings of law and security. But Ferguson also understood that such civilisation was more than mere laws, it depended on a population disposed to orderly behaviour, and that this, in turn, was a historically evolved achievement that had to be understood and defended. Far from being a sceptic about commercial modernity, Ferguson sought to diagnose its potential weaknesses and set out a system of moral science that could defend a civil society.

Notes

1. For discussions of Ferguson's reaction to the French Revolution see McDaniel (2013a) and Plassart (2015).
2. Camic (1983: 71) argues that Ferguson's patriotism and partisanship for the British cause sets him apart from his peers. This seems hard to sustain given that all of the Scots were committed Unionists and that several of them, notably Kames, attempt analyses of patriotism. John Robertson (1985: 122 n. 13) argues, against Richard Sher, that the

notion of patriotism involved in the militia debate is more complex than a vindication of Scotland's pride, a point we will return to below.

3. The same definition appears in the *Institutes* where Ferguson uses it to distinguish between the nation and the state: 'A nation is any independent company or society of men acting under a common direction.' 'The united force of numbers, and the direction under which they act, is termed *the state*' (*Institutes* 263). The term nation was 'an ambiguous and fluctuating term' at this time (Sebastiani 2014: 595). Lehmann (1930: 83) points out that Ferguson traces the original rise of nations to the barbaric age, which places his treatment of group cohesion in the same era as his fellow four-stage Scots.

4. See also *Principles* (1: 35), *Militia* (26), *Manuscripts* (137).

5. For a discussion of Ferguson's notion of civilised warfare see Buchan (2006, 2009) and Smith (2014).

6. Smith invokes a similar stadial analysis of war in Book V of the *Wealth of Nations* and parallel arguments can be found in Kames and Robertson.

7. It is also worth noting that Ferguson, for all of his stress on the potentially beneficial functions of warfare, had a genuine horror of the idea of civil war (Kettler 2005: 256). Ferguson's hardline opposition to the Jacobites and the American colonists shows that there were limits to his valorisation of warfare.

8. 'Hence the sacred regard that is paid to cartels, respecting the treatment or exchange of Prisoners, the capitulations or treaties of surrender which take place in the midst of military operations, the quarter granted to an enemy who lays down his arms, or the freedom that is given to a prisoner, upon his parole of honour not to serve until he is fairly exchanged' (*Principles* 2: 304).

9. It need hardly be said that the account of war offered by Ferguson sounds hopelessly naive in the light of later major conflicts. Bruce Buchan (2009: 26) notes that Ferguson's admiration for modern war traces back to its status as an example of civilisation and is one of the features that leads to his ambivalence about the ancients versus moderns comparisons.

10. For a discussion of Ferguson's *History of Rome* as a contribution to the debate over the danger of 'Caesarism' see Iain McDaniel (2013a).

11. See *Essay* (191–3). Ferguson also examines another product of this tradition that he believes is a manifestation of natural sociability combined with a concern for reputation among a group. In several

places (*Principles* 2: 281–2; *Essay* 103) Ferguson discusses duelling as an indication of the functional inefficiency of using law to defend honour and reputation.

12. For Ferguson's class analysis of the Roman civil wars see *Rome* (38, 95, 112, 225).

13. We can also find traces of this argument in Ferguson's discussion of the Covenanters (*Principles* 2: 296).

14. See *Essay* (123, 208).

15. For a discussion of which see Allan (2008a: 23–38).

16. For a discussion of Ferguson's relationship with Montesquieu see Allan (2006: 48–9), Mason (1988) and Broadie (2012).

17. See Montesquieu (1989: 310). It is also worth noting that Hegel cites Montesquieu on this point in a number of places, notably (1991: 29, 283–4, 310–11). A number of writers have discussed the influence of Montesquieu's idea of spirit on Hegel's development of the idea of *Geist*. For a summary of the debate see Michael Mosher (1984).

18. Though once again Ferguson's looseness with terminology produces several places where he both appears to defend Empire against the claims of the American colonists for example (*Price* 19) and where he seems to apply the term Empire to Great Britain without concern (*Price* 32).

19. *Correspondence* (2: 378).

20. *Principles* (2: 292).

21. David Raynor (2008: 72) refers to this as a 'backward-looking socially conservative' vision of the militia, while Donald Winch (1978: 175) stresses Ferguson's attempts to invoke patriotic political action in the aristocracy. In what follows here I will suggest that the vision is indeed socially conservative but far from backward-looking and that the argument is aimed at a wider class range than just the aristocracy.

22. See *Essay* (256). In *Sister Peg* he expands on this and argues that a disarmed population is a population ripe to be enslaved. A further argument used to supplement this is that ownership of arms is the 'great distinction between masters and slaves' (*Sister Peg* 92).

23. *Militia* (4).

24. *Militia* (20, 31, 35, 50).

25. *Militia* (36–40).

26. The predominantly military nature of Ferguson's concerns over the militia are noted by David Raynor (2008: 71), John Robertson (1985: 175) and Emma McLeod (2015: 368).

27. The discussion of Rome turns critical on precisely this point. In

his discussion of Coriolanus he notes that: 'Their civil and military transactions were constantly blended together. The senate frequently involved the state in war, in order to suspend its intestine division, and the people as often took occasion, from the difficulties in which the community was involved by its enemies, to extort a compliance with their own demands' (*Rome* 17). This indicates the potential danger that the combination of statesmen and warriors can produce.

28. Forbes (1967: 45) and Gellner (1994: 75) stress that Ferguson's concerns are about the very specific separation of citizen and soldier.

29. He repeats the point at *Manuscripts* (150).

30. 'It is impossible, without violating the principles of human nature to prevent some permanent distinction of ranks' (*Principles* 2: 463).

31. It is interesting to consider whether this arose from Ferguson's reading of Roman history or from his awareness of the reality of late eighteenth- and early nineteenth-century British politics with the likes of Walpole, the Pitts and Dundas, and military figures such as Wolfe and, later, Nelson and Wellington rising from relatively modest social backgrounds to great prominence through public service.

32. Iain McDaniel (2013a: 157–9) suggests that Ferguson is drawing on the Germanic ideal of a military nobility as a solution to the danger faced by Britain, but it seems equally likely that the sources for this argument are classical, such as Aristotle and Cicero, coupled with the contemporary Whig arguments, such as Hume and Smith, on the significance of the middle classes. Ferguson's middle-class professionals seem closer to the muscular bourgeois of the nineteenth century than they do to the Teutonic knights.

33. When writers such as Merolle (2009) argue for Ferguson as a proto-Romantic they realise that there is something different and new about Ferguson's analysis of the emotional dynamics of national belonging. The felt experience of national sentiment and the attempt to capture national spirit are both innovations in his analysis.

Bibliography

Ahnert, Thomas (2011) 'The Moral Education of Mankind: Character and Religious Moderation in the Sermons of Hugh Blair', in T. Ahnert and S. Manning (eds), *Character, Self, and Sociability in the Scottish Enlightenment*. London: Palgrave Macmillan, pp. 67–83.

Ahnert, Thomas (2014) *The Moral Culture of the Scottish Enlightenment 1690–1805*. New Haven, CT: Yale University Press.

Ahnert, Thomas and Manning, Susan (2011) 'Introduction', in T. Ahnert and S. Manning (eds), *Character, Self, and Sociability in the Scottish Enlightenment*. London: Palgrave Macmillan, pp. 1–30.

Allan, David (1993) *Virtue, Learning and the Scottish Enlightenment*. Edinburgh: Edinburgh University Press.

Allan, David (1998) 'Protestantism, Presbyterianism and National Identity in Eighteenth-Century Scottish Historiography', in I. McBride and A. Claydon (eds), *Protestantism and National Identity: Britain and Ireland c.1650–1850*. Cambridge: Cambridge University Press, pp. 185–205.

Allan, David (2006) *Adam Ferguson*. Aberdeen: AHRC Centre for Scottish and Irish Studies.

Allan, David (2008a) 'Ferguson and Scottish History: Past and Present in an Essay on the History of Civil Society', in Eugene Heath and Vincenzo Merolle (eds), *Adam Ferguson: History, Progress and Human Nature*. London: Pickering & Chatto, pp. 23–38.

Allan, David (2008b) *Making British Culture: English Readers and the Scottish Enlightenment 1740–1830*. New York: Routledge.

Amoh, Yasuo (2008) 'Ferguson's Views on the American and French Revolutions', in Eugene Heath and Vincenzo Merolle (eds), *Adam Ferguson: History, Progress and Human Nature*. London: Pickering & Chatto, pp. 73–86.

Arbo, Matthew B. (2011) 'Adam Ferguson's Sermon in the Ersh Language:

A Word from 2 Samuel on Martial Responsibility and Political Order',
Political Theology, 12 (6), pp. 894–908.

Arbo, Matthew B. (2014) *Political Vanity: Adam Ferguson on the Moral Tensions of Early Capitalism*. Minneapolis, MN: Fortress Press.

Aristotle (1998) *Nicomachean Ethics*, trans. D. Ross. Oxford: Oxford University Press.

Aurelius, Marcus (1930) *The Meditations and other Texts*, trans. C. R. Hines, Cambridge, MA: Harvard University Press.

Bello, Xandra (2017) 'Adam Ferguson's History of the Progress and the Termination of the Roman Republic. Passions, Epistemology, and Politics in the Late Scottish Enlightenment'. Unpublished PhD Thesis, University of Aberdeen.

Benton, Ted (1990) 'Adam Ferguson and the Enterprise Culture', in P. Hulme and L. Jordanova (eds), *The Enlightenment and Its Shadows*. London: Routledge, pp. 101–20.

Bernstein, John Andrew (1978) 'Adam Ferguson and the Idea of Progress', *Studies in Burke and His Time*, 19 (2), pp. 99–118.

Berry, Christopher J. (1974) 'Climate in the Eighteenth Century: James Dunbar and the Scottish Case', *Texas Studies in Literature and Language*, XVI (2), pp. 281–92.

Berry, Christopher J. (1994) *The Idea of Luxury: A Conceptual and Historical Investigation*. Cambridge: Cambridge University Press.

Berry, Christopher J. (1997) *Social Theory of the Scottish Enlightenment*. Edinburgh: Edinburgh University Press.

Berry, Christopher J. (2003) 'The Scottish Enlightenment and the Idea of Civil Society', in A. Martinos (ed.), *Sociadade Civil – Entre Miragen e Oportunidade*. Coimbra: Faculdade de Lettres, pp. 99–115.

Berry, Christopher J. (2004) 'Smith under Strain', *European Journal of Political Theory*, 3 (4), pp. 455–63.

Berry, Christopher J. (2009) 'But Art itself is Natural to man': Ferguson and the Principle of Simultaneity', in Eugene Heath and Vincenzo Merolle (eds), *Adam Ferguson: Philosophy, Politics and Society*. London: Pickering & Chatto, pp. 143–53.

Berry, Christopher J. (2013) *The Idea of Commercial Society in the Scottish Enlightenment*. Edinburg: Edinburgh University Press.

Berry, Christopher J. (2015) 'The Rise of the Human Sciences', in A. Garrett and J. A. Harris (eds), *Scottish Philosophy in the Eighteenth Century*. Oxford: Oxford University Press, pp. 283–322.

Beveridge, Craig and Turnball, Ronnie (1997) *Scotland After the Enlightenment*. Edinburgh: Polygon.

Bottomore, Tom and Nisbet, Robert (1978) *A History of Sociological Analysis*. London: Heinemann.

Bowden, Brett (2004) 'The Idea of Civilisation: Its Origins and Socio-political Character', *Critical Review of International Social and Political Theory*, 7 (1), pp. 25–50.

Bowles, Paul (1985) 'The Origin of Property and the Development of Scottish Historical Science', *Journal of the History of Ideas*, 46, pp. 197–209.

Boyd, Richard (2000) 'Reappraising the Scottish Moralists and Civil Society', *Polity*, XXXIII (1), pp. 101–25.

Boyd, Richard (2004) *Uncivil Society: The Perils of Pluralism and the Making of Modern Liberalism*. Lanham, MD: Lexington Books.

Brewer, A. (1999) 'Adam Ferguson, Adam Smith and the Concept of Economic Growth', *History of Political Economy*, 31 (2), pp. 237–55.

Brewer, John D. (1986) 'Adam Ferguson and the Theme of Exploitation', *British Journal of Sociology*, 37 (4), pp. 461–78.

Brewer, John D. (1989) 'Conjectural History, Sociology and Social Change in Eighteenth Century Scotland: Adam Ferguson and the Division of Labour,' in D. McCrone, S. Kendrick and P. Straw (eds), *The Making of Scotland: Nations, Culture and Social Change*. Edinburgh: Edinburgh University Press, pp. 13–30.

Brewer, John D. (2007) 'Putting Adam Ferguson in his place', *British Journal of Sociology*, 58 (1), pp. 105–22.

Brewer, John D. (2008) 'Ferguson's Epistolary Self', in Eugene Heath and Vincenzo Merolle (eds), *Adam Ferguson: History, Progress and Human Nature*. London: Pickering & Chatto, pp. 7–22.

Broadie, Alexander (1990) *The Tradition of Scottish Philosophy*. Edinburgh: Polygon.

Broadie, Alexander (2001) *The Scottish Enlightenment*. Edinburgh: Birlinn.

Broadie, Alexander (2009) *A History of Scottish Philosophy*. Edinburgh: Edinburgh University Press.

Broadie, Alexander (2012) *Agreeable Connexions: Scottish Enlightenment Links with France*, Edinburgh: John Donald.

Brooke, Christopher (2012) *Philosophic Pride: Stoicism and Political Thought from Lipsius to Rousseau*. Princeton, NJ: Princeton University Press.

Bryson, Gladys (1945) *Man and Society: The Scottish Inquiry of the Eighteenth Century*. Princeton, NJ: Princeton University Press.

Buchan, Bruce (2005) 'Enlightened Histories: Civilisation, War and the Scottish Enlightenment', *European Legacy*, 10 (2), pp. 177–99.

Buchan, Bruce (2006) 'Civilisation, Sovereignty and War: The Scottish

Enlightenment and International Relations', *International Relations*, 20 (2), pp. 175–92.

Buchan, Bruce (2009) 'Adam Ferguson, The 43rd, and the Fictions of Fontenoy', in Eugene Heath and Vincenzo Merolle (eds), *Adam Ferguson: Philosophy, Politics and Society*. London: Pickering & Chatto, pp. 25–43.

Buchan, Bruce (2011) 'Civilised Fictions: Warfare and Civilisation in Enlightenment Thought', *Alternatives: Global, Local, Political*, 36 (1), pp. 64–71.

Buchan, James (2003) *Crowded with Genius: The Scottish Enlightenment, Edinburgh's Moment of the Mind*. New York: Harper Collins.

Burke, Edmund (1987) [1790] *Reflections on the Revolution in France*, ed. J. G. A. Pocock. Indianapolis, IN: Hackett.

Camic, Charles (1983) *Experience and Enlightenment: Socialisation for Cultural Change in Eighteenth Century Scotland*. Edinburgh: Edinburgh University Press.

Carey, Daniel (2015) 'Francis Hutcheson's Philosophy and the Scottish Enlightenment: Reception, Reputation, and Legacy', in A. Garrett and J. A. Harris (eds), *Scottish Philosophy in the Eighteenth Century*. Oxford: Oxford University Press, pp. 36–76.

Chen, Jeng-Guo S. (2008) 'Providence and Progress: The Religious Dimension in Ferguson's Discussion of Civil Liberty', in Eugene Heath and Vincenzo Merolle (eds), *Adam Ferguson: History, Progress and Human Nature*. London: Pickering & Chatto, pp. 171–86.

Chitnis, Anand C. (1976) *The Scottish Enlightenment: A Social History*. London: Croom Helm.

Cicero, Marcus T. (1913) *On Duties*, trans. Walter Miller. Cambridge, MA: Harvard University Press.

Clark, Ian D. C. (1970) 'From Protest to Reaction: The Moderate Regime in the Church of Scotland, 1752–1805,' in N. T. Phillipson and R. Mitchieson (eds), *Scotland in the Age of Improvement*. Edinburgh: Edinburgh University Press, pp. 200–24.

Cohen, J. and Arato, A. (1992) *Civil Society and Political Theory*. Cambridge, MA: MIT Press.

Colley, Linda (2009) *Britons: Forging the Nation 1707–1837*. New Haven, CT: Yale University Press.

Dwyer, John (1998) *The Age of the Passions: An Interpretation of Adam Smith and Scottish Enlightenment Culture*. East Linton: Tuckwell Press.

Ehrenberg, J. (1999) *Civil Society: The Critical History of an Idea*. New York: New York University Press.

Elazar, Yiftah (2014) 'Adam Ferguson on Modern Liberty and the Absurdity of Democracy', *History of Political Thought*, XXXV (4), pp. 768–87.

Elias, Norbert (1982) *The Civilising Process*, trans. E. Jephcott. New York: Pantheon.

Emerson, R. L. (1984) 'Conjectural History and the Scottish Philosophers', *Canadian Historical Association Historical Papers*, pp. 63–90.

Emerson, Roger (2008) *Academic Patronage in the Scottish Enlightenment: Glasgow, Edinburgh and St Andrews Universities*. Edinburgh: Edinburgh University Press.

Emerson, Roger (2015) 'The World in which the Scottish Enlightenment Took Shape', in A. Garrett and J. A. Harris (eds), *Scottish Philosophy in the Eighteenth Century*. Oxford: Oxford University Press, pp. 16–35.

Epictetus (1925) *Discourses Books 1–2*, trans. W. A. Oldfeather. Cambridge, MA: Harvard University Press.

Fagg, Jane B. (1968) 'Adam Ferguson: Scottish Cato'. Unpublished PhD dissertation, University of North Carolina at Chapel Hill.

Fagg, Jane B. (1994) 'Complaints and Clamours: The Ministry of Adam Fergusson, 1700–1754', *Records of the Scottish Church History Society*, 25, pp. 283–308.

Fagg, Jane B. (1995) 'Introduction', in Vincenzo Merolle (ed.), *The Correspondence of Adam Ferguson*, Vol. 1. London: William Pickering, pp. xx–cxvii.

Fagg, Jane B. (2000) 'An Ingenious Literary Production: Adam Ferguson and the Carlisle Commission Manifesto', *Scotia*, 24, pp. 1–14.

Fagg, Jane B. (2008) 'Ferguson's Use of Edinburgh University Library: 1764–1806', in Eugene Heath and Vincenzo Merolle (eds), *Adam Ferguson: History, Progress and Human Nature*. London: Pickering & Chatto, pp. 39–64.

Ferguson, Adam (1756) *Reflections Previous to the Establishment of a Militia*. London: R. & J. Dodsley.

Ferguson, Adam (1760) *Of Natural Philosophy*. Edinburgh.

Ferguson, Adam (1766) *Analysis of Pneumatics and Moral Philosophy*. Edinburgh: A. Kincaid & J. Bell.

Ferguson, Adam (1856) *The History of the Progress and Termination of the Roman Republic*. New York: J. C. Derby; University of Michigan: Historical Reprint Series.

Ferguson, Adam (1973) [1792] *Principles of Moral and Political Science*, 2 Vols. New York: AMS Press.

Ferguson, Adam (1994) [1769] *Institutes of Moral Philosophy*. London: Routledge/Thoemmes Press.

Ferguson, Adam (1995) [1767] *An Essay on the History of Civil Society*, ed. Fania Oz-Salzberger. Cambridge: Cambridge University Press.

Ferguson, Adam (1995) *The Correspondence of Adam Ferguson*, 2 Vols, ed. Vincenzo Merolle, London: William Pickering.

Ferguson, Adam (2006) *The Manuscripts of Adam Ferguson* (ed.), Vincenzo Merolle. London: Pickering & Chatto.

Finlay, Christopher (2006) 'Rhetoric and Citizenship in Adam Ferguson's Essay on the History of Civil Society', *History of Political Thought*, 27 (1), pp. 27–49.

Forbes, Duncan (1954) 'Scientific Whiggism: Adam Smith and John Millar', *Cambridge Journal*, VII (II), pp. 643–70.

Forbes, Duncan (1966) 'Introduction' to Adam Ferguson, *An Essay on the History of Civil Society 1776*, ed. D. Forbes. Edinburgh: Edinburgh University Press, pp. xii–xli.

Forbes, Duncan (1967) 'Adam Ferguson and the Idea of Community', in D. Young (ed.), *Edinburgh in the Age of Reason*. Edinburgh: Edinburgh University Press, pp. 40–7.

Forbes, Duncan (1975) *Hume's Philosophical Politics*. Cambridge: Cambridge University Press.

Forbes, Duncan (1982) 'Natural Law and the Scottish Enlightenment', in R. H. Campbell and A. Skinner (eds), *The Origins and Nature of the Scottish Enlightenment*. Edinburgh: John Donald, pp. 186–204.

Fry, Michael (2009) 'Ferguson the Highlander', in Eugene Heath and Vincenzo Merolle (eds), *Adam Ferguson: Philosophy, Politics and Society*. London: Pickering & Chatto, pp. 9–24.

Garrett, Aaron (2014) 'Introduction', in A. Garrett (ed.), *The Routledge Companion to Eighteenth Century Philosophy*. London: Routledge, pp. 1–27.

Garrett, Aaron and Hanley, Ryan (2015) 'Adam Smith: History and Impartiality', in A. Garrett and J. A. Harris (eds), *Scottish Philosophy in the Eighteenth Century*. Oxford: Oxford University Press, pp. 239–82.

Garrett, Aaron and Heydt, Colin (2015) 'Moral Philosophy: Practical and Speculative', in A. Garrett and J. A. Harris (eds), *Scottish Philosophy in the Eighteenth Century*. Oxford: Oxford University Press, pp. 77–130.

Gellner, Ernest (1994) *Conditions of Liberty: Civil Society and Its Rivals*. Harmondsworth: Penguin.

Geuna, M. (2002) 'Republicanism and Commercial Society in the Scottish Enlightenment: The Case of Adam Ferguson', in M. van Gelderen and Q. Skinner (eds), *Republicanism: A Shared European Heritage*, 2 Vols. Cambridge: Cambridge University Press, Vol. 2, pp. 177–95.

Goldsmith, M. M. (1988) 'Regulating Anew the Moral and Political Sentiments of Mankind: Bernard Mandeville and the Scottish Enlightenment', *Journal of the History of Ideas*, 49 (4), pp. 587–606.

Graham, Gordon (2007) 'The Ambition of Scottish Philosophy', *The Monist*, 90, pp. 157–69.

Graham, Gordon (2013) 'Adam Ferguson as a Moral Philosopher', *Philosophy*, 88 (4), pp. 511–25.

Haakonssen, Knud (1996) *Natural Law and Moral Philosophy from Grotius to the Scottish Enlightenment*. Cambridge: Cambridge University Press.

Hamowy, Ronald (1968) 'Adam Smith, Adam Ferguson, and the Division of Labour', *Economica*, XXXV, pp. 249–59.

Hamowy, Ronald (1986) 'Progress and Commerce in Anglo-American Thought: The Social Philosophy of Adam Ferguson', *Interpretation*, 14 (4), pp. 61–87.

Hamowy, Ronald (1987) *The Scottish Enlightenment and the Theory of Spontaneous Order*. Carbondale, IL: Southern Illinois University Press.

Hamowy, Ronald (2005) 'Two Whig Views of the American Revolution: Adam Ferguson's Response to Richard Price', in R. Hamowy (ed.), *The Political Sociology of Freedom: Adam Ferguson and F. A. Hayek*. Cheltenham: Edward Elgar, pp. 159–82.

Harris, James A. (2015) *Hume: An Intellectual Biography*. Cambridge: Cambridge University Press.

Harris, James A. and Tolonen, Mikko (2015) 'Hume In and Out of Scottish Context', in A. Garrett and J. A. Harris (eds), *Scottish Philosophy in the Eighteenth Century*. Oxford: Oxford University Press, pp. 163–95.

Hayek, F. A. (1960) *The Constitution of Liberty*. London: Routledge & Kegan Paul.

Hayek, F. A. (1967) 'The Results of Human Action not Human Design', in *Studies in Philosophy, Politics, and Economics*. London: Routledge & Kegan Paul, pp. 96–105.

Heath, Eugene (2006) 'Ferguson's Moral Philosophy', in Vincenzo Merolle (ed.), *The Manuscripts of Adam Ferguson*. London: Pickering & Chatto, pp. xlvii–lxxvi.

Heath, Eugene (2009) 'Ferguson and the Unintended Emergence of Social Order', in Eugene Heath and Vincenzo Merolle (eds), *Adam Ferguson: Philosophy, Politics and Society*. London: Pickering & Chatto, pp. 155–68.

Heath, Eugene (2015) 'In the Garden of God: Religion and Vigour in the

Frame of Ferguson's Thought', *Journal of Scottish Philosophy*, 13 (1), pp. 55–74.

Heath, Eugene and Merolle, Vincenzo (2009) 'Introduction', in Eugene Heath and Vincenzo Merolle (eds), *Adam Ferguson: Philosophy, Politics and Society*. London: Pickering & Chatto, pp. 1–8.

Hegel, G. W. F. (1991) *The Philosophy of Right*, trans. H. B. Nisbet, ed. A. W. Wood. Cambridge: Cambridge University Press.

Hill, Jack A. (2013) 'Marx's Reading of Adam Ferguson and the Idea of Progress', *Journal of Scottish Philosophy*, 11 (2), pp. 167–90.

Hill, Jack A. (2017) *Adam Ferguson and Ethical Integrity: The Man and His Prescriptions for the Moral Life*. Lanham, MD: Lexington Books.

Hill, Lisa (1997) 'Adam Ferguson and the Paradox of Progress and Decline', *History of Political Thought*, 18 (4), pp. 677–706.

Hill, Lisa (1998) 'The Invisible Hand of Adam Ferguson', *European Legacy*, 3 (6), pp. 42–64.

Hill, Lisa (2001) 'Eighteenth-Century Anticipations of the Sociology of Conflict: The Case of Adam Ferguson', *Journal of the History of Ideas*, 62 (2), pp. 281–99.

Hill, Lisa (2006) *The Passionate Society: The Social, Political and Moral Thought of Adam Ferguson*. Dordrecht: Springer.

Hill, Lisa (2007) 'Adam Smith, Adam Ferguson and Karl Marx on the Division of Labour', *Journal of Classical Sociology*, 7 (3), pp. 339–66.

Hill, Lisa (2009) 'A Complicated Vision: The Good Polity in Adam Ferguson's Thought', in Eugene Heath and Vincenzo Merolle (eds), *Adam Ferguson: Philosophy, Politics and Society*. London: Pickering & Chatto, pp. 107–23.

Hont, Istvan (2005) *The Jealousy of Trade: International Competition and the Nation-State in Historical Perspective*. Cambridge, MA: Belknap Press.

Hont, Istvan (2015) *Politics in a Commercial Society: Jean-Jacques Rousseau and Adam Smith*, ed. B. Kapossy and M. Sonennscher. Cambridge, MA: Harvard University Press.

Hope, Vincent M. (1989) *Virtue by Consensus: The Moral Philosophy of Hutcheson, Hume, and Adam Smith*. Oxford: Clarendon Press.

Höpfl, H. M. (1978) 'From Savage to Scotsman: Conjectural History in the Scottish Enlightenment', *Journal of British Studies*, XVII (2), pp. 19–40.

Hume, David (1976) [1739] *A Treatise of Human Nature*, ed. L. A. Selby-Bigge, rev. P. H. Nidditch. Oxford: Clarendon.

Hume, David (1985) *Essays Moral, Political, and Literary*, ed. Eugene F. Miller. Indianapolis, IN: Liberty Fund.

Hutchinson, Terence (1990) 'History and Political Economy in Scotland: Alternative "Inquiries" and Scottish Ascendancy', in D. Mair (ed.), *The Scottish Contribution to Modern Economic Thought*. Aberdeen: Aberdeen University Press, pp. 61–80.

Kalyvas, Andreas and Katznelson, Ira (1998) 'Adam Ferguson Returns: Liberalism Through a Glass, Darkly', *Political Theory*, 26 (2), pp. 173–97.

Kalyvas, Andreas and Katznelson, Ira (2008) 'Agonistic Liberalism: Adam Ferguson on Modern Commercial Society and the Limits of Classical Republicanism', in Andreas Kalyvas and Ira Katznelson (eds), *Liberal Beginnings: Making a Republic for the Moderns*. Cambridge: Cambridge University Press, pp. 51–87.

Kames, Henry Home, Lord (1776) *Historical Law Tracts*, 3rd edn. Edinburgh.

Keane, J. (1988) 'Despotism and Democracy', in J. Keane (ed.), *Civil Society and the State: New European Perspectives*. London: Verso, pp. 35–71.

Kettler, David (1977) 'History and Theory in Ferguson's Essay on the History of Civil Society', *Political Theory*, 5 (4), pp. 437–60.

Kettler, David (2005) *Adam Ferguson: His Social and Political Thought*. New Brunswick, NJ and London: Transaction Press.

Kettler, David (2008) 'Political Education for Empire and Revolution', in Eugene Heath and Vincenzo Merolle (eds), *Adam Ferguson: History, Progress and Human Nature*. London: Pickering & Chatto, pp. 87–114.

Kidd, Colin (1993) *Subverting Scotland's Past: Scottish Whig Historians and the Creation of an Anglo-British Identity 1689–1830*. Cambridge: Cambridge University Press.

Kidd, Colin (1996) 'North Britishness and the Nature of Eighteenth-Century British Patriotisms', *Historical Journal*, 39 (2), pp. 361–82.

Kugler, Michael (1994) 'Savagery, Antiquity, and Provincial Identity: Adam Ferguson's Critique of Civilisation'. Unpublished PhD thesis, University of Chicago.

Kugler, Michael (1996) 'Provincial Intellectuals: Identity, Patriotism, and Enlightened Peripheries', *Eighteenth Century: Theory and Interpretation*, 37 (2), pp. 156–73.

Kugler, Michael (2006) 'Book Review of Lisa Hill's The Passionate Society, Ronald Hamoway's The Political Sociology of Freedom and David Allan's Adam Ferguson', *Eighteenth-Century Scotland*, 21, Spring, pp. 30–1.

Kugler, Michael (2009) 'Adam Ferguson and Enlightened Provincial

Ideology in Scotland', in Eugene Heath and Vincenzo Merolle (eds), *Adam Ferguson: Philosophy, Politics and Society*. London: Pickering & Chatto, pp. 125–42.

Kugler, Michael (2017) 'Book Review of Jack Hill's Adam Ferguson and Ethical Integrity', *Eighteenth-Century Scotland*, 31, Spring, pp. 15–16.

Laski, Harold (1920) *Political Thought in England: Locke to Bentham*. Oxford: Oxford University Press.

Lehman, W. C. (1930) *Adam Ferguson and the Beginnings of Modern Sociology*. New York: Columbia University Press.

Livingston, Donald W. (1990) 'Hume's Historical Conception of Liberty', in Nicholas Capaldi and Donald W. Livingston (eds), *Liberty in Hume's History of England*. Dordrecht: Kluwer, pp. 105–53.

McArthur, Neil (2005) 'Laws Not Men: Hume's Distinction Between Barbarian and Civilised Government', *Hume Studies*, 31 (1), pp. 123–44.

McArthur, Neil (2014) 'Civil Society', in A. Garrett (ed.), *The Routledge Companion to Eighteenth Century Philosophy*. London: Routledge, pp. 643–62.

McDaniel, Iain (2008) 'Ferguson, Roman History and the Threat of Military Government in Modern Europe', in Eugene Heath and Vincenzo Merolle (eds), *Adam Ferguson: History, Progress and Human Nature*. London: Pickering & Chatto, pp. 115–30.

McDaniel, Iain (2013a) *Adam Ferguson in the Scottish Enlightenment: The Roman Past and Europe's Future*. Cambridge, MA: Harvard University Press.

McDaniel, Iain (2013b) 'Philosophical History and the Science of Man in Scotland: Adam Ferguson's Response to Rousseau', *Modern Intellectual History*, 10 (3), pp. 543–68.

McDowell, Gary L. (1983) 'Commerce, Virtue, and Politics: Adam Ferguson's Constitutionalism', *Review of Politics*, XLV, pp. 536–52.

Machiavelli, Niccolò (1987) *The Discourses*, trans. Leslie Walker, ed. Bernard Crick. Harmondsworth: Penguin.

McLeod, Emma (2015) 'Revolution', in A. Garrett and J. A. Harris (eds), *Scottish Philosophy in the Eighteenth Century*. Oxford: Oxford University Press, pp. 361–403.

MacRae, Donald G. (1969) 'Adam Ferguson', in T. Raison (ed.), *The Founding Fathers of Social Science*. Harmondsworth: Penguin, pp. 17–26.

Marx, Karl (1975) *Early Writings*, ed. Lucio Colletti. Harmondsworth: Penguin.

Mason, Sheila (1988) 'Ferguson and Montesquieu: Tacit Reproaches?', *British Journal for Eighteenth Century Studies*, 11 (2), pp. 193–203.

Meek, Ronald (1967) 'The Scottish Contribution to Marxist Sociology', in R. L. Meek (ed.), *Economics and Ideology and Other Essays*. London: Chapman & Hall, pp. 34–50.

Meek, Ronald L. (1976) *Social Science and the Ignoble Savage*. Cambridge: Cambridge University Press.

Merolle, Vincenzo (1994) *Saggio su Ferguson: con un saggio su Millar*. Rome: Gangeri Editione.

Merolle, Vincenzo (2006) 'Introduction', in *The Manuscripts of Adam Ferguson*, ed. Vincenzo Merolle. London: Pickering & Chatto, pp. xi–xlv.

Merolle, Vincenzo (2009) 'Hume as a Critic of Ferguson's Essay', in Eugene Heath and Vincenzo Merolle (eds), *Adam Ferguson: Philosophy, Politics and Society*. London: Pickering & Chatto, pp. 73–87.

Meyer, Annette (2008) 'Ferguson's "Appropriate Stile" in Combining History and Science: The History of Historiography Revisited', in Eugene Heath and Vincenzo Merolle (eds), *Adam Ferguson: History, Progress and Human Nature*. London: Pickering & Chatto, pp. 131–45.

Mitchieson, Rosalind (1978) 'Patriotism and National Identity in Eighteenth-Century Scotland', in T. W. Moody (ed.), *Nationality and the Pursuit of National Independence*. Belfast: Appletree Press, pp. 73–95.

Mizuta, Hiroshi (1981) 'Two Adams in the Scottish Enlightenment: Adam Smith and Adam Ferguson on Progress', *Studies in Voltaire*, 191, pp. 182–99.

Montesquieu, C. (1965) [1748] *Considerations on the Causes of the Greatness of the Romans and Their Decline*, trans. David Lowenthal. Ithaca, NY: Cornell University Press.

Montesquieu, C. (1989) [1748] *The Spirit of the Laws*, trans. and ed. Anne M. Cohler, Basia Carolyn Miller and Harold Samuel Stone. Cambridge: Cambridge University Press.

Moore, Dafydd (2005) 'Adam Ferguson, The Poems of Ossian and the imaginative life of the Scottish Enlightenment', *History of European Ideas*, 31, pp. 277–88.

Moore, James (2009) 'Montesquieu and the Scottish Enlightenment', in R. E. Kingston (ed.), *Montesquieu and his Legacy*. Albany, NY: SUNY Press, pp. 179–95.

Moran, Mary Catherine (2000) 'The Commerce of the Sexes: Gender and the Social Sphere in Scottish Enlightenment Accounts of Civil

Society', in Frank Trentmann (ed.), *Paradoxes of Civil Society: New Perspectives on Modern German and British History*. New York: Berghahn, pp. 61–85.

Mosher, Michael A. (1984) 'The Particulars of a Universal Politics: Hegel's Adaptation of Montesquieu's Typology', *American Political Science Review*, 78, pp. 179–88.

Murdoch, Alexander (1980) *The People Above: Politics and Administration in Mid-Eighteenth Century Scotland*. Edinburgh: John Donald.

Nicolai, Katherine (2011) 'The Scottish Cato? A Re-examination of Adam Ferguson's Engagement with Classical Antiquity'. Unpublished PhD thesis, University of Edinburgh.

Nicolai, Katherine (2014) 'Adam Ferguson: Pedagogy and His Engagement with Stoicism', *Journal of Scottish Philosophy*, 12 (2), pp. 199–212.

O'Brien, Karen (1997) *Narratives of Enlightenment: Cosmopolitan History from Voltaire to Gibbon*. Cambridge: Cambridge University Press.

O'Brien, Karen (2009) *Women and the Enlightenment in Eighteenth-Century Britain*. Cambridge: Cambridge University Press.

Oz-Salzberger, Fania (1994) 'Introduction', in *An Essay on the History of Civil Society* (ed.), F. Oz-Salzberger. Cambridge: Cambridge University Press.

Oz-Salzberger, Fania (1995) *Translating the Enlightenment: Scottish Civic Discourse in Eighteenth-Century Germany*. Cambridge: Cambridge University Press.

Oz-Salzberger, Fania (2001) 'Civil Society in the Scottish Enlightenment', in K. Kaviraj and S. Khilnani (eds), *Civil Society: History and Possibilities*. Cambridge: Cambridge University Press, pp. 58–83.

Oz-Salzberger, Fania (2003) 'The Political Theory of the Scottish Enlightenment', in A. Broadie (ed.), *The Cambridge Companion to the Scottish Enlightenment*. Cambridge: Cambridge University Press, pp. 157–77.

Oz-Salzberger, Fania (2008) 'Ferguson's Politics of Action', in Eugene Heath and Vincenzo Merolle (eds), *Adam Ferguson: History, Progress and Human Nature*. London: Pickering & Chatto, pp. 147–56.

Pagden, Anthony (1988) 'The "Defence of Civilisation" in Eighteenth-Century Social Theory', *History of the Human Sciences*, 1 (1), pp. 33–45.

Pettit, Phillip (1997) *Republicanism: A Theory of Freedom and Government*. Oxford: Oxford University Press.

Phillips, Mark Salber (2000) *Society and Sentiment: Genres of Historical Writing in Britain 1740–1820*. Princeton, NJ: Princeton University Press.

Phillipson, Nicholas (1981) 'The Scottish Enlightenment', in R. Porter and M. Teich (eds), *The Enlightenment in National Context*. Cambridge: Cambridge University Press, pp. 19–40.

Phillipson, Nicholas (1983) 'The Pursuit of Virtue in Scottish University Education', in N. Phillipson (ed.), *Universities, Society and the Future*. Edinburgh: Edinburgh University Press, pp. 87–109.

Phillipson, Nicholas (1987) 'Politics, Politeness and the Anglicisation of Early Eighteenth Century Scottish Culture', in R. Mason (ed.), *Scotland and England 1286–1815*. Edinburgh: John Donald, pp. 226–46.

Pitts, Jennifer (2005) *A Turn to Empire: The Rise of Imperial Liberalism in Britain and France*. Princeton: Princeton University Press.

Plassart, Anna (2015) *The Scottish Enlightenment and the French Revolution*. Cambridge: Cambridge University Press.

Pocock, J. G. A. (1975) *The Machiavellian Moment: Florentine Political Thought and the Atlantic Republican Tradition*. Princeton, NJ: Princeton University Press.

Pocock, J. G. A. (1983) 'Cambridge Paradigms and Scottish Philosophers: A Study of the Relations between the Civic Humanist and Civil Jurisprudential Interpretations of Eighteenth-century Thought', in I. Hont and M. Ignatieff (eds), *Wealth and Virtue: The Shaping of Political Economy in the Scottish Enlightenment*. Cambridge: Cambridge University Press, pp. 235–52.

Pocock, J. G. A. (1999) *Barbarism and Religion: Narratives of Civil Government*, Vol. II. Cambridge: Cambridge University Press.

Poovey, Mary (1998) *A History of the Modern Fact: Problems of Knowledge in the Sciences of Wealth and Society*. Chicago: University of Chicago Press.

Putnam, Robert (2001) *Bowling Alone: The Collapse and Revival of American Community*. New York: Simon & Schuster.

Raphael, D. D. (1994) 'Adam Ferguson's Tutorship of Lord Chesterfield', *Studies on Voltaire and the Eighteenth Century*, 323, pp. 209–23.

Raphael, D. D., Raynor, D. and Ross, I. S. (1990) '"This Very Awkward Affair": An Entanglement of Scottish Professors with English Lords', *Studies on Voltaire and the Eighteenth Century*, 278, pp. 419–63.

Raynor, David (2008) 'Ferguson's Reflections Previous to the Establishment of a Militia', in Eugene Heath and Vincenzo Merolle (eds), *Adam Ferguson: History, Progress and Human Nature*. London: Pickering & Chatto, pp. 65–72.

Raynor, David (2009) 'Why did David Hume Dislike Adam Ferguson's An Essay on the History of Civil Society', in Eugene Heath and Vincenzo Merolle (eds), *Adam Ferguson: Philosophy, Politics and Society*. London: Pickering & Chatto, pp. 45–72.

Reid, Thomas (1997) [1764] *An Inquiry into the Human Mind on the Principles of Common Sense*, ed. Derek R. Brookes. Edinburgh: Edinburgh University Press.

Rendall, Jane (1978) *The Origins of the Scottish Enlightenment 1707–1776*. London: Macmillan.

Rendall, Jane (2008) 'The Progress of Civilisation: Women, Gender, and Enlightened Perspectives on Civil Society c. 1750–1800', in G. Budde, K. Hagemann and S. Michel (eds), *Civil Society and Gender Justice: Historical and Comparative Perspectives*. New York: Berghahn, pp. 59–78.

Robertson, John (1983a) 'The Scottish Enlightenment at the Limits of the Civic Tradition', in I. Hont and M. Ignatieff (eds), *Wealth and Virtue: The Shaping of Political Economy in the Scottish Enlightenment*. Cambridge: Cambridge University Press, pp. 137–78.

Robertson, John (1983b) 'Scottish Political Economy beyond the Civic Tradition: Government and Economic Development in the Wealth of Nations', *History of Political Thought*, VI (3), pp. 451–82.

Robertson, John (1985) *The Scottish Enlightenment and the Militia Issues*. Edinburgh: John Donald.

Sabine, G. H. (1957) *A History of Political Theory*. London: George Harrap.

Sampson, R. V. (1956) *Progress in the Age of Reason*. London: Heinemann.

Schliesser, Eric (2014) 'Newton and Newtonianism', in A. Garrett (ed.), *The Routledge Companion to Eighteenth Century Philosophy*. London: Routledge, pp. 62–90.

Schneider, Louis (1980) 'Introduction' to Adam Ferguson's *An Essay on the History of Civil Society*. New Brunswick, NJ: Transaction Press, pp. v–xxviii.

Sebastiani, Silvia (2011) 'National Character and Race: A Scottish Enlightenment Debate', in T. Ahnert and S. Manning (eds), *Character, Self, and Sociability in the Scottish Enlightenment*. London: Palgrave Macmillan, pp. 187–205.

Sebastiani, Silvia (2013) *The Scottish Enlightenment: Race, Gender, and the Limits of Progress*. London: Palgrave Macmillan.

Sebastiani, Silvia (2014) 'Nations, Nationalism and National Character', in A. Garrett (ed.), *The Routledge Companion to Eighteenth Century Philosophy*. London: Routledge, pp. 593–617.

Sebastiani, Silvia (2015) 'Barbarism and Republicanism', in A. Garrett and J. A. Harris (eds), *Scottish Philosophy in the Eighteenth Century*. Oxford: Oxford University Press, pp. 323–60.

Sher, Richard B. (1982) 'Those Scotch Imposters and their Cabal: Ossian and the Scottish Enlightenment', *Man and Nature*, 1, pp. 55–63.

Sher, Richard B. (1985) *Church and University in the Scottish Enlightenment: The Moderate Literati of Edinburgh*. Edinburgh: Edinburgh University Press.

Sher, Richard B. (1989) 'Adam Ferguson, Adam Smith and the Problem of National Defence', *Journal of Modern History*, 61, June, pp. 240–68.

Sher, Richard B. (1990) 'Professors of Virtue: The Social History of the Edinburgh Moral Philosophy Chair in the Eighteenth Century', in M. A. Stewart (ed.), *Studies in the Philosophy of the Scottish Enlightenment*. Oxford: Oxford University Press, pp. 87–126.

Sher, Richard B. (1991) 'Percy, Shaw, and the Ferguson "Cheat": National Prejudice in the Ossian Wars', in H. Gaskill (ed.), *Ossian Revisited*. Edinburgh: Edinburgh University Press, pp. 207–45.

Sher, Richard B. (1994) 'From Troglodytes to Americans: Montesquieu and the Scottish Enlightenment on Liberty, Virtue, and Commerce', in D. Wooton (ed.), *Republicanism, Liberty and Commercial Society*. Stanford, CA: Stanford University Press, pp. 368–402.

Sher, Richard B. (2006) *The Enlightenment and the Book: Scottish Authors and Their Publishers in Eighteenth-Century Britain, Ireland, and America*. Chicago: University of Chicago Press.

Shils, Edward (1997) *The Virtue of Civility: Selected Essays on Liberalism, Tradition, and Civil Society*, ed. Steven Grosby. Indianapolis, IN: Liberty Fund.

Simpson, K. (1988) *The Protean Scot: The Crisis of Identity in Eighteenth-Century Scottish Literature*. Aberdeen: Aberdeen University Press.

Skinner, Andrew (1967a) 'Natural History in the Age of Adam Smith', *Political Studies*, XV, (1), pp. 32–48.

Skinner, Andrew (1967b) 'Adam Ferguson: The History of Civil Society', *Political Studies*, XV (2), pp. 219–21.

Skinner, Andrew (1982) 'A Scottish Contribution to Marxist Sociology?', in I. Bradley and M. C. Howard (eds), *Classical and Marxian Sociology*. London: Macmillan, pp. 95–121.

Skjönsberg, Max (2017) 'Adam Ferguson on Partisanship, Party Conflict, and Popular Participation', *Modern Intellectual History*, doi: 10.1017/S1479244317000099, pp. 1–28.

Smith, Adam (1976a) [1759] *The Theory of Moral Sentiments*, ed. D. D. Raphael and A. L. Macfie. Oxford: Oxford University Press.

Smith, Adam (1976b) [1776] *An Inquiry into the Nature and Causes of the Wealth of Nations*, ed. R. H. Campbell, A. S. Skinner and W. B. Todd. Oxford: Oxford University Press.

Smith, Adam (1978) *Lectures on Jurisprudence*, ed. R. L. Meek, D. D. Raphael and P. G. Stein. Oxford: Oxford University Press.

Smith, Craig (2006) 'Adam Ferguson and the Danger of Books', *Journal of Scottish Philosophy*, 4 (2), pp. 93–109.

Smith, Craig (2008) 'Ferguson and the Active Genius of Mankind', in Eugene Heath and Vincenzo Merolle (eds), *Adam Ferguson: History, Progress and Human Nature*. London: Pickering & Chatto, pp. 157–70.

Smith, Craig (2013) 'Adam Ferguson and Ethnocentrism in the Science of Man', *History of the Human Sciences*, 26 (1), pp. 52–67.

Smith, Craig (2014) 'We have mingled politeness with the use of the sword': Nature and Civilisation in Adam Ferguson's Philosophy of War', *European Legacy*, 19 (1), pp. 1–15.

Sorenson, Roy (2002) 'Fame and the Forgotten Philosopher: Meditations on the Headstone of Adam Ferguson', *Philosophy*, 77, pp. 109–14.

Starobinski, J. (1993) *Blessings in Disguise; or the Morality of Evil*, trans. A. Goldhammer. Cambridge, MA: Harvard University Press.

Stephen, Leslie (1902) *A History of English Thought in the Eighteenth Century*. London: Smith, Elder & Co.

Swingewood, Alan (1970) 'Origins of Sociology: the Case of the Scottish Enlightenment', *British Journal of Sociology*, 21, pp. 164–80.

Taylor, Jacqueline (2014) 'Moral Sense and Sentiment', in A. Garrett (ed.), *The Routledge Companion to Eighteenth Century Philosophy*. London: Routledge, pp. 421–41.

Testa, Denise Ann (2007) 'A Bastard Gaelic Man: Reconsidering the Highland Roots of Adam Ferguson'. Unpublished PhD thesis, University of Western Sydney.

Towsey, Mark (2010) *Reading the Scottish Enlightenment: Books and their Readers in Provincial Scotland, 1750–1820*. Leiden: Brill.

Turner, Brandon P. (2012) 'Adam Ferguson on "Action" and the Possibility of Non-political Participation', *Polity*, 44, pp. 212–33.

Varty, John (1997) 'Civic or Commercial? Adam Ferguson's Concept of Civil Society', in R. Fine and S. Rai (eds), *Civil Society: Democratic Perspectives*. London: Frank Cass, pp. 29–48.

Waszek, Norbert (1986) *Man's Social Nature: A Topic of the Scottish Enlightenment in Its Historical Setting*. Frankfurt am Main: Peter Lang.

Waszek, Norbert (1988) *The Scottish Enlightenment and Hegel's Account of Civil Society*. Dordrecht: Kluwer Academic.

Weinstein, J. R. (2009) 'The Two Adams: Ferguson and Smith on Sympathy and Sentiment', in Eugene Heath and Vincenzo Merolle (eds), *Adam Ferguson: Philosophy, Politics and Society*. London: Pickering & Chatto, pp. 89–106.

Winch, Donald (1978) *Adam Smith's Politics: An Essay in Historiographic Revision*. Cambridge: Cambridge University Press.

Wood, Paul B. (1989) 'The Natural History of Man in the Scottish Enlightenment', *History of Science*, 27, pp. 89–123.

Wood, Paul B. (2015a) 'Thomas Reid and the Common Sense School', in A. Garrett and J. A. Harris (eds), *Scottish Philosophy in the Eighteenth Century*. Oxford: Oxford University Press, pp. 404–52.

Wood, Paul B. (2015b) 'Postscript: On Writing the History of Scottish Philosophy in the Age of Enlightenment', in A. Garrett and J. A. Harris (eds), *Scottish Philosophy in the Eighteenth Century*. Oxford: Oxford University Press, pp. 453–67.

Index